CHICAGO PUBLIC LIBRARY

D1611610

Chicago Public Library
C
P
L
REFERENCE
Form 178 rev. 1-94

# An Argument of Images

*The Poetry of Alexander Pope*

# An Argument of Images

## *The Poetry of Alexander Pope*

*Patricia Meyer Spacks*

*Harvard University Press*
*Cambridge, Massachusetts*
*1971*

*Printed in the United States of America*

*Library of Congress Catalog Card Number 77–154499*
*SBN 674–04485–1*

For Nancy Nichols, M.D.

"And all our Knowledge is, OURSELVES TO KNOW."

*"Art does not reproduce the visible, it makes visible."*

*—Paul Klee*

*"Thus, by a fine Taste and happy Management of Nature, you are presented with an undistinguishable Mixture of Realities and Imagery."*

*—Anon. letter on Pope's garden and grotto,* The Newcastle General Magazine, or Monthly Intelligencer, *1748*

Acknowledgments

Most of Chapter 2, in slightly different form, appeared in "Imagery and Method in *An Essay on Criticism*," *PMLA*, 85 (1970), 97–106. Part of the discussion of the *Epistle to Arbuthnot* in Chapter 5 was incorporated, in different form, in "In Search of Sincerity," *College English*, 29 (1968), 591–602, and is reprinted with permission of the National Council of Teachers of English.

I am grateful to the John Simon Guggenheim Foundation and to the Trustees of Wellesley College for the support, in the form of a fellowship and a sabbatical leave, which made possible the completion of this study.

My debt to my husband is too large and inclusive for adequate statement. He has been the critic and the friend of this study in all its stages; without him, it could not have been written.

*Contents*

# An Argument of Images

*The Poetry of Alexander Pope*

## One

# The Controlling Image

One function of the poet may be, as Ezra Pound suggested, to present the image that his age demands. Each new generation requires new self-representation, summarizing ideas or emblematic personalities to embody its vision of itself. But what "the age demands" depends on who is looking at it, critic or apologist. The English Augustans might see themselves in the Horatian spokesmen of the period's urbane satires, but such figures viewed in historical perspective seem to reflect more fantasy than reality: they were dreams of what the age might have been, not convincing versions of actuality. Swift's Modest Proposer, on the other hand, is equally far from being an adequate emblem for his age. The early eighteenth century, like every other period, required ambivalent rendition: no single image could contain it. The varied imagery of Alexander Pope's poetry, including both Horatian idealizations and their embodied opposites, supplies an index to the complexity of his time.

Twentieth century criticism has demonstrated that one can use a poet's images to "prove" almost anything, to show him as either simpler or more complex than he immediately appears. Now, as in the eighteenth century, no clear consensus exists even about the meaning of the word *image*, which may designate a simile or metaphor, any concrete representation, or the vaguest of symbols. In all their varied definitions, however, images remain the raw material of poetry; and the poet's choice of this material must reflect, however obliquely, his values. A study of Pope's images—including his objectifications of idea, impulse, and feeling, as well as his less highly-charged concrete details—illuminates both his assumptions and those of his period. They are precisely the assumptions one would expect, which is to say that imagery reveals the obvious. But what it reveals is less important than how. The ways in which Pope converts conventional images to new purposes, as well as his invention of new kinds of imagery, display an intricate balance of oppositions, an awareness of contradictory values and of the possibility of their harmonious coexistence more subtle than direct statement can render.

The central problem, both moral and aesthetic, on which Pope's imagery focuses is one of control—a problem crucial to the thought of the early eighteenth century. During this period, the sense of possibility bore an intimate relation to the sense of restriction: energy demanded control, while control became meaningless without energy. Spontaneity was attractive, but so was discipline. As a result, praise for one often implied praise for its opposite. Pope and his contemporaries, highly conscious of the value of discipline—the discipline of God's law and of man's, of self and of society—often seemed unaware of the obsessiveness of this concern. Erik Erikson, in a psychiatrist's version of Pound's dictum, has written: "Exactly what image of human life appears in a given age and culture, an image so conscious and obvious that no explanation seems necessary, or what image is . . . so much 'in a man's bones' that he need not be conscious of it—*that* must be put into words in each age."[1] Pope, speaking the assumptions of his time in the patterns of his imagery, reveals not only the "conscious and obvious" ethical image of life as an orderly sequence, man as a responsible being, but also the degree to which that same vision had penetrated beneath the conscious level.

A concern with control as an ethical issue is perhaps most striking in Pope's handling of traditional, even hackneyed images, which he often uses to original purpose. The image of life as a river, for example, which lends itself naturally to a view of man as subject to forces beyond himself, is transformed at Pope's hands into a metaphor for achieved rather than "natural" life. Because the flow of water is normally controlled not by man but by God, man's ordering propensities would seem to have little scope in this metaphor. Samuel Johnson's version of the water image, for instance, depends on this implication: "Must helpless man, in ignorance sedate, / Roll darkling down the torrent of his fate?"[2] In his *Imitations of Horace, Epistle* I, i, Pope hints a similar view, describing himself parenthetically as having "each Opinion with the next at strife, / One ebb and flow of follies all my life."[3] Yet he insists that this state of affairs is for him neither necessary nor desirable, that his "Guide, Philosopher, and Friend" (177) should "mend" him (178) and "make" him into "That Man divine whom Wisdom calls her own" (179–80). The river's flux can be controlled. Uncontrolled, it is incomprehensible:

> Our depths who fathoms, or our shallows finds,
> Quick whirls, and shifting eddies, of our minds?
> Life's stream for Observation will not stay,
> It hurries all too fast to mark their way.
> (*Epistle to Cobham,* 29–32)

But inconsistency is only apparent; we are, after all, "Consistent in our follies and our sins" (226), and insight into the principle of the ruling passion can calm troubled waters. In Pope's *Essay on Man,* the "virtuous mind" is a "peaceful lake" (IV, 363–364): self-love may stir it like a dropped pebble, but that pebble produces an orderly series of concentric circles, "Wide and more wide" (369), embracing more and more of mankind. Man must "steer" (379) "along the stream of Time" (383); steering, he dominates disorder. The possibilities of control always combat the incipience of chaos, this being the central drama of existence.

Another elaboration of the metaphor of life as water suggests the depth of Pope's commitment to the recurrent notion that life is a sequence which can and should be ordered:

> I love to pour out all myself, as plain
> As downright *Shippen,* or as old *Montagne.*
> In them, as certain to be lov'd as seen,
> The Soul stood forth, nor kept a Thought within;
> In me what Spots (for Spots I have) appear,
> Will prove at least the Medium must be clear.
> In this impartial Glass, my Muse intends
> Fair to expose myself, my Foes, my Friends . . .
> My Head and Heart thus flowing thro' my Quill,
> Verse-man or Prose-man, term me which you will.
> (*Imitations of Horace, Satire* II, i, 51–58, 63–64)

The "water" that the poet "pours out" by acts of choice and personal commitment becomes a medium of reflection, as earlier in *Spring* and *Windsor-Forest* he had unified art and nature through the device of images reflected in water.[4] Now he perceives his life and his art as a single entity, and he expresses their unity through the complicated imagery of water. A Twickenham note to this passage quotes from Pope's prose *Thoughts on Various Subjects:* "The best way to prove the clearness of our mind, is by shewing its faults; as when a stream discovers the dirt at the bottom, it convinces us of the transparency and purity of the water."[5] The "transparency" that the poet claims for his life is identical with the revelatory power of his verse; the moral force of the good life "flows through his quill" to generate the force of poetry or prose.

An equally traditional metaphor for human life is the play, which carries more obvious implications of the necessity of discipline. To regard life as a play is to manifest belief in an operative principle of control in the universe, for a play must have shape and meaning. The "shape" of the individual human drama is that of the inevitable sequence of life's stages, with the activities and appurtenances appropriate to them, from the rattle of infants to the beads and prayer books of old age (*Essay on Man*, II, 275–282). The shape of the human drama considered on a larger scale is more difficult to discern, because Pope's "optimism" does not extend to a conviction of historical progress. Yet to see life as analogous to a work of art implies a deeper kind of optimism than any common to the twentieth century. It is nevertheless true that the play's stage manager may be a "great Anarch" who "lets the curtain fall" to bring "Universal Darkness" on the world (*Dunciad*, IV, 655–656). On the individual level, moreover, one can sum up the human drama as "Life's poor play" (*Essay on Man*, II, 282), from which the poet warns men to "Walk sober off; before a sprightlier Age / Comes titt'ring on, and shoves you from the stage" (*Imitations of Horace, Epistle* II, ii, 324–325).[6] Pope's sense of endings is tragic, though he imagines his own life as a farce and that of "graver Mortals" as "A long, exact, and serious Comedy" (*Epistle to Miss Blount, with the Works of Voiture*, 21, 22, 25). Nonetheless, some faith in a cosmic plan and purpose underlies such a choice of metaphor.

As Pope employs it, the image of life as a play also expresses his concern for ethical responsibility. Although the length of each individual human comedy is a matter of divine dispensation, its exactness and seriousness are within the control of the actors, who also participate in the authorship of their parts. When Pope imagines himself as acting in a farce, he specifies that it should be "innocent," "gay," "And more Diverting still than Regular" (25–26)—all characteristics within his own control. The actors in life's drama will be shoved from the stage if they refuse to leave it, but they retain the power to "Walk sober off" at the dictates of their own will. According to this eighteenth century style of "living theater," the overall course of action is established from without, but the actors, by their mode of acting, can display creative power, and by what they create they may be judged. The anarchy of dullness that brings the curtain down on the universe is a projection of the inertia of individual minds;[7] human actions generate their own punishments.

Life, in other words, is to Pope a meaningful sequence of events. That sequence is universal and predictable, moving inevitably through stages of experience from childhood to age. Until the nineteenth century, a social historian has written, "the division of life into periods had the same fixity as the cycle of Nature or the organization of society."[8] The comparison is suggestive in relation to Pope, whose perception of order in society resembles his awareness of the order in individual lives. In both cases, the incipience of chaos is a salient fact. Man's intelligence, moral commitment, and ethical perception enable him to preserve, both individually and in society, an order that is analogous to the great pattern of nature. But human passion, vacillation, and blindness are equally real, so that the drama of life often verges on meaningless melodrama. The need for ethical control is manifest.

Pope's central poetic subject is the intricacies of right conduct, and of deviations from it. His images, trite or original, reflect this concern. He steadily insists on the moral necessity of living a disciplined life and of freely accepting restrictions as a means to growth. He maintains that the laws of conduct are both discoverable and satisfying. The sequence of experiences that composes an individual's life is moral as well as psychological. Pope's imagery stresses the corollary fact that individuals must struggle to achieve order and clarity through their own experience.

Not only does the mythology of control rendered by his images reflect the values of his time, but its relevance is also compellingly personal. The diminutive hunchback, afraid of feminine mockery, tormented by illness, impeded by religion and filial piety, as well as by personal inclination and literary tradition, from assuming any important public role in which he could direct meaningful happenings in the life of the country—such a figure might be expected to harbor fantasies of control that would express themselves through his art. Control, after all, implies power as well as restriction. One could account for the persistence of imagery of control in Pope's work through biography alone: his letters and, as Maynard Mack has recently demonstrated, his private history reveal his insistent construction of a larger-than-life self-image for his own contemplation and that of his friends.[9] "My Infirmities increase ev'ry year," he writes to Ralph Allen: "Tho my Spirit be prompt; my Flesh is weak. I have two great Tasks on my hands: I am trying to benefit myself, and to benefit Posterity; not by Works of my own God knows: I can but Skirmish, & maintain a flying Fight with Vice: its Forces augment, & will drive me off the Stage, before I shall see the Effects complete, either of Divine Providence or Vengeance: for sure we can be quite Saved only by the One, or punished by the other: the Condition of Morality is so desperate, as to be above all Human Hands."[10] The metaphor of life as drama here combines with the poet's awareness of life as battle. Despite his declaration of the weakness of his flesh and the powerlessness of human effort, Pope considers himself, through his poetry, to be the agent or ally of Divine Providence and Vengeance. Again, he writes to Swift: "let Philosophy be ever so vain, it is less vain now than Politicks, and not quite so vain at present as Divinity: I know nothing that moves strongly but Satire, and those who are asham'd of nothing else, are so of being ridiculous."[11] Poetry is an instrument of moral power.

Although he is proud of his force as a poet, he also claims the strength of personal virtue: "It is Truth and a clear Conscience that I think will set me above all my Enemies, and make no Honest man repent of having been my Friend."[12] In a letter to his friend William Fortescue, the lawyer, he attests his devotion to friends, concluding, "when shall you & I sit by a Fireside, without a Brief or a Poem in our hands, & yet not idle, not thoughtless, but as Serious, and more so, than any Business ought to make us, except the great Business, that of enjoying a reasonable Being, & regarding its End. The sooner this is our case, the better: God deliver you from Law, me from Rhime! and give us leisure to attend what is more important."[13] His concern with ethics both surpasses and justifies his concern with poetry. He offers an image of himself as holding power over himself, over nature, and through poetry, over the minds and hearts of others. The manifest simplifications of this version of his own character support an ideal of ethical control comparable to that conveyed by Pope's poetic imagery.

Aesthetic discipline was as pressing an issue for the eighteenth century as was its moral counterpart.
The extravagances of the poetic imagination must always lie under the control of literary tradition and of reality, the ultimate source of all imagery. When Johnson summarized—as well as anyone has ever done—the nature of Pope's poetic gifts, he stressed the ways in which actuality had disciplined his imagination:

> Pope had, in proportions very nicely adjusted to each other, all the qualities that constitute genius. He had Invention, by which new trains of events are formed and new scenes of imagery displayed . . . and by which extrinsick and adventitious embellishments and illustrations are connected with a known subject. . . he had Imagination, which strongly impresses on the writer's mind and enables him to convey to the reader the various forms of nature, incidents of life, and energies of passion . . . he had Judgement, which selects from life or nature what the present purpose requires, and, by separating the essence of things from its concomitants, often makes the representation more powerful than the reality; and he had colours of language always before him ready to decorate his matter with every grace of elegant expression.[14]

The poet's invention enables him to connect the unknown with the known; his imagination and linguistic powers are the means of conveying truth; and his judgment's selectivity helps him to increase the power of reality in representing it. "Nothing but Nature can give a sincere pleasure," wrote Dryden.[15] To Pope, nature was reality, the necessary and assumed foundation of poetry, the source of aesthetic effect.

But to specify the proper relation between image and "reality" is a complex undertaking, particularly in dealing with eighteenth century poetry, written by men who assumed that analogy was a primary method of God, the first Maker, as well as of His poet-imitators. The universe was itself a great system of analogies, from which men might learn. Aesthetics and science were thus closely allied. Addison's essays on the pleasures of the imagination, which consider the various sources of imaginative stimulation, includes a long, rhapsodic passage on the wonders of the physical universe:

> Nothing is more pleasant to the fancy, than to enlarge itself, by degrees, in its contemplation of the various proportions which its several objects bear to each other, when it compares the body of man to the bulk of the whole earth, the earth to the circle it describes round the sun, that circle to the sphere of the fixed stars, the sphere of the fixed stars to the circuit of the whole creation, the whole creation itself to the infinite space that is everywhere diffused about it . . . But if, after all this, we take the least particle of . . . animal spirits, and consider its capacity of being wrought into a world, that shall contain within those narrow dimensions a heaven and earth, stars and planets, and every different species of living creatures, in the same analogy and proportion they bear to each other in our own universe; such a speculation, by reason of its nicety, appears ridiculous to those who have not turned their thoughts that way, though, at the same time, it is founded on no less than the evidence of a demonstration.[16]

The belief that the order of the universe could be perceived and expressed in terms of analogy and proportion was a fundamental article of faith. And when Addison considers metaphor, his tone is similar:

> A noble metaphor, when it is placed to an advantage, casts a kind of glory round it, and darts a lustre through a whole sentence . . . It is this talent of affecting the imagination, that gives an embellishment to good sense, and makes one man's compositions more agreeable than another's. It sets off all writings in general, but is the very life and highest perfection of poetry. Where it shines in an eminent degree, it has preserved several poems for many ages, that have nothing else to recommend them; and where all the other beauties are present, the work appears dry and insipid, if this single one be wanting. It has something in it like creation; it bestows a kind of existence, and draws up to the reader's view several objects which are not to be found in being.[17]

The poet's power to create metaphor is the heart of his mystery. "Imaging is, in itself, the very height and life of Poetry," wrote Dryden.[18] And late in the eighteenth century, John Aikin referred to "that variety, novelty, and distinctness of imaging which constitute the true riches of poetry."[19] In creating illustrative images, the poet uses his perception of the external world to enlarge the perceptions of others. Revealing new structures of analogy, he thus heightens awareness of the subtleties inherent in God's patterns, for the connections he makes convey his understanding of reality and affect the reader's understanding. Every new metaphor modifies the "real world" because the linkage it asserts, once perceived, seems actually to exist.

Such statements are truer of eighteenth century poetry than of more recent verse because—to use Meyer Abrams' terminology—the "mirror" aspect of the poet's function was then more important than the "lamp."[20] Poetry, like the other arts, was assumed to be imitative and therefore to reflect reality. The poetic imagination provided a way of seeing, and of conveying what was seen; it was not a form of private inspiration but a means of public revelation. Physical perception was the necessary basis for imagination. As Addison wrote, "We cannot indeed have a single image in the fancy that did not make its first entrance through the sight."[21] An image that revealed the peculiarities of the poet's mind without conveying a larger truth would have been incomprehensible. Until late in the eighteenth century, critical commentary on imagery rested on the assumption that the universally-recognized emotional power of the image derived from its foundation in sense impressions and from its capacity to expand the reader's awareness of connections. "Genius is delighted with what thrills the senses powerfully and vividly," wrote Thomas Tickell.[22] And well chosen images, wrote William Duff, "impart a pleasing gratification to the mind, arising from the discovery of the resemblance betwixt the similitude and the object to which it is compared; they . . . are a principal source of those exquisite sensations, which [poetry] is calculated to inspire."[23]

Addison's implicit definition of an image as a visual sense impression and Duff's as a metaphor or simile, differ radically, but both critics agree that the fundamental controlling element of poetic language is the poet's perception of the real world. Pope's imagery gives clues as to what constitutes and limits that real world. It is not necessarily the physical world alone:

> See the same man, in vigour, in the gout;
> Alone, in company; in place, or out;
> Early at Bus'ness, and at Hazard late;
> Mad at a Fox-chace, wise at a Debate;
> Drunk at a Borough, civil at a Ball,
> Friendly at Hackney, faithless at Whitehall.
> (*Epistle to Cobham,* 130–135)

The introductory imperative "See" prepares one for a series of visual presentations, and each of the evoked states of being suggests plausible physical correlatives: one can summon up scenes to give solidity to "Early at Bus'ness, and at Hazard late." Earliness and lateness, madness and wisdom, drunkenness and civility, friendliness and faithlessness—each characteristic has a socially sanctioned appropriateness to a special context which the reader can readily imagine. But these "images" are more psychic than physical: the locus of reality is interior. They function not quite as metaphors but as emblems. In their neat contrasting pairings they sum up the orderly inconsistencies that compose a man. Their concreteness derives from precise observation not of the physical world but of its psychic significance.

G. Wilson Knight has written, "Pope is not a pre-eminently visual poet; rather he tells facts, names concrete objects, attaches needed epithets."[24] He is a poet of imagery without being primarily a poet of the visual. Many of his images stress function rather than appearance. Often they record activity:

> The hog, that plows not nor obeys thy call,
> Lives on the labours of this lord of all. . .
> Who bid the stork, Columbus-like, explore
> Heav'ns not his own, and worlds unknown before?
> (*Essay on Man,* III, 41–42, 105–106)

The hog is defined by an implied negative simile (he is not like an ox or a dog), the stork by a daring and provocative positive one; both creatures, their importance established by the nature and attributed meaning of their activities, supply images of action. The comparisons depend more on the poet's capacity to abstract than on his perception of concrete reality. He sees essence beneath appearance, and uses his vision to reveal a dynamic universe.

Physical observation is only the beginning of insight. Even Pope's physical imagery may depend for effect on the known falseness of physical perception: "Nature well known, no prodigies remain, / Comets are regular, and Wharton plain" (*Epistle to Cobhan,* 208–209). Comets appear to the eye and to the uninformed mind as phenomena outside the established order of things, but knowledge alters perception. The implied comparison between Wharton and the comet rests on the relation between what can be apprehended at different levels of perception.

Pope's imagery, then, rests on a foundation of philosophical and psychological as well as physical perception. But perception is not the only controlling force of imagery. Two other distinct intellectual faculties are involved in the creation of images: wit, the eighteenth century equivalent to what is today called imagination, which unifies the disparate and makes new connections; and judgment, which discriminates. These three faculties, with varying degrees of relative importance in the development of images, exist in varying relation to one another. The differences in their functions depend on the purpose as well as the nature of the images they create. Poetic imagery can be merely decorative or illustrative; it may create meaning or amplify meanings previously stated; it can provide emotional or intellectual emphasis or clarification. For different purposes, different kinds and degrees of control are appropriate: extravagance and restraint are both poetic resources.

It is usually impossible to isolate imagery's functions from one another, and always impossible to determine the exact relation of forces involved in their creation. An image based largely on simple perception may seem to be the product of wit; to discriminate between wit's discipline and judgment's often requires supernatural intuition. But it is important to realize that the nature of the human mind as well as of the external world can provide a check on poetic extravagance. Pope's experimentation with imagery involves apparent efforts to exploit various kinds of intellectual resources as well as diverse areas of reference.

The aesthetic problem of control is not only how to discipline imagery but how to use imagery itself to discipline emotion. The expressive functions of imagery are manifest: through images, a poet conveys feeling. Imagery also, as most eighteenth century critics explicitly recognized, generates or intensifies emotion in the reader. But the image provides a mode of containment as well as of expression; it orders feeling, organizes it into comprehensible patterns, and gives it larger than personal meanings. It makes feeling visible. Imagery thus may itself provide a principle of control. If many of Pope's images refer directly to the issue of control, in their functioning in the poems they also reveal the subtle operation of controls, which can intensify as well as limit meaning.

Verbal commitment to the classical ideal of "decorum" or fitness, with its implications of discipline, was well-nigh universal in Pope's time. In practice, control often meant limitation. W. J. Bate has commented, "It is always easier, as Johnson said, to throw out or forbid than to incorporate—'to take away superfluities than to supply defects.' In the title of George Granville's *Essay upon Unnatural Flights in Poetry* (1701), with all that it suggests, we sense the relief that neoclassic theory could provide: something still remained to be done, and the difficulties were not insuperable. In the very limitation, in other words, lay much of the attraction."[25] But the implication of power in the idea of control is also relevant. Both power and restriction are important to Pope, who seeks in his poetry aesthetic and moral power, and recognizes that its source may be the acceptance of limitation.

The problem, theoretical and practical, is to determine which modes of restriction are desirable. As early as the *Essay on Criticism*, Pope makes clear his uneasiness with the idea that codified rules can provide an adequate aesthetic guide. On the one hand, he argues, the rules of poetry derive from and reflect nature and are therefore final and inescapable. Yet great artists may in fact transgress the rules, which increases the power of their art. "Nature to all things fix'd the Limits fit" (52), but no system of rules is identical with Nature. Although moderns should "beware" (163) of offending against the rules, they may properly violate a precept if they "ne'er transgress its *End*" (164).

In matters of conduct, fundamental laws reflecting the natural order also exist, but whether one may disobey a rule while desiring its end is more problematical. To discover the right laws, of wit and of conduct, can be difficult, although common assumption may still be accepted as a fairly comfortable guide. To follow these laws without being destructively hampered by them is another problem. Pope's artistic practice duplicates the complexity of his ethical assertions. In his use of the heroic couplet he demonstrates the expressive possibilities of self-discipline; in his use of imagery he shows how the freedom of wit can express both fantasy and control.

Pope's images "express" control in two ways: they are means of conveying his ideas about the value of ethical control, or they embody principles of aesthetic control. Frequently they fill both functions simultaneously. His use of people as images of virtue and vice, for example, which is a common, perhaps even necessary, satiric practice, exhibits a striking deftness in elevating individuals to symbolic status. The aesthetic simplifications of the device create clarity, while the figures themselves embody or oppose the ethical ideal that underlies the poet's stress on discipline as a high value. Images from inanimate nature can similarly unite aesthetic and ethical suggestion to convey a sense of double discipline. Thus, a couplet about the sun from *The Rape of the Lock* establishes an image of harmonious competition between man and nature; its selectivity creates a miniature order while at the same time criticizing it. "*Sol* thro' white Curtains shot a tim'rous Ray, / And op'd those Eyes that must eclipse the Day" (I, 13–14). The sun, traditional image of divine power, source of light, energy, and growth, shrinks to timorousness in the presence of Belinda, the poem's operative image of divinity. That it is muffled by white curtains suggests the delicate obscuring of reality characteristic of a society in which the sun's burning rays can signal judges to sentence their victims so that jury men may dine. Belinda's power is greater, her light brighter, the second line seems to suggest, than the sun's. But a less complimentary interpretation is possible. An eclipse is literally a blocking out of light; Belinda's eyes, like her curtains, may metaphorically darken the sun, a fact that symbolizes her lack of awareness. The discipline of detail creates an aesthetic order and illuminates its ethical implications.

No single example can suggest the intricacy with which Pope manipulates his principles of aesthetic and ethical control: both subjects require detailed investigation. Analyzing Pope's imagery as it embodies principles of aesthetic control is the more complicated problem of the two. Although his poetic practice becomes more sophisticated with time, his general mode of using imagery to express ethical ideas does not markedly develop: an image of gardening is likely to fill the same kind of function in an early Pope poem as in a late one. In his use of imagery as an expression of aesthetic control, however, there appears to have been a developmental sequence, which is the concern of the first half of this book. Pope's two long didactic poems, the *Essay on Criticism* and the *Essay on Man,* and his most ambitious satiric effort, *The Dunciad,* suggest a sequence of ideas about imagery deriving from different degrees of emphasis on the various determining forces of the image. The *Essay on Criticism,* a poem largely about wit, explores the possibilities of wit as an energy of control. The *Essay on Man,* with its insistence that man should "see" widely and deeply, concentrates more intensely on perception as a possible control. *The Dunciad,* a vision of society as a hell of irrationality, implies that reason, judgment, and knowledge—significantly including knowledge of tradition—are the necessary controlling powers, for poetry as for life. In each instance, the aesthetic choice has ethical implications as well. To examine Pope's different bases for imagery is thus to learn something about his developing sense of moral possibility and necessity.

There is no inevitable reason why "perception" should provide a more sophisticated and flexible principle of control than "wit," or why the idea of "judgment" should organize Pope's greatest poem. But the sequence of these three poems—didactic, philosophic, satiric—is one of gathering mastery, which suggests that only with his discovery of a full commitment to intellect could Pope achieve his triumphs. The comparative inadequacies of the earlier poems may derive partly from the restrictions implicit in the principles guiding the selection and use of their imagery.

The second half of this exploration of Pope's imagery examines in detail the ways in which he employs characters as images, along with other methods of focusing through imagery the problems of ethical control. Through images Pope displays his ethical convictions, indicating the nature and limits of proper discipline, the difficulties and terrors of achieving it, the forces opposing it, and the reasons for valuing it. In this book I concentrate on images from three areas of reference: imagery of character, including the peculiarly emblematic technique of personification; imagery that directly alludes to or defines standards and limits; and imagery of madness, symbolizing the terrors of failed control. All three suggest the close relation between vitality and control. The vigor of passion and will makes human character absorbing but creates dangers that must be opposed by steady discipline; the principles of limitation embody positive standards but create a threat of sterility; and madness represents unchecked vitality with the attendant possibilities of either insight or destruction. By surveying these three modes of allusion through imagery, one may understand more precisely how Pope's imagery embodies and enforces his ideas about ethical power and limitation, and how those ideas relate to his aesthetic principles.

Varied problems are apparent in every image. To define the attitudes and assumptions revealed by Pope's imagery, one must consider how the images work as well as what they say, the kinds of intellectual force that produced them, the meaning of large image-patterns as well as of individual metaphors, and the relations between the principle of control through imagery and other forces of control or liberation. The labels applied are necessarily arbitrary: even the meaning of "image" varies from one instance to another. And none of the questions produce definitive answers. They lend themselves rather to speculation, which may suggest something about the ways in which poetry works.

# Two

# Wit Governing Wit

## *An Essay on Criticism*

*An Essay on Criticism* is the most daring, if perhaps the least successful, of Pope's attempts to discover a viable principle of artistic control. It is a young man's poem, a display piece, but the mode of display, random though it may seem, implies a serious aesthetic principle. Here, as in his later works, Pope tries to achieve both exuberance and discipline, in addition to demonstrating the relation between them.

Two critical comments will illuminate the method of the *Essay*: Byron's statement that there is "more *imagery* in twenty lines of Pope than in any equal length of quotation in English poetry," and T. E. Hulme's pronouncement that poetry "always endeavours to arrest you, and to make you continuously see a physical thing, to prevent you gliding through an abstract process."[1] Though Pope's assumptions about poetry are far removed from Hulme's, in this versified investigation of abstractions he does not permit the reader to skim over familiar doctrine. His method depends on voluminous imagery, a product of the "wit" which is, with "Nature," a presiding power of the poem.

One of the *Essay's* famous cruxes suggests the nature of its author's intent:[2]

> Some to whom Heav'n in Wit has been profuse,
> Want as much more, to turn it to its use.
>
> (80–81)

The poetic ambition of the *Essay on Criticism* centers on an attempt to demonstrate how wit can provide a controlling power for what wit creates. And since this poem asserts as firmly as any of the

Horatian imitations the association between good poetry and the life of virtue, the method implies that imaginative energy may be a source of moral discipline as well. Some of Pope's later imagery suggests that control can create freedom; here he explores the converse of the paradox, demonstrating that the freedom of wit's inventiveness may provide disciplinary principles.

That wit is the image-making faculty is stressed in some of Pope's prose comments.[3] In his notes to *The Iliad,* for example, he remarks, "There cannot be a truer kind of Wit, than what is shewn in apt Comparisons."[4] Wit is equivalent to invention, the power of poetic discovery and creativity for which Pope admired Homer.[5] Homer's invention displays itself in his imagery: "If we observe his *Descriptions, Images,* and *Similes,* we shall find the Invention still predominant. To what else can we ascribe that vast Comprehension of Images of every sort, where we see each Circumstance of art and Individual of Nature summon'd together by the Extent and Fecundity of his Imagination?"[6]

It is less obvious that this aspect of wit can supply control as well as energy. Pope's use of metaphor is, from one point of view, orthodox and ordinary, decorative rather than argumentative. Thus, Jacob Adler has written of the technique of the *Essay on Criticism* and *Essay on Man*: "The Essays depend upon comparisons to an extent which no other of Pope's poems can very well claim. In Pope's day there were of course two perfectly good reasons for this: first, didactic poems were cast in the 'middle' style, avoiding both the epic 'high' and the satirical 'low,' and were hence to be dignified but not elaborately adorned; second, the comparisons considered (and surely properly considered) essential to illustrating and illuminating precepts and theories could adorn or amuse as well as instruct, could appropriately provide the *dulce* as well as confirm the *utile.*"[7] Pope's imagery in the *Essay on Criticism* fulfills these standard functions; but the poet strives to make it do more. If wit can control wit, imagery can supply poetic organization. The structure of the *Essay* has long been an issue in evaluating the poem. Aubrey Williams has argued that Pope tried to supply the "larger design" he found missing in Horace, and he has demonstrated how that design manifests itself in the poem's broad divisions and in some of its details.[8] In contrast, Donald Greene earlier pointed out, with equal truth, that the main heads alone of the *Essay on Criticism* reveal that "there is no real logical order in the poem at all, beyond that of simple enumeration."[9] It is my contention that Pope wished to enlarge imagery's function, to supply a logic of metaphor, so as to achieve an organic unity that would demonstrate wit's power to organize as well as to decorate didacticism. The nature of the *Essay's* imagery, the complexity of its interrelations and of its moral and emotional implications, all support this thesis.

Early in Horace's *Ars Poetica* a passage occurs that widens the physical, philosophical, and emotional scope of the poem:

Ut silvae foliis pronos mutantur in annos,
Prima cadunt, ita verborum vetus interit aetas,
Et juvenum ritu florent modo nata vigentque.
Debemur morti nos nostraque, sive receptus
Terra Neptunus classes Aquilonibus arcet,
Regis opus, sterilisve diu palus aptaque remis
Vicinas urbes alit et grave sentit aratrum,
Seu cursum mutavit iniquum frugibus amnis,
Doctus iter melius, mortalia facta peribunt,
Nedum sermonum stet honos et gratia vivas.
(60–69)

(As forests change their leaves with each year's decline, and the earliest drop off: so with words, the old race dies, and, like the young of human kind, the new-born bloom and thrive. We are doomed to death—we and all things ours; whether Neptune, welcomed within the land, protects our fleets from northern gales—a truly royal work—or a marsh, long a waste where oars were plied, feeds neighbouring towns and feels the weight of the plough; or a river has changed the course which brought ruin to corn-fields and has learnt a better path: all mortal things shall perish, much less shall the glory and glamour of speech endure and live.[10])

Man, his works, and his language are all part of a natural process, according to the poet. Thus, the elegiac note is as appropriate to a consideration of the death of words as to contemplating the transience of other noble accomplishments. The tone and reference of this passage establish a new context for Horace's consideration of poetic minutiae, insisting that the value of iambic meter or the proper relation of beginning, middle, and end can be understood as a concern of high seriousness. The relevance of criticism, Horace suggests, is finally human, not technical.

Although the *Essay on Criticism* rises to astonishing heights of poetic dignity and passion, its expansion of reference—equivalent to that achieved by Horace—depends less on individual passages than on the cumulative effect of its multitudinous imagery. Like Horace, Pope wished to demonstrate that his concerns were human, that criticism was in the fullest sense a moral activity. The poem itself, considered as an essay *in* as well as *on* criticism, demonstrates what criticism can be, and how it can unite with poetry and morality. Its technique of employing images asserts the relatedness of all endeavor; the intricacies of the poem reflect those of human experience.

The special insistence of Pope's imagery derives partly from its repetitiousness. Maynard Mack has called attention to the patterns underlying references to physiological and institutional health or sickness. "Literary norms, these images suggest, are not ultimately dissociable from greater norms. A perverse criticism and a corrupt art are equivalent in their own way to other symptoms and symbols of deterioration: tyranny in the state; bigotry and schism in the church; impotence, nausea, flatulence, jaundice, in the individual organism."[11] Implicit reference from limited to greater norms occurs as well in other image clusters. One may instance the frequent allusions to art and architecture, to sex, and to military activity.

The reason for the association between art and criticism lies in their origins. Throughout the poem, Pope maintains that "wit," the faculty that produces criticism, is like the genius that makes art: mysterious, powerful, creative. The analogies to sex associate that most "natural" of human activities with a more sophisticated form of literary behavior, which is also natural in that it is dedicated to following nature. The sexual metaphors frequently refer to perversions or distortions of natural sex: to eunuchs, mules, "equivocal" generation, the wooing of maids when one cannot win mistresses, the wife enjoyed by other men. In a striking simile, Pope suggests that dullness in combination with obscenity is "As Shameful sure as *Impotence* in *Love*" (533): failure in the attempt at wit, equivalent to sexual failure, should be felt as a comparable disgrace. The vulgar treat the muse like a mistress: "This hour she's *idoliz'd*, the next *abus'd*" (433). Wit and judgment are "meant each other's Aid, like *Man* and *Wife*" (83), though the rest of the poem stresses how seldom this simple sexual mutuality obtains. If sex is natural and universal, its misuses are correspondingly abundant; the misuses of wit, as easy to fall into as those of sex, are equally destructive—and like sexual misbehavior, they hinder generation.

Sexual metaphors stress creativity and its failure, whereas military references emphasize the precariousness of power. For instance, wits are said to turn poets' own arms against them. The productions of wit involve awareness of military strategy, for "Those oft are *Stratagems* which *Errors* seem" (179). The rewards of literature once resembled those of war, in that those who excelled were honored. Now "ratling Nonsense" breaks out from time to time "in full *Vollies*" (628). Efforts to consolidate literary gains, like their military equivalents, may fail, so that "Like Kings we lose the Conquests gain'd before" (64). The weak heads of the vulgar resemble "Towns unfortify'd" (434). The rules and method prescribed by Quintilian are like properly arranged arms, ordered "less to please the Eye, than arm the Hand" (673). "Natural" though it is, criticism—like art and love—is also a struggle, in which victory is possible but probably fleeting.

Through metaphors of this sort the poet conveys an attitude toward the experiences from which his images derive as well as toward those to which they allude. He indicates his high sense of the importance of art, his fastidious distaste for the misuse of sexuality, and his Horatian awareness of the precariousness of human glory. In his view, criticism is one of the many possible human enterprises, to be attempted and judged always in the richest available context. But through imagery, he also makes the reader aware of the complex bases of judgment and of a hierarchy of values.

The interaction of imagery in the *Essay on Criticism* is as functional as the repeated emphasis on specific areas of reference. Images grow out of, comment on, modify one another. As a consequence, their felt significance may increase between one appearance and another. A case in point is the passage containing the perplexing definition of "*True Wit.*"

> Some to *Conceit* alone their Taste confine,
> And glitt'ring Thoughts struck out at ev'ry Line;
> Pleas'd with a Work where nothing's just or fit;
> One *glaring Chaos* and *wild Heap* of *Wit:*
> Poets like Painters, thus, unskill'd to trace
> The *naked Nature* and the *living Grace,*
> With *Gold* and *Jewels* cover ev'ry Part,
> And hide with *Ornaments* their *Want of Art.*
> *True Wit* is *Nature* to Advantage drest,
> What oft was *Thought,* but ne'er so well *Exprest,*
> *Something,* whose Truth convinc'd at Sight we find,
> That gives us back the Image of our Mind:
> As Shades more sweetly recommend the Light,
> So modest Plainness sets off sprightly Wit:
> For *Works* may have more *Wit* than does 'em good,
> As *Bodies* perish through Excess of *Blood* . . .
> . . . true *Expression,* like th' unchanging *Sun,*
> *Clears,* and *improves* whate'er it shines upon,
> It *gilds* all Objects, but it *alters* none.
> Expression is the *Dress* of *Thought,* and still
> Appears more *decent* as more *suitable.*
> (289–304, 315–319)

In this sample showing the range of the poem's pervasive light imagery, "glitt'ring" and "*glaring*" describe the false; true wit is simple "Light"; true expression, more specifically, resembles "th' unchanging *Sun.*"[12] Almost as emphatic are the metaphors from painting (the four-line comparison of poets and painters, the suggested manipulation of shadow and light in line 301, the reference to gilding in line 317) and the two important metaphors of dress. Then there is an implicit metaphor of building in line 292, a mirror image in lines 299–300, a submerged analogy to people in line 302, and a blood simile in lines 303–304.

The multiplicity of reference in twenty-one lines is bewildering and compelling. John Aden has demonstrated, with special reference to "Nature," how elaborate a battery of poetic devices Pope brings to bear in this poem to make sure of engaging the reader's attention.[13] Such a multiplicity of imagery makes it difficult to paraphrase Pope's meaning but adds to their richness of implication.

In the passage quoted above, the first painting metaphor is crucial to an understanding of the "*True Wit*" couplet that develops from it. The antithesis is not, as might appear at first glance, between the skilled painter who can trace "The *naked Nature*" and the unskilled one who loads her with jewels; rather, it is, between the painter skilled enough to dress her properly—"to Advantage"—and the mere decorator. No painter, no poet, is sufficiently deft to duplicate nature without alteration; his choice concerns only the nature of the alteration. Wit's mirror does not reflect the truth of the outside world, only "the Image of our Mind."

The mirror and the lamp are often associated with opposed views of the creative process: the mirror-metaphor is more classic, the lamp more romantic in implication.[14] It is characteristic of Pope to define wit as both a light-giving and a reflective power. Many metaphors in the *Essay on Criticism* invite a view of Pope as a kind of Ur-Coleridge, full of awe for a creative power that he associates with the sun and with divinity, urging reverence for genius and its mysterious force. But other metaphors always qualify such images, or in their elaboration these images qualify themselves.[15] Wit concerns itself with "The *naked Nature* and the *living Grace*," is equated with the vast energy of Nature, and is analogous to blood, the vital fluid. Substitute "imagination" for "wit" in these instances, and they suggest the romantics. But wit can also produce the "*glaring Chaos*" for which the poet has only contempt; it creates proper dress, not the nakedness which the romantics would have found more glamorous; it concerns itself more with relatively superficial expression than with thought, and it can (like blood) produce disease if its excessive energy is not controlled. The antiromantic images that stress the necessity of control qualify the conception. Wit's function as ordering power is as important as its creative force; different sets of images stress each aspect.

Pope's awareness of the value of multiple analogies emerges in many of his notes to the *Iliad.* Although he admits the possibility that an object may be "lost amidst too great a Variety of different Images," he points out that in Homer "the principal Image is more strongly impress'd on the Mind by a Multiplication of Similes."[16] His effort to impress the idea of wit on the mind by multiplication of similies is different in technique from the predecessors he may have used as direct models. The Duke of Buckingham and the Earl of Roscommon, with whose accomplishments Addison equated Pope's,[17] spell out to the point of tedium the implications of a single metaphor; rarely do they rely on diversity of reference. When they do, their purposes are simpler than Pope's. A sample passage from Buckingham's *Essay on Poetry* concerns "genius":

> A Spirit which inspires the Work throughout,
> As that of Nature moves the World about;
> A Flame that glows amidst Conceptions fit;
> Ev'n something of Divine, and more than Wit;
> It self unseen, yet all things by it shown,
> Describing all Men, but describ'd by none.
> Where dost thou dwell? What Caverns of the Brain
> Can such a vast and mighty thing contain?
> When I, at vacant Hours, in vain thy Absence mourn,
> Oh where dost thou retire? and why dost thou return,
> Sometimes with pow'rful Charms to hurry me away,
> From Pleasures of the Night, and Bus'ness of the Day?
> Ev'n now too far transported, I am fain
> To check thy Course, and use the needful Rein.[18]

The difference between this and the passage quoted above from the *Essay on Criticism* is the difference between good poetry and bad; but the role of imagery in creating that difference is instructive. Here, too, is a variety of reference. Genius is a spirit analogous to the divine spirit, a flame, a light, a "vast and mighty thing," a possessor of magic power, a horse. But the multiplicity creates confusion rather than clarification, emphasized by the vagueness of "Ev'n something of Divine, and more than Wit" and of "a vast and mighty thing." The inadvertent effect of the poet's references to himself is to suggest that his lines demonstrate what they in part describe: the effect of genius's absence.

Pope's metaphors reinforce one another; Buckingham's cancel one another out. If a reader is troubled, in the lines from *An Essay on Criticism,* by a sense that the dress metaphor is unduly "low," or that it does not relate coherently to the exalted imagery of light, the poet deals with such an objection by using one dress metaphor to explain the other. In the second use of the image, the power of dress is directly associated with that of the sun,which "*gilds* all Objects, but it *alters* none." Typographical stress on the verbs directs attention to a vital antithesis and recalls the more elaborate contrast between the painter who loads a human figure with jewels and the true wit that dresses reality to advantage—gilded rather than altered. The dress metaphors, light metaphors, and art metaphors have close relationships, which Pope demonstrates and emphasizes. In contrast, Buckingham's metaphors are desperate gropings at a glimpsed idea. Even if the horse of genius signifies Pegasus, it is hard to feel any coherence between genius as flame and as steed.

"Images have efficacy to move a reader's affections, to quite properly affect his judgments; they move him to feel intensely, to will, to act, to understand, to believe, to change his mind."[19] Miss Tuve's summary of the Renaissance view sheds light also on Pope's poetic practice. His purposes are emotional and moral as well as narrowly didactic. The conjunctions of imagery in the *Essay on Criticism* lend density to the poetry and deepen its philosophic and emotional implications. Individual images participate in this process as well. Such an image is Pope's figure of the "good man," who emerges gradually through the *Essay,* and who demonstrates wit's controlling power by giving reality and substance to abstract ideas. The poem's central abstractions—wit, nature, sense, judgment—achieve solidity through a variety of imagery, but its general moral doctrine depends heavily on human embodiment to generate the emotional energy to make it real to the reader.

The human image—a simplified human being who embodies and summarizes a set of moral qualities—is peculiarly important in Pope's work. In his late satiric poetry—the moral epistles, the Horatian imitations, *The Dunciad*—he turns people into images by an artificial isolation and heightening of characteristics. "The *Poem was not made for these Authors, but these Authors for the Poem,*" Pope would write of his victims in the appendix to the 1728 *Dunciad.* He thus suggests how living people became in his hands poetic devices: "And I should judge they were clapp'd in as they rose, fresh and fresh, and chang'd from day to day, in like manner as when the old boughs wither, we thrust new ones into a chimney."[20] In the *Essay on Criticism,* his primary purpose is not satiric, but his technique bears affinities to his later method. Here, too, the good man through activity exemplifies positive values. It is possible to study the way in which Pope converts a general moral idea—the notion that the good poet or critic must be a good man—into a concrete embodiment of that idea: an idealized, heightened figure, appearing in several guises, who exemplifies the virtues Pope advocates.

This figure has no physical substance; its function as image does not depend on direct sensuous appeal. Yet the way it works in the poems is the way images work. Critics who have tackled the painful task of defining imagery usually try to avoid limiting their definition to objects of sensuous reality. Caroline Spurgeon's attempt is typical. An image, she writes, "is a description or an idea, which by comparison or analogy, stated or understood, with something else, transmits to us through the emotions and associations it arouses, something of the 'wholeness,' the depth and richness of the way the writer views, conceives or has felt what he is telling us."[21] The vagueness of this definition acknowledges the difficulty of pinning down the term, as well as the fact that other forms of embodiment than physical ones ("idea" as well as "description") may solidify or enlarge the poet's statement. The solidity that Pope's virtuous figures (and for that matter his vicious ones) possess is moral solidity. By summing up and balancing moral qualities in an imagined individual, the poet gives them greater imaginative reality than they can have when their value is suggested only by sententious adjuration.

In Boileau, one of Pope's models, the idea of a connection between the creation of literature and personal uprightness took the form of general moral injunctions:

> Que les vers ne soient pas votre eternel emploi;
> Cultivez vos amis, soyez homme de foi.
> C'est peu d'etre agreable et charmant dans un livre,
> Il faut savoir encore et converser et vivre.[22]

(Don't let verse be your eternal occupation; cultivate your friends, be an honorable man. It is little enough to be agreeable in a book; one must still know how to converse and how to live.)

The lines imply a possible antithesis between the good man and the good poet: one can be agreeable and charming in a book without being so in life; to devote oneself to the eternal occupation of verse is to neglect the responsibilities of personal morality. For Pope, no such antithesis exists: the identity between the good critic and the good man is not just possible but almost necessary. Early in the *Essay*, he refers to "a Critick's noble Name" (47); the phrase's justification is moral, not literary. A succession of metaphors associates wit with good breeding. As Pope develops injunctions for the conduct of criticism, his language becomes increasingly moral, though it still concentrates on the promulgation rather than the embodiment of doctrine:

> Avoid *Extreams*; and shun the Fault of such,
> Who still are pleas'd *too little*, or *too much*.
> At ev'ry Trifle scorn to take Offence,
> That always shows *Great Pride*, or *Little Sense*.
> (384–387)

The conduct of the good critic is that of the good man. After Pope warns that one should not "let the *Man* be lost" in the critic, he adds, "*Good-Nature* and *Good-Sense* must ever join; / To Err is *Humane*; to Forgive, Divine" (524–525). He is urging his readers—in their roles as men and as critics—to partake of divinity through high morality. One is to "make each Day a *Critick* on the last" (571). This line exemplifies the union of literary and human concern. One need not choose between human and literary activity; the two are identical.

None of these references gives concrete form to the notion of the good man. Even the metaphors of good breeding are so general that they lack the force of images: "As Men of Breeding, sometimes Men of Wit, / T'avoid *great Errors,* must the *less* commit" (259–60). Yet an image lurks behind the moral injunctions, and it finally achieves reality, strengthened by the broad religious context earlier established. The last lines of the poem's first section enunciate a mythology of art in the most exalted terms:

> Still green with Bays each *ancient* Altar stands,
> Above the reach of *Sacrilegious* Hands,
> Secure from *Flames,* from *Envy's* fiercer Rage,
> Destructive *War,* and all-involving *Age* . . .
> Hail *Bards Triumphant*! born in *happier Days*;
> *Immortal Heirs* of *Universal* Praise!
> Whose Honours with Increase of Ages *grow,*
> As Streams roll down, *enlarging* as they flow!
> Nations *unborn* your might Names shall sound,
> And Worlds applaud that must not yet be *found*!
> Oh may some Spark of *your* Coelestial Fire,
> The last, the meanest of your Sons inspire,
> (That, on weak Wings, from far, pursues your Flights;
> *Glows* while he *reads,* but *trembles* as he *writes*)
> (181–184, 189–198)

The tone resembles that of the visionary ending of *Windsor-Forest,* but the vision is artistic, not political, and it concentrates on the past more than the future. The energy of the account derives from the tension between Pope's sense of the permanence of these deities and their monuments, and his awareness of the unbridgeable gap between past and present. The restoration of order depends on looking to the past, to which alone can be applied the emphatic language of permanence. Always adorned, always young, always marked with emblems of honor, the poetry of the past looms above the poets of the present, impregnable and universal: "above the reach," "secure," "triumphant," "immortal," "universal." As time passes, the bards become only more secure, their fame enlarging like a flowing stream.

The result of contemplating the "monuments of unaging intellect" is new moral awareness. The speaker understands precariousness as well as permanence; he knows the forces of destruction, including natural energies (flames); human passion, individual and collective (envy and war); the mortality of people and objects ("all-involving *Age*"). Sacrilegious hands always reach to destroy. Praise of "*happier Days*" also implies an unhappy present. Because the possibility of enduring fame is therefore slender, the poet must find a position that justifies his vocation independently of the hope of fame.

It is in this context that Pope introduces into the poem a version of himself—a preliminary and vague image. The exaggerated humility of his pose ("The last, the meanest of your Sons") is justified by the dilemma that produces it: humility is the moral doctrine of this religion of art. The resolution of the poet's problem is moral, not artistic; the speaker declares his aspiration "To teach vain Wits a Science *little known, / T'admire* Superior Sense, and *doubt* their own!" (199–200). Having learned humility from contemplating the past, he proposes to teach it. The identification of poet-critic-good man derives from the moral necessity created by the gap between present and past. Thomas Edwards, discussing the writer's role as hero in this poem, has remarked: "by his continuation of an 'epic' literary past, by his demonstration that the present need not be wholly worthless when measured by classical standards, the writer-hero in his own person reconciles the actual and the ideal. His craft perpetuates values, and it proves that time can be challenged, if not conquered."[23] The writer's perpetuation of values, however, comes less from his craft than from his character—character which must, Pope suggests, both form and be formed by his vocation. This is precisely the notion conveyed by his self-portrayal in his letters. Commitment to wit, like commitment to God, requires discipline, self-knowledge, relinquishment of lesser ideals. Such a commitment, its full range and weight recognized, is an important subject of the *Essay*.

Toward the end of the poem, Pope gives his moral doctrine a

local habitation and several names. Now the standard of virtue takes form in a hypothetical figure, whose characteristics must be familiar to any reader of Pope's later satiric poetry.

> But where's the Man, who Counsel *can* bestow,
> Still *pleas'd* to *teach,* and yet not *proud* to *know?*
> Unbiass'd, or by *Favour* or by *Spite;*
> Not *dully prepossest,* nor *blindly right;*
> Tho' Learn'd, well-bred; and tho' well-bred, sincere;
> Modestly bold, and Humanly severe . . .
> Blest with a *Taste* exact, yet unconfin'd;
> A *Knowledge* both of *Books* and *Humankind;*
> *Gen'rous Converse;* a *Soul* exempt from *Pride;*
> And *Love to Praise,* with Reason on his Side?
> (631–636, 639–642)

Compare this later version:

> The Sense to value Riches, with the Art
> T'enjoy them, and the Virtue to impart,
> Not meanly, nor ambitiously pursu'd,
> Not sunk by sloth, nor rais'd by servitude;
> To balance Fortune by a just expence,
> Join with Oeconomy, Magnificence;
> With Splendour, Charity; with Plenty, Health;
> Oh teach us, BATHURST! yet unspoil'd by wealth!
> (*Epistle to Bathurst,* 219–226)

In one case criticism is the subject; in the other, wealth. More than twenty years lie between the composition of the two poems; yet the form of the moral ideal remains the same. In both poems, Pope values the balancing of extremes, the virtue of the middle way, taking in and giving out as complementary activities. And the function of the figure who embodies the ideal is the same in the satiric and the nonsatiric poem, although in one case he is a hypothesis from the past ("Such once were *Criticks,*" 643), and in the other he has a specific modern identity. Both figures function as images rather than realities—like reverses of the images of Sporus and Bufo in the *Epistle to Dr. Arbuthnot.* Pope's portrayals of those he admires and those he detests alike are heightened to emblematic proportions. They provide the most forceful indications of his standards and values.

Beginning at line 724 of the *Essay on Criticism,* Pope names two writers who embody the union of intellectual and moral value suggested by the earlier idealized portrait and by the moral stress of the entire poem. They are Wentworth Dillon, fourth Earl of Roscommon ("not more *learn'd* than *good,*" 725) and William Walsh ("The *clearest Head,* and the *sincerest Heart,*" 732). Then he returns to self-description, personifying himself as a muse. This is a daring way to end the poem, and an appropriate one. Pope himself becomes an image, as he was to do again in the Horatian imitations, and demonstrates, through his capacity to fictionalize in this way, his determination to embody the fusion of criticism, poetry, and morality that has been the ideal throughout the poem. Declaring his intention to confine himself to "low Numbers," he elaborates:

> Content, if hence th' Unlearn'd their Wants may view,
> The Learn'd reflect on what before they knew:
> Careless of *Censure,* nor too fond of *Fame,*
> Still pleas'd to *praise,* yet not afraid to *blame,*
> Averse alike to *Flatter,* or *Offend,*
> Not *free* from Faults, nor yet too vain to *mend.*
>
> (739–744)

The antithetical form of the verse heightens awareness of the affinities between this description and the earlier account of the ideal man. This mortal muse is subject to criticism himself, in his role as poet ("Careless of *Censure,* nor too fond of *Fame*"); he is also a critic, who praises and blames; but his ultimate concerns are moral ("Not *free* from Faults, nor yet too vain to *mend*"). In fact, the "faults" of the final line may be moral, poetic, or critical, it hardly matters, for all three, the poem's imagery has demonstrated, are finally the same.

The idea that the poet must be a good man[24] is less important in the poem than the way in which it is propounded, through embodiment in images that engineer the reader's assent to the proposition by making him feel the fusion of the qualities. The poet-critic-hero emerges only gradually, but by the end of the poem he is a well-defined figure, both the poet's *persona* and his central subject.

The complex relations among Pope's images involve variations of form as well as content. For example:

> Others for *Language* all their Care express,
> And value *Books,* as Women *Men,* for *Dress*:
> Their Praise is still—*The Stile is excellent*:
> The *Sense,* they humbly take upon Content.
> Words are like *Leaves*; and where they most abound,
> Much *Fruit* of *Sense* beneath is rarely found.
> *False Eloquence,* like the *Prismatic Glass,*
> Its gawdy Colours spreads on *ev'ry place.*
>
> (305–312)

In this profusion of imagery, one image merges with or yields to another: a sexual implication combines with a reference to dress; both give way to an image from external nature, then to a simile about the division of light (the poem's primal power), in which science becomes art as the prism spreads gaudy color like a poor painter. Equally important is the intricate relation between metaphor and simile. Three of the four couplets contain both devices (the second couplet, which elaborates the meaning of the first, has neither). The effect is to make the metaphors seem like literal statements, and thus greatly to increase their force. That man regards books as dress; that sense is the proper fruit of wit (a fresh approach to the generation theme); that eloquence displays gaudy colors—these are the truths to which Pope's technique calls special attention. The similes, by comparison, seem decorative. They broaden the context and display a limited version of the poet's wit; most of all, they heighten the significance of the accompanying metaphors and direct awareness to them.

It may be argued that there is no essential difference of effect between "Words are like *Leaves*" and "Much *Fruit* of *Sense* beneath is rarely found," that the kind of meaning is in both instances essentially the same. Certainly the distinction between metaphor and simile is tenuous at best, and difficult to generalize about even within an individual poem. In this case, the context rather than the substance of metaphor and simile demands that a distinction be made between them. The juxtaposition of contrasting syntactical modes forces awareness of their differences. Pope's more detailed development of the metaphors, in conjunction with the manifest artificiality of the similes, suggests that the metaphors carry more important messages.

It is notable that the pattern of equivalences established by the crucial light imagery depends largely on metaphor rather than simile, a fact that reinforces the sense of value created by the religious implications of many of the equivalences. Two exceptions have already been quoted:

> As Shades more sweetly recommend the Light,
> So modest Plainness sets off sprightly Wit.
> ( 301–302)

> But true *Expression,* like th' unchanging *Sun,*
> *Clears,* and *improves* whate'er it shines upon.
> (315–316)

In both instances, the reference of the light imagery is less weighty than in the dominant structure of metaphors. The kind of "Wit" referred to in the first couplet is not the transcendent creative power but a relatively trivial deftness and economy of expression. The power of "*Expression*" is important—bad expression can nullify good thought—but perhaps less vital than the vast forces that light as metaphor defines. In both cases the similes establish an analogy, not only between the two terms compared but between them and the other forces that have been defined in terms of light. They also support a hierarchy. In the metaphors, analogy moves toward identity. The similes, by their connecting terms, insist that they describe *only* analogies, and thus remind the reader that lesser powers, though resembling greater ones, remain lesser.

It is through the light metaphors that Pope makes the boldest suggestions in the poem. "And indeed," he was later to write, "they who would take Boldness from Poetry, must leave Dulness in the room of it."[25] By a series of equations he indicates that "Heav'n" (or alternately "Nature") is the source of light, then that Nature itself, "divinely bright," is "One *clear, unchang'd,* and *Universal* Light" (71). Truth, another source of light, is therefore equivalent to Nature ("*Truth* breaks upon us with *resistless Day,*" 212), and Wit is equivalent to both (470–473, 648, 659). Wit, the imagery suggests, has a lower position in the hierarchy than the cosmic forces; it is identified with "fire" and "light" more often than with the sun and, in one important metaphor, is produced by rather than identical with the "sun" of Nature or Heaven:

> Meanly they seek the Blessing to confine,
> And force *that Sun* but on a *Part* to Shine;
> Which not alone the *Southern Wit* sublimes,
> But ripens Spirits in cold *Northern Climes.*
> (398–401)

The human creative force partakes of the divine nature but does not duplicate it, although it may be seen as itself a sun which "too powerful Beams displays" (470), producing by its energy the clouds that obscure it.

The association of wit with divinity, substantiated by the poem's many references to religion, exemplifies the way in which Pope uses imagery to make precise a set of complex implications concerning value as well as meaning. William Empson has commented, "The performance inside the word *wit,* I should maintain, was intended to be quite obvious and in the sunlight, and was so for the contemporary reader; that was why he thought the poem so brilliant."[26] Imagery elucidates this performance, as Empson's own discussion makes clear. Evaluative as well as explanatory, the imagery becomes almost unimaginably complex. Considering only the term *wit* in connection with the images that describe it, one discovers a bewildering range. At one extreme, wit is associated with divinity; at another, it becomes:

The *Owner's Wife*, that *other Men* enjoy,
Then most our *Trouble* still when most *admir'd*,
And still the more we *give*, the more *requir'd*;
Whose Fame with *Pains* we guard, but lose with *Ease*,
Sure *some* to *vex*, but never *all* to *please*.
(501–505)

The difference between the two versions of wit is less in definition than in evaluation. Wit from the point of view of its inventor is an awe-inspiring power, a duplication of the divine creative force. Considered from a broader, "public" point of view, its value is ambiguous. Its audience may value it highly but misapprehend its nature; it may be a burden to its possessor because it cannot remain private; and once displayed, it may be misunderstood.

The sensitivity to varying possibilities demonstrated by the poem's metaphoric implications gives energy, complexity, and authority to *An Essay on Criticism*. It is tempting to speculate about whether Pope's mode of imagery represents a new eighteenth-century direction. Though the images in their variety and inventiveness recall the extravagances of metaphysical poetry, the poem as a whole does not. Considering it in comparison with such a predecessor as Abraham Cowley's *Ode: Of Wit*, one discovers that Pope has employed many specific images from the past, but changed the method of using them.

Pope's early letters reveal his preoccupation with the relation between wit's method and its extravagances. His comments on the metaphysical poets suggest that he finds in them a troublesome lack of discipline; yet their creative energy makes it difficult for him to arrive at a negative final judgment of them. "Donne," he writes in 1706," . . . had infinitely more Wit than he wanted Versification: for the great dealers in Wit, like those in Trade, take least Pains to set off their Goods; while the Haberdashers of small Wit, spare for no Decorations or Ornaments."[27] To "set off one's goods" properly is desirable; yet one would rather be a "great dealer in Wit" than a mere "Haberdasher." Four years later, Pope is more unambiguously negative about Richard Crashaw: "All that regards Design, Form, Fable, (which is the Soul of Poetry) all that concerns exactness, or consent of parts, (which is the Body) will probably be wanting; only pretty conceptions, fine metaphors, glitt'ring expressions, and something of a neat cast of Verse, (which are properly the dress, gems, or loose ornaments of Poetry) may be found in these verses."[28] Like Johnson after him, he notes that Crashaw's thoughts, though pretty, are "oftentimes far fetch'd" (p. 110); he objects most of all to the apparent carelessness of his writing. Care in poetry—as he was to insist in the *Essay on Criticism*—is an important desideratum. Even at the age of nineteen, he refuted Wycherley's suggestion that "The sprightliness of Wit despises method." "This is true enough," Pope replied, "if by *Wit* you mean no more than *Fancy* or *Conceit*; but in the better notion of *Wit*, consider'd as propriety, surely *Method* is not only necessary for Perspicuity and Harmony of parts, but gives beauty even to the minute and particular thoughts, which receive an additional advantage from those which precede or follow in their due places."[29]

The metaphor of expression as "the dress, gems, or loose ornaments of Poetry," prominent in the *Essay on Criticism*, appears also in Cowley's poem. Superabundance of wit, the piling up of decoration, is as distasteful to Cowley as to Pope. Working toward a definition of true wit, Cowley writes:

> Yet 'tis not to adorn, and gild each part;
> That shows more Cost, then Art.
> Jewels at Nose and Lips but ill appear;
> Rather then all things Wit, let none be there.
> Several Lights will not be seen,
> If there be nothing else between.
> Men doubt, because they stand so thick i' th' sky,
> If those be Stars which paint the Galaxie.[30]

Both the metaphors and the use made of them strikingly foreshadow Pope. The jewel metaphor pays due deference to the surface effect of wit's displays while reinforcing a negative value judgment through its implication of vulgarity and barbarism. It yields gracefully to the light metaphor through the visual nature of the images: jewels, tiny sparkles of light, prepare for the idea of light in general and of stars in particular. The movement, as often in Pope, is from a trivial to a serious metaphor; and, as in Pope, images explain and define abstract statements ("Rather then all things Wit, let none be there"). The entire poem resembles the *Essay on Criticism* in its varied but often related metaphor, its fluctuating movement between abstract and concrete. Yet the most superficial reading reveals that this poem is radically different in kind from Pope's, and that the difference has something to do with the handling of imagery.

Design and form compose the soul of poetry, while consent of parts is the body. The soul and body of Pope's poem differ so radically from Cowley's that the dress, gems, and loose ornaments appear different as well. Cowley's poem exists for its metaphors. The subject of wit is a pretext for witty display, and the poem's interest derives from the ingenuity with which various metaphoric definitions are proposed and rejected. No structure, no argument, exists other than the one shaped by images. When the poet asks, "What is it, then, which like the Power Divine / We only can by Negatives define?" (55–56), one admires the ingenuity that led him to this crucial analogy and recognizes its linguistic appropriateness, but nothing in the poem's texture or substance leads one to take the comparison more seriously than the earlier reference to jewels. The ode's penultimate stanza develops comparisons between wit and the results of divine power, but their force is self-contained; "earned" only by the rejection of the preceding series of extravagant images, they grow out of no substantial development. The poem in its final lines explicitly denies the possibility of meaning contained in language. Moving back toward the complimentary tone of his opening, the speaker concludes that if anyone asks him "What thing right Wit, and height of Genius is, / I'll only shew your Lines, and say, 'Tis This." Wit can only be displayed, not discussed, as borne out by the entire poem.

Although Pope's poem, too, is an exuberant outburst of imaginative energy, its prose table of contents describes a scheme bearing little obvious relation to its structure of imagery. The relation of substance to metaphor is thus more complicated than in Cowley's ode. The "design" of the poem, the consent of its parts, involves a set of paraphrasable ideas that offer more than definitions. Here, as in Cowley, definition emerges through metaphor, but the purpose of the poem is more complex. The poet wishes to show "that most men are born with some Taste, but spoil'd by false *Education*," or to suggest "When Severity is chiefly to be used by Critics," or to offer "Rules for the *Conduct* of *Manners* in a Critic." He also wishes to make the reader respond to these ideas, suggestions, rules, and to make him understand the assumptions and convictions that lie behind them and the ramifications buried within them. The poem in a sense has two designs: to promulgate a body of doctrine, and to convey a system of feeling and belief concerning broader issues than doctrine.

Rosemond Tuve, writing of the traditional metaphor of style as dress, has explained that one meaning derives from "the notion of style as a garment in the sense that the flesh is the soul's garment, its bodying-forth or manifestation."[31] The ideal relation between metaphor and substance, Pope suggests in the *Essay on Criticism,* is of this kind. The *Essay* is an ambitious attempt to unite the disparate by the operations of wit, traditionally considered a unifying power. Pope starts with an intellectual subject and a traditional set of attitudes toward it. By the resources of figurative language, he attempts to connect this subject with the widest reaches of human experience. The images have a logic and energy more compelling than the structure of ideas about criticism that they are intended to support; the relation between the pattern of intellectual discourse and the pattern of imagery is not always perfectly lucid and expressive. Yet Pope here demonstrates through his poetic practice that wit can be a principle of control, that imagery can create as well as express ideas, and that metaphor can provide organization without comprising the sole substance of a poem.

In contrast, the sense of disjunction between the ideas outlined in Pope's prose table of contents and those conveyed by the poem itself suggests the problems inherent in making wit the primary poetic principle of control. That wit can indeed control wit, the *Essay on Criticism* triumphantly demonstrates. The authority of wit dominates the poem, enforces fine discriminations, and reveals the emotional energy of ideas. Reuben Brower has pointed out that the *Essay*'s "shiftings and turnings do not produce mere confusion, because of the control with which Pope poises his contrasts of phrase and rhythmic stress. As in the dialogue of Jane Austen, the reader finds not a blur, but alternatives distinctly defined."[32] The contrasts, the control, the distinct definitions, are to a considerable extent results of the play of imagery, which does much of the poem's work. But if wit can control wit, can it control judgment as well, reversing the traditional arrangement in which judgment is the presiding power? And what does it mean for wit, the imaginative power, to "control" the rational force of judgment?

To say that wit "enforces discriminations" is to say that it fulfills a function of judgment. But at some points in the *Essay on Criticism,* wit seems to control judgment rather in the sense of overruling it. The table of contents, as Donald Greene has pointed out, is itself fairly incoherent; it does not proceed by clear logical progression. It does, however, state explicitly a series of judgments that are the nominal subject matter of the *Essay,* which is concerned with the proper nature of criticism as judgmental activity. Though the text of the *Essay* proceeds through the headings indicated in the contents, this outline of ideas is manifestly less important than the ways in which they are presented and elaborated—ways that themselves become the poem's true subject. The section in which Pope illustrates by example while simultaneously condemning a sequence of poetic faults is one of the most memorable in the poem—but memorable for the brilliance of its display, not for its contribution to an argument. The poet describes how "*Expletives* their feeble Aid *do* join, / And ten low Words oft creep in one dull Line" (345–346). The couplet flawlessly manifests Pope's absolute control and clarity, imitating what it mocks and thus justifying the mockery. Its wit exemplifies the poet's power and declares the validity of his constant assertion that wit is a high value. Inasmuch as the purpose of the *Essay on Criticism* is to do precisely these things, it is almost always successful.

But its declared purpose is also to promulgate a body of traditional doctrine, and the brilliance of the performance interferes with the fulfillment of that end. The couplet about expletives purportedly contributes to a demonstration of the inadequacy of critics concerned with language and versification alone. In fact, it tells nothing about critics but something about poets; and what it tells most clearly is that Alexander Pope is a very skillful poet. That, in fact, is what much of the poem conveys more convincingly than anything else. To describe the *Essay* as brilliant indicates its inadequacy as well as its triumph. The *Essay on Criticism* leaves one with a sense of judgments incompletely integrated into a poetic texture. Never again would Pope give this kind of importance to imagery; never again would so much depend on the power of wit. That wit here achieves so much, functions so complexly, is the wonder of the poem.

## Three

# Word and Vision

## Donne's *Anniversarie* Poems and *An Essay on Man*

*An Essay on Man,* like *An Essay on Criticism,* has suffered because of its subject matter. Like the earlier poem, it is rich in memorable quotations, and its content too has provided material for scholarly controversy. Is its philosophy commonplace? Are its inconsistencies reconcilable? The question of whether it is really a poem at all has been relatively neglected until recently, when the commentary of Maynard Mack, Reuben Brower, and Thomas Edwards has called attention to some of its poetic brilliancies. But brilliancies alone do not make a poem. Since Martin Kallich's attempt to reveal a coherent structure of imagery in the *Essay* was only a dubious success, the problem remains of defining its sources of poetic (as opposed to philosophic) coherence.[1]

Seen as part of Pope's sequence of experiments in control, the *Essay on Man* represents an attempt to use the powers of human perception, physical and metaphysical, both as subject matter and as organizing device. The concentration on perception and its objects provides for the poem exactly the kind of coherence that has often been denied by its critics. A single aesthetic approach organizes the wealth of detail and of idea incorporated in a loose philosophic framework. The poet now turns his attention outward. Wit's assertion of connections depends on the ingenuity and energy of the creator's mind, whereas to base imagery on perception implies belief in the reality of relationships in the external world. In this sense the movement from stress on wit to emphasis on perception represents a poetic progression: not a widening range of concern, but an increasing grasp on actuality. The poet, rejecting the centrality of his own cleverness, asserts the aesthetic and philosophic vitality of the created universe. The assertion may produce an air of overinsistence, which sometimes weakens the *Essay on Man,* but also accounts for its striking increase in poetic density over the *Essay on Criticism.*

One aspect of the *Essay*'s concentration on perception is its almost obsessive concern with "seeing," as both fact and metaphor. Josephine Miles has observed that the generation of poets writing at the beginning of the eighteenth century was characterized by their "abrupt abandoning of a conceptual vocabulary in favor of a sensory descriptive one."[2] The change is most often ascribed to Locke: "The objective quality of Eighteenth-Century literature is certainly owing in part to the fact that Locke's demonstration that all ideas originate in sensation induced writers to give almost undue attention to the external world."[3] By the middle of the century, it was possible to assert that description—meaning visual description—produced virtually all emotional power in poetry.

> The power of description in poetry is very great, and there is more use made of it than is generally imagined; for however the modes of expression have been multiplied, many of them will be found to be little more than descriptions: thus images are descriptions only heightened and animated; allusions and similes, descriptions placed in an opposite point of view; epithets are generally descriptions of the substantives they precede, or some of their properties; every metaphor is a short description and comparison united; and the hyperbole is often no more than a description carried beyond the bounds of probability; and it is chiefly owing to their descriptive power that these figures strike the imagination so forcibly, and impress such lively images on the mind.[4]

The reason for the peculiar dominion of description over the emotions, unspecified in this passage, is surely that description recalls and enlarges man's perception of reality. The poet, reminding the reader of the richness of external things, demonstrates that his work is rooted in the real, although it may transform one's understanding of the outer world.

For Pope, writing a didactic philosophical poem, the problem of "reality" was acute. Thomas Tickell, who believed didactic poetry as a form was "second to Epic alone," defined its special difficulty: "To Philosophical Themes there is attached, by an inevitable bond, Obscurity, which of all qualities is most incongruous with the Nature of Poetry, since, unless Poetry is taken in at the first glance, it immediately loses its force and point."[5] Pope's statement on his "Design" for the *Essay on Man* reflects his awareness of this problem. He claims to have written his "system of Ethics" in verse rather than prose because "principles, maxims, or precepts so written, both strike the reader more strongly at first, and are more easily retained by him afterwards."[6] But he confesses that he "was unable to treat this part of my subject more in detail, without becoming dry and tedious; or more *poetically*, without sacrificing perspicuity to ornament, without wandering from the precision, or breaking the chain of reasoning." The notion of imagery as ornament here implied suggests a potential weakness of the poem; and one critic has argued that the text indeed shows an "attitude to imagery . . . strictly incompatible with the seriousness of the theme."[7]

The most important imagery of the *Essay on Man,* however, is functional, essential to the poem's argument and to its commitment to the real. The imagery's source lies in perception rather than wit—if such a distinction can be made about images existing as verbal constructs. Unlike the crucial images of the *Essay on Criticism,* those in the *Essay on Man* exist less to draw together ideas than directly to depict reality. Maynard Mack has referred to the "remarkable width of imagery and allusion . . . whose inclusion in the poem's universe dramatizes the infinite variety comprehended and reconciled in God's."[8] The poem's imagery exposes the world, illustrates the meaning of "perception," and defines perception's limits.

The main insistence of this imagery is on man's struggle to understand and accept his place in the universe, a struggle embodied as a drama of seeing. To see properly, with the artist's vision and the moralist's, is to understand—an equation characteristic of Pope's period, in which, as one commentator has put it, "unless we can understand this conception of simple seeing by a clear light as reasoning . . . we cannot fully understand . . . why description for its own sake, the setting forth of simple images, is a paramount activity of poetry."[9] The abundance of "simple images" that comprise much of the substance of the *Essay on Man* is accounted for in part by the assumed identity between seeing and reasoning, ultimately between seeing and understanding.

The natural world, as Pope presents it, contains those "who blindly creep, or sightless soar" (I, 12). These are alternate possibilities of action, but not of perception. Man "sees" little to provide solid foundation for philosophic speculation:

> Of Man what see we, but his station here,
> From which to reason, or to which refer?
> Thro' worlds unnumber'd tho' the God be known,
> 'Tis ours to trace him only in our own.
>
> (I, 19–22)

In contrast, the God he contemplates can "pierce" through immensity, "See worlds on worlds compose one universe, / Observe how system into system runs" (I, 24–25). This emblematic contrast of capacities is at the heart of the human struggle.

In Epistle I of *An Essay on Man*, an insistent series of verbs concerning sight—*see* and *observe* being most important among them—directs the reader's attention to the conflict of perspective between God and man that is the book's subject. Man aspires proudly to a greater vision than he has been given or can properly use. Yet to write a philosophic poem asserts the possibility of metaphysical vision, so that the speaker's expressed scorn for blind mortals implies—although it fails to explain—his superiority to them. Vision, however, is not an unequivocal good; this fact generates intellectual and emotional tension.

> The lamb thy riot dooms to bleed to-day,
> Had he thy Reason, would he skip and play?
> Pleas'd to the last, he crops the flow'ry food,
> And licks the hand just rais'd to shed his blood.
> Oh blindness to the future! kindly giv'n,
> That each may fill the circle mark'd by Heav'n;—
> Who sees with equal eye, as God of all,
> A hero perish, or a sparrow fall,

> Atoms or systems into ruin hurl'd,
> And now a bubble burst, and now a world.
>
> (I, 81–90)

Man does not have a microscopic eye because he is not a fly; he also lacks transcendent vision because he is not a god. But God's vision depends on the rejection of morality as man understands it, in a cosmic scheme where worlds count no more than bubbles, with God seeing "likeness in shape and destiny" where men perceive only "disparity in size and substance."[10] In this scheme partial evil contributes to universal good. The implications, while contributing to the poem's philosophical optimism, suggest its personal pessimism. If man foresaw his fate, he would see suffering and, more bitter still, suffering's unimportance. Doomed to limitation, man struggles to extend his boundaries, but extension of perception means enlargement of misery. The place of the individual in Pope's benign universe, a place in which man is defined by his blindness, is not a happy one. But then, happiness is irrelevant in the cosmic, though not the social, order.

Epistle I ends with stress on the necessity of accepting human incapacity, imagined in terms of physical metaphor:

> Know thy own point: This kind, this due degree
> Of blindness, weakness, Heav'n bestows on thee.
> Submit—
>
> (I, 283–285)

Human blindness is God's gift. The ambiguity of feeling implicit in this way of describing blindness helps to account for the atmosphere of emotional tension that provides much of the poem's energy. The argument, for all its surface assurance, dramatizes the speaker's struggle to accept. And the power to accept depends on one's way of "seeing," a fact that becomes increasingly apparent as the poem continues.

The lines of the drama sketched in Epistle I help to shape subsequent epistles as well. The second book begins with a description of the proper object of vision: "Know then thyself, presume not God to scan." The epistle's subject, its Argument asserts, is "the Nature and State of *Man*, with respect to *Himself*, as an Individual." Examining human nature, Pope concentrates on the problem of moral vision, for which he offers constant physical metaphors.

> This light and darkness in our chaos join'd,
> What shall divide? The God within the mind.
> (II, 203–204)
>
> Vice is a monster of so frightful mien,
> As, to be hated, needs but to be seen.
> (II, 217–218)
>
> Mean-while Opinion gilds with varying rays
> Those painted clouds that beautify our days.
> (II, 283–284)

Man's visual capacities provide him with a way of coming to terms, through analogy, with vital abstractions.

This epistle, too, ends with an injunction to "see," which stresses the identity of vision and understanding and the metaphorical connection between physical and metaphysical perception:

> See! and confess, one comfort still must rise,
> 'Tis this, Tho' Man's a fool, yet *God is wise*.
> (II, 293–294)

Although this resolution implies some equanimity, it reveals the same ambivalence of feeling found in the first epistle. The assertion that to know man's folly brings "comfort," in the context of awareness of God's wisdom, resembles the attribution of benevolence to God's gift of blindness. One may gain security by accepting existential ambiguities as the product of divine wisdom, yet belief in that wisdom does not entirely compensate for the bitterness of recognizing human folly.

Other parts of the second epistle, like the first, use the metaphor of physical vision to suggest discontent with the divine dispensation:

See the blind beggar dance, the cripple sing.
The sot a hero, lunatic a king;
The starving chemist in his golden views
Supremely blest, the poet in his muse.
(II, 267–270)

Such a specific evocation of human folly, introduced by the suggestion that "The fool is happy that he knows no more" (II, 264), hints by its grotesqueness the horror of the human condition. Literally it demonstrates that everyone is content with his own limitations and develops individual compensations for them. But the thesis is questionable, and its suggestions of extreme neurotic or even psychotic compensation undermine the literal assertion. The fact that the figure of the poet appears in this company is more than a joke. The poet's commitment to the imagination here seems equivalent to the illusion of the chemist who believes himself about to create gold, and it is closely related to the self-deceptions of the drunkard who fancies himself a hero, or of the beggar who pretends that musical ability makes up for blindness. Physical reality always contradicts psychic illusion. Once more, the images convey the ambiguous value of perception. Reality is blindness, lameness, drunkenness, madness, starvation; opposed to it are the mechanisms of self-deception; and the poet who hopes to substitute verbal for physical reality is, like the rest, an escapist. The *Essay*'s stress on the substantiality and significance of the physical universe implies a belief, here reflected in practice, that the poet's full responsibility is to the world without as well as the one within. Yet the poet who sees reality, sees also the necessity for escape, which is his constant temptation. However useful it may be in the short run, escape is essentially grotesque, and the poetic variety, in spite of being more sophisticated and more appealing than the others, more useful to the world at large, yet resembles them.

What there is to see in the realm of reality, physical and metaphysical, is a kind of horror, particularly when man is examined "with respect to *Himself*, as an Individual." The third epistle, however, which concerns "the Nature and State of *Man*, with respect to

*Society,*" achieves a more optimistic view of the possibilities for man's visual capacities:

> Look round our World; behold the chain of Love
> Combining all below and all above.
> See plastic Nature working to this end . . .
> See Matter next, with various life endu'd,
> Press to one centre still, the gen'ral Good.
> See dying vegetables life sustain,
> See life dissolving vegetate again.
>
> (III, 7–9, 13–16)

Man, invited to "see" and glory in his own progress, "from Nature rising slow to Art!" (III, 169), does not find his progress uninterrupted, as much of Epistle III demonstrates. But no matter what catastrophes interfere with humanity's development, the poet fills an important function in generating political improvements, always possible despite the forces of destruction:

> Poet or Patriot, rose but to restore
> The Faith and Moral, Nature gave before;
> Relum'd her ancient light, not kindled new;
> If not God's image, yet his shadow drew.
>
> (III, 285–288)

The poet's duty is to restore ancient light, to imitate the divine act of creation, by creating, if not God's image and likeness, at least His shadow. Such an act is in essence political—the function of the patriot as well as the poet—because it involves the only meaningful movement toward the public good, which, like private, depends on insight. The true light that makes vision possible is Nature's: man is dependent on the universe, which the poet interprets.

Epistle IV, concerned with the subject of happiness, again stresses an ethical context, the limitations of man's vision as opposed to God's. Happiness is "O'er-look'd, seen double, by the fool, and wise" (6); "the Learn'd are blind" (19), but so are the unlearned. Anyone may be "blind to truth, and God's whole scheme below" (93); the test of virtue is the degree of spiritual vision:

> Who sees and follows that great scheme the best,
> Best knows the blessing, and will most be blest.
> (IV, 95–96)

Blessing, Martin Kallich has pointed out, has three distinct meanings in Pope's usage: "contentment with one's place in the divine system . . . hope for a life after death, and, conventionally, exaltation or salvation in the immortal state."[11] The first meaning is primary in this couplet, but the others reverberate in the background, suggesting that precise knowledge—the knowledge implicit in the best "seeing"—teaches man to hope and promises that hope's fulfillment. The poet repeatedly invites his reader to "see" various models of virtue (as in 99–101) and urges him "To see all others faults, and feel our own" (262). The man of full vision "looks thro' Nature, up to Nature's God" (332). The importance of "seeing" emerges fully when placed in a crucial moral progression, in which the good man:

> Sees, that no being any bliss can know,
> But touches some above, and some below;
> Learns, from this union of the rising Whole,
> The first, last purpose of the human soul;
> And knows where Faith, Law, Morals, all began.
> (IV, 335–339)

From seeing to learning to knowledge, the progression is from less to more inclusive, from concrete to abstract. "God loves from Whole to Parts: but human soul / Must rise from Individual to the Whole" (361–362). Pope's stress on vision is a mode of attending to the parts, a way of emphasizing the importance of the concrete, specific, individual reality that must support wider understanding. Man rises to his greatest height through proper use of the senses, which also constitute his necessary limitation.

William Bowman Piper has written that Pope's perfected couplet form "carries a philosophical, a didactic implication: that it is necessary for limits to be put on human intellectual ambitions and, contrariwise, that the human mind, working within its proper limits, has tremendous powers . . . If a man will confine himself to the limited area of his understanding . . . he can organize and judge the totality of his knowledge and derive from it a lucid and sufficient understanding of his condition, his duties, and his destiny."[12] "Lucid and sufficient understanding" is the human goal defined in the *Essay on Man;* the process by which it is achieved is one of the poem's central concerns. And a belief in the necessity and potential power of recognized limits, which Professor Piper finds implicit in the couplet form, is explicit in the text, which asserts and demonstrates how much man sees, and how little, as well as dramatizing ways in which limited vision can provide a substructure for understanding the cosmos.

"It is . . . in the Anatomy of the Mind as in that of the Body," Pope writes in his "Design" for the *Essay;* "more good will accrue to mankind by attending to the large, open, and perceptible parts, than by studying too much such finer nerves and vessels, the conformations and uses of which will for ever escape our observation."[13] More than a hundred years earlier, John Donne, also writing about metaphysics, had taken the metaphor of the anatomy more seriously. In his two *Anniversarie* poems he anatomizes a world strikingly different from the one Pope sees. Donne's is a moral universe with physical trappings; Pope's has physical solidity and moral vagueness. If imagery for Pope is a way of seeing, it is for Donne a way of saying.

The distinction between these forms of action as realized in poetry may seem arbitrary or tenuous. "A poet's way of seeing becomes his way of saying," writes a recent critic. "To imitate and to make new is the simultaneous gesture of the poem."[14] It is true that seeing produces saying, yet something very like the converse is also true. To examine in detail how Donne presents and justifies his imagery helps to define Pope's presentation of external reality. The difference in function and nature between Donne's and Pope's imagery both reflects and conveys a different view of the universe. In both poets it is easy to perceive the essential links between rhetorical patterning and intellectual structure.

The sense of a mind in action so often commented on as integral to Donne's imagery derives partly from the special relation he notes between linguistic and existential reality. The profuse metaphors of the *Anniversarie* poems call attention to their own artifice; an insistent structure of reference to naming, singing, and the writing of poetry demands the reader's awareness of linguistic artifice.

"Her name defin'd thee, gave thee forme and frame," the speaker tells the world in *The First Anniversarie: An Anatomy of the World.*[15] Mankind, after the loss of Elizabeth Drury, "spoke no more / Then tongues, the soule being gone, the losse deplore" (53–54). Language is a source of order, a giver of form, the direct expression of soul. The death of Elizabeth Drury, whatever she represents—the Catholic Church, Queen Elizabeth, the principle of divine wisdom—was among other things a loss of speech. The "anatomy" the poet provides is necessarily verbal rather than physical; toward the end of the poem he stresses the implications of this point:

> But as in cutting up a man that's dead,
> The body will not last out to have read
> On every part, and therefore men direct
> Their speech to parts, that are of most effect;
> So the worlds carcasse would not last, if I
> Were punctuall in this Anatomy.
> Nor smels it well to hearers, if one tell
> Them their disease, who faine would think they're wel.
> Here therefore be the end: And, blessed maid,
> Of whom is meant what ever hath beene said,
> Or shall be spoken well by any tongue,
> Whose name refines course lines, and makes prose song.
> (435–446)

*Read, speech, tell* remind one of the verbal form of this "dissection." In their context they also suggest that even a literal dissection is significant largely because of accompanying words, which provide necessary interpretation of observed phenomena. The last three lines reiterate the point that the "blessed maid" sums up all verbal reality, recalling the connection between the poem as formal structure and the larger forms of the universe. A sense of this connection leads the poet to conclude that poetry is God's chosen mode of communication:

> God did make
> A last, and lastingst peece, a song. He spake
> To *Moses*, to deliver unto all,
> That song: because he knew they would let fall,
> The Law, the Prophets, and the History,
> But keepe the song still in their memory.
> (461–466)

The incomprehensibility of Elizabeth Drury's meaning does not deter the poet from believing that it is his responsibility to preserve her memory for the world: "Verse hath a middle nature: heaven keepes soules, / The grave keeps bodies, verse the fame enroules" (473–474). These concluding lines emphasize the verbal construct as well as its meaning. By preserving "fame," the valuable essence of reputation, the poet participates in the divine work of leading man toward heaven. His re-creation of essence, an ordering, form-giving activity, asserts continuing value in a devalued world.

Early in *The Second Anniversarie: Of the Progres of the Soule*, the poet addresses Elizabeth Drury, the "Immortal Mayd" who is his subject: "Thou seest mee strive for life; my life shalbe, / To bee hereafter prais'd, for praysing thee" (31–32). The value of poetry has become more personal than in the previous elegy; now the poet's search for salvation depends on his verbal activity. His emphatic insistence on the spiritual importance of poetry as act, as saying, occupies fourteen lines (31–44). Much of the poem consists of an elaborate verbal exercise (85–218), in which the speaker urges his soul to "think" through a series of vivid images of its potential experience. The joy of heaven as here evoked is partly that of losing the limitations of sense perception:

> When wilt thou shake off this Pendantery,
> Of being taught by sense, and Fantasy?
> Thou look'st through spectacles; small things seeme great,
> Below; But up unto the watch-towre get,

And see all things despoyld of fallacies:
Thou shalt not peepe through lattices of eies.

(291–296)

One thus achieves a new mode of understanding, in which the means and the object of perception are united:

Onely who have enioyd
The sight of God, in fulnesse, can thinke it;
For it is both the object, and the wit.

(440–442)

And at the end of the poem, in the earthly rather than heavenly sphere:

The purpose, and th' Autority is his [God's];
Thou art the Proclamation; and I ame
The Trumpet, at whose voice the people came.

(526–528)

In heaven, means and end are united; on earth, separation serves the purposes of ultimate unity. The poet feels himself God's trumpet, his song proclaiming what Elizabeth Drury embodied. The poem, only a verbal construct, is yet somehow identical with its subject; the poet, manipulator of words, is the instrument of God, who dictates form and meaning.

The series of references to the poet as "sayer," to the idea of poetry as a spiritual instrument, and to the importance of moving beyond commitment to data of the senses implies an awareness of artifice, which dictates not only the form but much of the meaning of the *Anniversarie* poems. Although a unified structure of allusion to sickness and health organizes a good deal of the imagery, the many images that do not fit this pattern often, by their jarringness, call attention to themselves. The rough edges of metaphysical imagery have frequently been noted, and critics have commented on the intellectual self-consciousness implicit in the creation of such imagery. "A mind as conscious of its own maneuvers as of the experience recovered thereby introduces this experience into the variables of the poem. One is aware of this mental quotient in Donne's poems both as a quality and as an efficient cause."[16] In Donne's meditations on the death of Elizabeth Drury, consciousness of the mind's maneuvers becomes an important element in the argument, for the poet's mind exemplifies the spiritual process that is the poem's subject.

The remarkable extended similes call special attention to the poet's artifice and verbal control. The comparisons in *The Second Anniversarie* that explain why the world continues though its soul has gone are so extravagant and disturbing that they demand speculation on their function:

> But as a ship which hath strooke saile, doth runne,
> By force of that force which before, it wonne,
> Or as sometimes in a beheaded man,
> Though at those two Red seas, which freely ran,
> One from the Trunke, another from the Head,
> His soule be saild, to her eternall bed,
> His eies will twinckle, and his tongue will roll,
> As though he beckned, and cal'd backe his Soul,
> He graspes his hands, and he puls up his feet,
> And seemes to reach, and to step forth to meet
> His soule; when all these motions which we saw,
> Are but as Ice, which crackles at a thaw:
> Or as a Lute, which in moist weather, rings
> Her knell alone, by cracking at her strings.
> So strugles this dead world, now shee is gone;
> For there is motion in corruption.
>
> (7–22)

"If one sets about comparing . . . the world to a beheaded man," Maynard Mack has written, "one is bound to specify in some detail the nature of the resemblances that make the image relevant; the value of the image is, as it were, generated in the process of constructing it. But it is also spent there."[17] Imagination does not continue to develop further connections. "Donne's images are for one thing a series of strenuous attempts to make us put our feet in exactly the path that will lead us through an inquiry."[18] The reader's consciousness of "strenuous attempts," of a process of construction as well as its results, is part of the meaning of the statement. He responds not only to the images directly presented, but to the way in which the presentation—so convoluted, so demanding—illuminates the power of human creativity to reshape and thus to recomprehend experience. The word is the divine creative force; by words man participates in the divine act. By imagery, which through verbal alignments reorders man's sense of meaning, he comes to understand the universe in new ways. Here he learns that the fallen world can be imagined as alive after its "death" in the teeming vermin of "corruption." What the reader is made to "see" is only incidental, whereas what the poet says, the ways his manipulation of language controls intellectual possibility, is crucial.

The distinction between the *Essay on Man* as a poem of seeing and *The Anniversaries* as poems of saying is a matter of emphasis, however, not of absolute divergence. In *The Dunciad* Pope was to demonstrate a concern with the possibilities of verbal control at least equal to Donne's, although used for very different purposes. But in the most literally metaphysical of his poems, his greater stress on perception both explains and reflects the *Essay's* special technique and purpose.

A simpler instance of Donne's concern with saying may clarify its implications. In *The First Anniversarie* two couplets comment on human birth:

> We are borne ruinous: poor mothers crie,
> That children come not right, nor orderly,
> Except they headlong come, and fall upon
> An ominous precipitation.
>
> (95–98)

Frank Manley cited a passage from the *Sermons* that elaborates the same point: "What miserable revolutions and changes, what downfals, what break-necks, and precipitations may we justly think our selves ordained to, if we consider, that in our comming into this world out of our mothers womb, we doe not make account that a childe comes right, except it come with the head forward, and thereby prefigure that headlong falling into calamities which it must suffer after?" He also points out that the word *precipitation* involves an etymological pun: *prae* plus *caput, headfirst*.[19] Donne's frequent use of serious puns reflects his concern with the verbal. The conceit about birth—in its prose and poetic versions alike—depends on a linguistic trick: the dual implications of *headlong*. It is an example of that false wit which Addison was to condemn, the kind depending on resemblance of words rather than of ideas;[20] but it is appropriate to Donne's purposes and to the meaning of his poem. Such verbal trickery demonstrates and illuminates the power of the word.

When Donne compares his subject's virtue to the serpent's poison, he provides a particularly dramatic instance of his way of using imagery:

> But as some Serpents poison hurteth not,
> Except it be from the live Serpent shot,
> So doth her vertue need her here, to fit
> That unto us; she working more then it.
> (409–412)

The wrenches of Donne's verbal manipulation lead to new modes of perception, though they are not visual. Since *working* can mean working like a poison or working like a virtuous woman, the snake's ejection of venom is understood as natural and hence proper, though not for this reason necessarily "good." On a further level of abstraction, based on the traditional symbolic value of the serpent, the ways in which evil operates may mysteriously parallel the ways in which goodness achieves its effects. The meaning if not the fact of head-first birth is understood in a new light. By being organized in new ways, the data of sense perception assume new meanings. But the progression from "seeing" to "knowing" is not inevitable for Donne, as it seems to be for Pope, who has faith that man can look "thro Nature, up to Nature's God" (IV, 332). In Pope, the development from visual to spiritual perception precedes and justifies its linguistic presentation. Donne's poems show a working out of individual perception understood more as a result of man's effort than of God's power; that is, God's power works through the medium of the poet's wit.

The density of texture that marks the *Anniversarie* poems depends heavily on abundant metaphors, often unstressed, which succeed one another rapidly and interact in complex and surprising ways. Their referents may be visual, but they often draw the reader's attention away from visual reality. "Neither is the *Imagination* simply and onely a Messenger," Bacon wrote; "but is invested with, or at least wise usurpeth no small authoritie in it selfe; besides the duty of the Message."[21] The imaginative authority of Donne's metaphors is so great that they seem to create a new kind of reality.

> But this were light, did our lesse volume hold
> All the old Text; or had we chang'd to gold
> Their silver; or dispos'd into lesse glas,
> Spirits of vertue, which then scattred was.
> But 'tis not so: w'are not retir'd, but dampt;
> And as our bodies, so our mindes are cramp't:
> 'Tis shrinking, not close-weaving, that hath thus,
> In minde and body both bedwarfed us.
> We seeme ambitious, Gods whole worke t'undoe;
> Of nothing he made us, and we strive too,
> To bring our selves to nothing backe; and we
> Do what we can, to do't so soone as hee.
>
> (*The First Anniversarie*, 147–158)

The first-person pronouns add special pressure to the argument here. To shift from seeing ourselves as books to understanding ourselves as alchemists, then as pieces of cloth, requires almost impossible mental agility. In a variation on the rhetorical technique of *praeteritio*, the poet rejects the first two metaphors in favor of the degrading third, with its emphatic series of denigrating verbs ("dampt," "cramp't," "bedwarfed"): in fact, the reader is required to accept it alone among the three possibilities. But all three have in common a peculiarity: while they unify the disparate, which is metaphor's traditional function, they also enforce an awareness of separation. They not only bring about an understanding of one thing in terms of another, but they at the same time insist on the divergence of the two things being compared ("A Metaphor is nothing but a comparison drawn into a word").[22] Specifically, while inviting one to think of (not "see") men as objects, they also require a continuing awareness of the literal nature of men. *Volume,* in addition to meaning "book," has specific reference to the smallness of human stature, which is here Donne's point of departure. In the second metaphor, men are imagined simultaneously as alchemists and as the object of their endeavors: they are "gold" or "silver" as well as workers on metal; they both embody and dispose "Spirits of vertue." Though the cloth metaphor seems more singly developed, the final verb, "bedwarfed," returns to a consciousness of people, not just substance. The poet thus reminds his readers steadily that his metaphors represent consciously selected ways of talking about things, a fact also conveyed by the rejection of two images in favor of a third. Metaphors are pieces of language more than of perception; their reality is linguistic and intellectual.

Words, however, and particularly metaphors, point to something outside themselves. It would be ridiculous to suggest that the effect of Donne's metaphors has nothing directly to do with external reality. But the difficulty of shifting ground as fast as the metaphors seem to demand moves the mind toward generalization and makes one struggle for a unifying idea. The metaphors just quoted all emphasize distinctions between appearance and function. Appearance, they reiterate, hardly matters; the meaning of appearance depends on the activity that produces it. If man's small stature means condensation rather than dispersion, or is the smallness appropriate to a precious metal, or represents a close weave rather than shrinkage—that is, if the action that creates the smallness is valuable, so is the smallness. The varied metaphors restate this single point, and after the series of concrete images, the final reiteration enlarges the terms to a cosmic scale. Man's obsessive self-destruction is hubristic, a proof of his pride and his insane competition with God. In the light of this assertion, the preceding metaphors, which have seemed to derive their contemptuous tone merely from the contrasts inherent in them, acquire new authority. Contempt is the only proper response, not only for man's pettiness—which each metaphor has called to the reader's attention—but for his presumptuousness, his effort to achieve dignity by destroying himself.

Despite their specificity and detail, Donne's images rarely direct attention to simple visual facts.Though imagery, he explicitly declares that other modes of reality are more significant:

> Sight is the noblest sense of any one,
> Yet sight hath onely color to feed on,
> And color is decayed: summers robe growes
> Duskie, and like an oft dyed garment showes.
> Our blushing redde, which us'd in cheekes to spred,
> Is inward sunke, and onely our soules are redde.
> Perchance the world might have recovered,
> If she whom we lament had not beene dead:
> But shee, in whom all white, and redde, and blue
> (Beauties ingredients) voluntary grew,
> As in an unvext Paradise; from whom
> Did all things verdure, and their lustre come,
> Whose composition was miraculous,
> Being all color, all Diaphanous,
> (For Ayre, and Fire but thicke grosse bodies were,
> And liveliest stones but drowsie, and pale to her,)
> Shee, shee is dead; shee's dead: when thou knost this,
> Thou knowst how wan a Ghost this our world is.
> (*The First Anniversarie*, 353–370)

The wan ghost of the final line has no physical existence, for the poet has systematically removed physical meaning from color terms. The red of the cheeks has become the red of sinful souls; literal color yields to metaphorical. The woman—or essence, or spirit—who is the source of "verdure" and "lustre," terms ordinarily describing physical phenomena, deprives those terms of sensuous content. They too seem like metaphors, as is the miraculous composition of the poet's subject, which is both "all color" and "all Diaphanous," making air and fire seem gross by comparison and brilliant jewels "drowsie, and pale." Truly knowing the death of which the poet writes leads to a new apprehension of the meaning of such a word as *wan,* which may concern the essence, not the accidents, of the human condition.

The process through which the soul transcends the need for physical seeing is a subject also of *The Second Anniversarie,* where the paradox that perfect sense-perception depends on liberation from the senses becomes explicit: "Hee that charm'd Argus eies, sweet Mercury, / Workes not on her, who now is growen all Ey" (199–200). She is "all Ey" because she no longer depends on eyes but "sees" in more immediate and spiritualized ways:

> For when our soule enjoyes this her third birth,
> (Creation gave her one, a second, grace,)
> Heaven is as neare, and present to her face,
> As colours are, and objects, in a roome
> Where darknesse was before, when Tapers come.
> (214–218)

The freedom of death is a freedom of illumination, in whicn spiritual reality becomes perceptible, as physical facts were before. Donne moves away from emphasis on seeing as the most crucial mode of perception but reveals its importance as metaphor. Representing man's physicality, the senses can also provide metaphors for his spiritual capacities, both analogous to and divergent from his bodily possibilities.

The distinction between "seeing" and "saying," which is crucial to an understanding of these very different poets, represents a kind of shorthand, reducing to single words a complex differentiation. Dealing with similar concepts, Jean Hagstrum has written, "The poet of the metaphysical and baroque seventeenth century tended to be emblematic and symbolic, to suggest the world of invisible reality, or to express private, esoteric, and individual meaning. The poet of the neoclassical eighteenth century tended to be pictorial and natural and to suggest, however briefly, the reality of nature and normative human experience."[23] This carefully balanced and exact statement contains, for most twentieth century minds, clear implications of value. Consider the relative excitement of "emblematic and symbolic" as opposed to "pictorial and natural," "invisible reality" versus "the reality of nature," "esoteric, and individual" in comparison with "normative." At every point, the critic seems to say, the seventeenth century poet provides something rich and demanding, while his eighteenth century counterpart offers what is apparent. Although it is possible to argue the complexity of the apparent, the fact remains that "metaphysical" poetry has qualities that one immediately responds to as "poetic," and that even as little quotation as here has been provided from the *Essay on Man* and the *Anniversarie* poems is likely to reinforce the assumption that "metaphysical" poetry is inherently more exciting than "neoclassical."

The reasons for that judgment deserve examination. Although Donne will triumph with most modern readers on the basis of his direct emotional appeal, there are other conceivable foundations for poetic value. When Pope remarked, "Donne had no imagination, but as much wit I think as any writer can possibly have," he may have meant approximately what Hagstrum meant, but with different evaluations (though his abstractions are hard to pin down).[24] Donne's poetry of "saying" is poetry of wit in several senses of that vexed term; and Pope's poetry of "seeing" is poetry of imagination in its common eighteenth century meaning ("by the pleasures of the imagination . . . I . . . mean such as arise from visible objects"[25]) and at its best in the Coleridgean sense as well. Donne, in his concentration on verbal reality, moved toward the situation of Swift's spider, spinning a creation out of his own guts, trying "to avoid not only the cloudy and the hackneyed but all images with familiar emotional associations."[26] Pope, that admirable bee, sought sweetness and light in the world without, making honey from existent flowers. But Swift's argument about the superiority of bees to spiders is more moral than aesthetic, as is Pope's tone when he explains his progression of concern "From sounds to things, from fancy to the heart" (*Essay on Man,* IV, 392). The problem remains whether the approach to art through perception—through metaphysical as well as physical perception—is aesthetically as well as morally viable.

The immediate justification for Pope's kind of perception is clearly moral. It is equally clear that moral and aesthetic justifications are difficult to distinguish from one another in the context he creates. Consider, for example, one of the great passages from Epistle III of the *Essay on Man,* which in its tonal complexity and condensation is characteristic of Pope's highest achievement in the poem. Tone and emotional power depend here, as always, on what is essentially a moral attitude toward physical phenomena:

> Is thine alone the seed that strews the plain?
> The birds of heav'n shall vindicate their grain:
> Thine the full harvest of the golden year?
> Part pays, and justly, the deserving steer:
> The hog, that plows not nor obeys thy call,
> Lives on the labours of this lord of all.
> Know, Nature's children all divide her care;
> The fur that warms a monarch, warm'd a bear.
> While Man exclaims, "See all things for my use!"
> "See man for mine!" replies a pamper'd goose;
> And just as short of Reason he must fall,
> Who thinks all made for one, not one for all . . .
> That very life his [man's] learned hunger craves,
> He saves from famine, from the savage saves;
> Nay, feasts the animal he dooms his feast,
> And, 'till he ends the being, makes it blest;
> Which sees no more the stroke, or feels the pain,
> Than favour'd Man by touch etherial slain.
> The creature had his feast of life before;
> Thou too must perish, when thy feast is o'er!
> (III, 37–48, 63–70)

This complex discussion of the relation between man and the lower animals gains force from the specificity—rarely visual—with which individual animals are imagined. The demonstrated imaginative power is situational: it consists in a capacity to conceive and render conjunctions, situations, possibilities with vividness and strength. The capacity to exploit verb tenses ("warms a monarch" versus "warm'd a bear"), unlikely alternatives to actuality (the glimpsed possibility of a hog that obediently plows and answers its master's call), and linguistic ambiguity ("pamper'd," containing within itself the opposed meanings of being cosseted for one's own pleasure or for someone else's) are all part of Pope's imaginative agility and his imaginative control. Delicately manipulated ironies keep one always slightly off-balance. Like so many crucial effects of the *Essay on Man,* they are ironies of perspective. Man "sees" all for his own use; the goose "sees" man as existing for his own convenience; and the thinker who "sees" all as made for one, is as short-sighted as they. Indeed, shortness of sight is the passage's theme; breadth of perspective belongs only to the poet.

The ironic conjunction of human and animal points of view was a conventional device in Pope's time. Just such a conjunction provides most of the comedy in the fourth book of *Gulliver's Travels.* Given Gulliver's account of the relation between men and horses in England, a Houyhnhmn can "see" clearly that horses are really the masters there that men suppose themselves to be. John Gay writes of a flea who urges man to "Be humble, learn thyself to scan," so that he can see that heaven and earth are "made only for our need; / That more important Fleas might feed."[27] Gay's other *Fables* provide repeated examples of how the world might look to the lower animals. Pope, unlike Gay but like Swift, pursues the implications of what might be merely a rhetorical device until it becomes philosophical. His imagery depends on an implicit syllogism: man has absolute power over animals; God has absolute power over man; therefore God is to man as man is to animals. First the poet fantasizes about animals with human rights and capacities: the steer is "deserving," the bear shares the monarch's luxury. Then he reduces human complexities to the animal level: man's life is only an extended "feast," in which he dies unknowing as the ox; metaphysics is a disguise for brutality. The meaning of everything depends on how one "sees" it. Through imagery, the exaltation of animals and the reduction of man becomes real. By imagery the poet controls the reader's vision, both of details and of wholes.

As Samuel Johnson pointed out, the paraphrasable content of these lines consists of truisms, yet Pope's technique ensures an emotional response to such commonplaces. Though the passage lacks the kind of surprises that Donne always provides, it offers surprises of its own. Its energy and economy hurry the reader along so that he is not aware of how complicated the argument, how ambiguous the tone. The first couplet ("Is thine alone the seed that strews the plain? / The birds of heav'n shall vindicate their grain") exemplifies the richness of implication achieved by the conjunction of points of view. Two images are suggested though not described: one of men seeding their fields, another of birds eating the seeds. The first image evokes an automatic and conventional set of feelings; the second undercuts those feelings. The imagery's emotional demands are quiet, but they determine the passage's effect. "Seed that strews the plain" conveys a human attitude toward a human activity: man strews seed with a plan to harvest. To birds, however, the seed man understands as potential grain represents actual sustenance. They are the "birds of heaven" not only because they fly, but because God watches over sparrows; their "vindication" is simpler but more telling than the poet's, consisting in action testifying to their position rather than in argument. Man, claiming sole rights to his seed, exemplifies the human tendency toward arrogance, which the birds in their naturalness rebuke. The couplet has delicately comic overtones, in its use of the verb *vindicate* and its indication that the plans of powerful man are inevitably thwarted by tiny birds. It enforces a serious point, yet suggests that one possible (though partial) response is amusement—at man's self-importance and at the ways it is reproved by the natural world.

The entire passage is rich in verbal ambiguities, both emotional and intellectual, which point to subleties of phenomenon and of appropriate response. Obvious examples are "learned," "blest," and "favour'd" in the last eight lines. Pope, who seems so much simpler than Donne, requires more explication. His demands on the reader are less apparent, for his images do not so clearly imply a process of thought and feeling. But ideas generate feelings, and the manipulation of the predictable deserves attention, as in the case of the inferiority of hogs to lords, of bears to monarchs, and the specially "blessed" state of man. The general or sum total of particulars can be moving, in that what one is able to "see" determines what he is able to feel.

Pope's imagery is often unassertive: the progress of a soul to heaven is inherently more interesting than the planting of wheat, and the relation between an animate corpse and a bereaved world is more compelling than the relation implied in the verb *vindicate* between what birds do and what philosophic poets do. But if one can accept the premise that the poet should present reality and his evaluations of it as a single act of perception, the rewards, in the *Essay on Man,* are subtly balanced, complexly felt structures of understanding and feeling, which achieve aesthetic effect from the philosophic basis of their conception, an assumption that perception is the necessary beginning of understanding.

What makes the repeated references to seeing, literal and metaphoric, in the *Essay on Man* more than a rhetorical trick, a mechanical unifying device, or a commonplace of Lockean psychology is the substantiality and multiplicity of the poem's imagery. Rightly understood, sense perception—particularly visual perception—is a means of learning. Acceptance, not transcendence, of experience must be the human goal.

Vision produces wisdom not only by example but by metaphor:

> There, in the rich, the honour'd, fam'd and great,
> See the false scale of Happiness complete! . . .
> Mark by what wretched steps their glory grows,
> From dirt and sea-weed as proud Venice rose;
> In each how guilt and greatness equal ran,
> And all that rais'd the Hero, sunk the Man.
> (IV, 287–288, 291–294)

One can "see the false scale of Happiness" only by understanding the simile that follows. In the demands made by the simile on the reader, it resembles Donne's images. Venice's rise on its particular foundations is a physical fact, but also a metaphysical one, having special meaning and implications. The tenor illuminates the vehicle: a comprehension of the relation between rising hero and sinking man helps the reader to judge the significance of Venice as a phenomenon. But the special effect of the simile depends on the degree to which Pope conveys the universality of rising and sinking as closely related forms of action, so that the Venice simile is not merely a poetic conceit but calls attention to one of the infinite analogies existing in the created universe. The connection between Venice and "the rich, the honour'd, fam'd and great," like the relation Pope asserts elsewhere between bees and men (III, 171-200), testifies to the constant duplication of universal moral patterns.

"There is nothing in Nature that is great and beautiful, without Rule and Order," wrote John Dennis, whose critical ideas often strikingly paralleled those of his enemy Pope; "and the more Rule and Order, and Harmony, we find in the Objects that strike our Senses, the more Worthy and Noble we esteem them. I humbly conceive, that it is the same in Art, and particularly in Poetry, which ought to be an exact Imitation of Nature."[28] To give preeminent poetic importance to "the Objects that strike our Senses," as Pope does in the *Essay on Man* (although without attempting or achieving much sensuous specificity), implies the commitment defined by Dennis of duplicating through poetic technique the order and harmony of external nature. But this ideal has further implications, which may be suggested by two other critical comments, one earlier, one later than Dennis'. The first is Bacon's famous declaration that poetry "was ever thought to have some participation of divinesse, because it doth raise and erect the Minde, by submitting the shewes of things to the desires of the Mind; whereas reason doth buckle and bowe the Mind unto the Nature of things."[29] The other comment, from the late eighteenth century, is by Daniel Webb: "The simplest truth is pleasing by its very nature; but this pleasure cannot be too much heightened: the force and surprise of imagery, the elegance of diction, the varied accords of harmony tend all to this point. Poetry is to the soul, what the sun is to nature; it calls forth, it cherishes, it adorns her beauties."[30]

The commitment to the realm of things, to Nature, to what perception teaches, involves a constant reference back to verifiable facts and subordination of speculation to observation, which protects against the temptation to philosophic abstraction. Although in the

*Essay on Man* Pope may soar into an *O altitudo* or occasionally flounder in a morass of theory, on the whole he exhibits the saving power of a determination to remain on the foundation of "nature." This commitment involves, as Dennis recognized, acceptance of the implications of what is perceived. The responsibility to create order grows from perception of it; the principle of control is implicit in the act of seeing.

But the analogical approach has expansive possibilities as well, as the quotations from Bacon and Webb suggest. Poetry may reflect nature in narrow as well as vast ways. Its power may resemble that of the sun, affecting the soul; or it may "imitate" the mind, as Bacon observes, or the heart, as one of Pope's own comments in the *Essay on Man* seems to indicate. He is praising Bolingbroke because:

> urg'd by thee, I turn'd the tuneful art
> From sounds to things, from fancy to the heart;
> For Wit's false mirror held up Nature's light . . .
> (IV, 391–393)

In the *Essay on Criticism* wit was both a source of light and a true mirror:

> *Something,* whose Truth convinc'd at Sight we find,
> That gives us back the Image of our Mind.
> (299–300)

But now the poet looks without, to a world of "things," creates his imagery from his "heart" rather than his "fancy," and refers to the ultimate sanction of "Nature" (which was also, of course, the source of true wit in the *Essay on Criticism*). Reuben Brower has suggested that the lines from the *Essay on Man* may be interpreted "in the language of the *Essay on Criticism*" as "saying that [Pope] has put behind him the 'wit' of fancy that distorts and decorates, and that he has now written a piece of 'true Wit.' "[31] But in fact the language of the *Essay on Man* is significantly different; and although what Pope here describes is indeed equivalent to the "true wit" of the earlier poem, it is important that he no longer calls it that. In an earlier passage, he refers to "wit oblique" as breaking the "steddy light" of "simple Reason" (III, 230–231). The standards of "nature" and "reason" now seem to supplant "wit," implying the poet's greater commitment to the external world, his wish to perceive and discriminate rather than merely to invent. And the lines about his progression "From sounds to things, from fancy to the heart" indicate that his new concern parallels a new responsiveness to feeling rather than fancy. It is therefore not necessarily true that Pope's reason must make him "buckle and bowe the Mind unto the Nature of things"; instead, his awareness of the nature of things may help him to render a world closer to the heart's desire. The *Essay on Man* describes things as they are; but much of its emotional power depends on its communication of the speaker's hopes and fears about the meaning of his perceptions—hopes and fears the more poignant because they are rendered through the firm control of reason.

One detailed example of the ways in which Pope conveys through imagery both his impressions of external reality and his attitude toward it is his great set-piece account of the Chain of Being:

> Far as Creation's ample range extends,
> The scale of sensual, mental pow'rs ascends:
> Mark how it mounts, to Man's imperial race,
> From the green myriads in the peopled grass:
> What modes of sight betwixt each wide extreme,
> The mole's dim curtain, and the lynx's beam:
> Of smell, the headlong lioness between,
> And hound sagacious on the tainted green:
> Of hearing, from the life that fills the flood,
> To that which warbles thro' the vernal wood:
> The spider's touch, how exquisitely fine!
> Feels at each thread, and lives along the line:
> In the nice bee, what sense so subtly true
> From pois'nous herbs extracts the healing dew:
> How Instinct varies in the grov'ling swine,
> Compar'd, half-reas'ning elephant, with thine.
> (I, 207–222)

The "vernal wood" of line 216 makes a conspicuous reappearance in English poetry in 1798 in the lines from Wordsworth:

> One impulse from a vernal wood
> May teach you more of man,
> Of moral evil and of good,
> Than all the sages can.[32]

In a sense, Pope's message is identical with Wordsworth's—but the classical poet also demonstrates what he affirms.

The appropriate gloss on Pope's lines is provided by the earlier couplet which comments on man's limitations of sense perception and concludes that they are appropriate to his station. Man lacks a microscopic eye for the plain reason that he is not a fly: "Say what the use, were finer optics giv'n, / T' inspect a mite, not comprehend the heav'n?" (I, 195–196). The antithesis of verbs is as important as that of their objects. To *inspect* is "to view closely and critically; to examine." To *comprehend* means "to grasp with the mind, conceive fully or adequately, understand," as well as "to grasp, take in, or apprehend with the senses, *esp.* sight" (O.E.D.). Comprehension is thus a crucial human power, implying both intellectual and physical control; in other words, the sensuous power of sight may provide, almost even contain, understanding. This kind of sight is an appropriate human goal, and as such it shapes much of the poem's visual imagery.

Pope's account of the Great Chain contains an occasional visual detail: "the green myriads," "the headlong lioness," "the grov'ling swine." Even these are not merely visual. The greenness of the "myriads" is part of their divinely ordained adjustment to their environment; the lioness' headlong activity suggests character as well as appearance; the swine grovels because of his low station in the scheme of things, not only because of his physical nature. The poet's presentation of mole, lynx, hound, spider, and bee depends on an almost kinesthetic perception of their physical natures merged with a sense of their philosophic significance. Made to respond to the "sensual, mental pow'rs" of such beings, the reader acquires a more than intellectual understanding of their emblematic and literal importance. For the spider there is no mental reality apart from sensuous reality; for the reader of Pope's poem the mental often derives from the sensuous. The purpose of much of the *Essay*'s nonmetaphoric imagery is to stress this fact. The Chain of Being becomes a physical reality, not just an abstraction; one sees—one *comprehends* —that its status as abstraction derives from its physical authenticity.

"Pope dispenses with the truth of the photographic epithet in favor of a truth of stricter relevance to central meaning."[33] His "vernal wood" teaches not only because it is "real" but because it is imagined in certain ways; and Pope's imagining in such a passage consists largely in his evaluation of its components. He does not merely locate them in a physical and metaphysical hierarchy; he also judges them. Such terms as "*imperial*," "*sagacious*," "*exquisitely*," "*nice*," and "*subtly true*" imply Pope's capacity not only to understand but to evaluate what he sees. His account of the Chain of Being exemplifies the poet's power to grasp and to communicate, the highest kind of human achievement. Poetry, Sir William Temple wrote in 1690, depends for its energy on the coexistence of opposites. The heat of invention must combine with the coldness of good sense, the liveliness of wit with the soundness of judgment, delicacy with force in expression.[34] Such a description points to the essential quality of the greatest passages in the *Essay on Man*, which combine passion with control, and even suggest that passion may derive from control. The imagery of Pope's account affirms the necessity of awareness, of seeing reality and also seeing through it. The reverberations that it sets up in the reader's mind do not derive from the emotional associations generated by visual exactitude. Their source is a more intellectual kind of complexity, which establishes its own emotional overtones. The images reflect a perception of order, an awareness of standards, proprieties, grounds for judgment. For Keats the poet's great gift was his negative capability, the power to suspend judgment in order to feel into the lives of people or objects. For Pope the central poetic gift is almost the reverse: the capacity to see, judge, and understand simultaneously. The double reference of the Chain of Being passage to both "nature" and "reason" explains its force.

Despite the heavy stress on the importance of the visual in the

*Essay on Man,* then, its memorable lines, its unforgettable details, rarely supply the illusion of sensuous substance. However, Pope seldom fails to offer some visual exemplification of his moral insights: "Fortune in Men has some small diff'rence made, / One flaunts in rags, one flutters in brocade" (IV, 195–196); "No less alike the Politic and Wise, / All sly slow things, with circumspective eyes" (IV, 225–226). In action, clothes, and facial expression, men reveal their natures. As the eye helps to comprehend truth, visual evidence helps to express it. Pope suggests that by "seeing" men's actions, one can judge them: "See, FALKLAND dies, the virtuous and the just! / See god-like TURENNE prostrate on the dust!" (IV, 99–100). He insists that the physical universe can be "seen" and understood: "See dying vegetables life sustain, / See life dissolving vegetate again" (III, 15–16). Vision as comprehension, not mere inspection, dominates the *Essay on Man.*

The illustrative images that give substance to Pope's argument merge easily into metaphors which enlarge the scope of implication. These metaphors frequently derive from and support the analogy between microcosm and macrocosm crucial in so much thought of Pope's time: "All are but parts of one stupendous whole, / Whose body, Nature is, and God the soul" (I, 267–268). But they also, like Donne's, suggest a view of human nature and responsibility:

> The rising tempest puts in act the soul,
> Parts it may ravage, but preserves the whole.
> On life's vast ocean diversely we sail,
> Reason the card, but Passion is the gale;
> Nor God alone in the still calm we find,
> He mounts the storm, and walks upon the wind.
> (II, 105–110)

Man's passions determine his action; he seems hardly a free agent. The weight of the metaphor is both physical and metaphysical. Its elaboration consistently stresses visually perceived facts—the ravaging of the tempest, the diverse course of man's voyage, the steersman's control, the wind's energy, calm and storm. It also develops a metaphysical conceit. Unlike Donne's elaborations, which may move away from the connections of a metaphor to dwell on its details, this development insists on ever more complex connections. Passions resemble winds in their ravaging power, then in their energizing force, then in their subservience to the will of God. Every physical truth in Pope's world has its metaphysical implications, but the metaphysical never denies by implication the importance of the physical.

Donne's imagery makes it clear that man's responsibility is to grow, to develop mental ingenuity and spiritual insight, in order to move closer, mind and soul, to heaven. His poems describe a soul's spiritual development, and the repeated discoveries and revelations of their imagery sustain an analogous process of growth in the reader's understanding. The mental agility the imagery demands—its shifts of emphasis and perspective, its stress on verbal as well as physical actualities—supports the emphasis on growth.

In comparable fashion, Pope's commitment to knowing as the fundamental duty of man dominates the structure of the *Essay on Man*. The *Essay* maintains that great men, poets and patriots, help one to learn; the poem itself is a means to knowledge and a reminder of other means. Its music, a reconciliation of jarring interests, exemplifies the harmony that must exist on larger scales and which can only be effected through understanding. The imagery embodies the rewards of knowing, the infinite riches of the created and perceived universe. Its complexities exist more in the poem's total plan than in individual metaphors. The imagery "proves" the poem's argument: that the proper study of mankind is man, but that man can study himself only by looking about him. It is true, Pope was to observe in his first moral epistle, "the diff'rence is as great between / The optics seeing, as the objects seen" (*Epistle to Cobham*, 23–24). The *Essay on Man*, with its insistence on significant analogies between large and small, between cosmic, political, and personal, suggests that differences in optics do not finally matter, that true perception and comprehension, as opposed to mere inspection, are possible to all.

Both the *Anniversarie* poems and the *Essay on Man* progress through the dynamic energy of their imagery, the different forms of that energy deriving in part from differences in psychological and philosophical assumptions. A single metaphor controls the large form of the *Anniversarie* sequence, giving to the poems' development a coherence and emphasis that Pope cannot so readily achieve. The symbolic relation of macrocosm and microcosm, long since explored in philosophic and literary discourse, involved a rich cluster of association and implication. Donne's way of using it was insistent and fresh, since the stress on the world as resembling a human body reversed the usual emphasis. Not only does a metaphor of the world as corpse, the poet as its anatomizer, order the two Donne poems, but in several instances the first poem also suggests the corollary, and more commonplace, metaphor of Elizabeth Drury as herself a world, but with the startling implication that the real world is microcosmic in comparison: "She to whom this world must it selfe refer, / As Suburbs, or the Microcosme of her" (235–236). She is a universe, a paradise, a sovereign state, a church: a whole that is greater than the sum of its parts. The metaphoric system involved in these references supplies a clear perspective on the poems. Through unifying metaphors the *Anniversarie* poems display a pattern of Christian assumption, which shapes their treatment of the problem of spiritual growth and stresses the singleness and ultimate clarity of the order controlling all. The metaphors thus duplicate in miniature the poems' larger statement.

Within the dominant metaphoric structure, one form of paradox recurs conspicuously three times. Elizabeth Drury is said to be "a part both of the Quire, and Song" (I, 10) and both "partaker, and a part" of heaven's joys (I, 434); the sight of God is "both the object, and the wit" of man's thoughts (II, 442). Each of these striking phrases asserts an identity of active and passive; action and its object are the same. The point is important in understanding the technique as well as the meaning of the poems, for it suggests a way of comprehending process. The specific process that interests Donne is one of spiritual growth, the development from *scientia*, knowledge of the world, to *sapientia*, heavenly wisdom.[35] In this process, as in the smaller actions suggested by individual metaphors, distinctions—Pope's great concern—are finally unimportant. Singing, partaking, exercising wit are significant acts, and the actors and the objects of action are vital as well, but to distinguish among them is not. The process of spiritual growth is in one sense a process of eliminating distinctions: one sees at last without need for eyes, apprehends through something larger and less limiting than intelligence. Through imagery one may come to understand the process that results in rejection of the need for imagery.

Imagery expresses the central paradox of these poems, a paradox central as well to much of Donne's work: the world must be both loved and rejected. The multiplicity, the insight, and the energy of the images declare their creator's involvement with phenomena. His mind, shifting, grasps one phenomenon and then another, sees kinds and degrees of relationship and the relevance of their diversity, glories in diversity and in his power to assert it. The body, Donne observes within a few lines, is a prison, a poor inn, a province packed up in two yards of skin, a rusty fowling piece, an egg. Each image, like Pope's images and most good images, evaluates and illuminates its subject. The images also demonstrate the scope of linguistic possibility and reveal the degree of human involvement with the things of the world, as well as the ways in which such involvement can lead beyond itself. The complexities of individual images and of their relationships demonstrate how man can create meaning, how his intellect enables him to value earthly experience in the act of rejecting it, for the capacity to reject depends on the ability to interpret. Here Donne's references are no more detailed than Pope's:

> Thinke, when t'was growne to most, t'was a poore Inne,
> A Province Pack'd up in two yards of skinne,
> And that usurped, or threatned with the rage
> Of sicknesses, or their true mother, Age . . .
> Thinke that a rusty Peece, discharg'd, is flowen
> In peeces, and the bullet is his owne,
> And freely flies: This to thy soule allow.
> (*The Second Anniversarie*, 175–178, 181–183)

They continually stress action, psychological or physical. Even when the comparison is simply to "a poore Inne," the psychological movement from expectation to disappointment underlies the phrase. If the body is a province, it is a province tensely contained and threatened by inevitable forces; if a gun, it is a gun that does something and to which something happens. The man beheaded is preeminently and horrifyingly a man in action. Even such a question as that of the shape and proportions of the earth finds images of action to explain it:

> Doth not a Tenarif, or higher Hill
> Rise so high like a Rocke, that one might thinke
> The floating Moone would shipwracke there, and sink?
> Seas are so deepe, that Whales being strooke to day,
> Perchance to morrow, scarse at middle way
> Of their wish'd journeys end, the bottom, dye.
> (*The First Anniversarie*, 286–291)

If process is, as I believe, the true subject of Donne's poems, it is appropriate that his imagery suggests universal participation in natural process. To be in motion is inevitable. Man's responsibility is to control the nature of moral process although he cannot interfere radically with its physical counterpart. He can transmute into its opposite the process that takes him from life to death: spiritual growth is thus allegorically related to and partly described by physical activity.

The imagery's pervasive vibrancy comes from its tonal complexity, from the tension between expressed rejection and felt love for the things of the world, conveyed, for example, by the exactitude of detail with which the beheaded man is pictured. Such exactitude, implying close observation, reflects the very dwelling on this world that the poem argues against. The details derive from and arouse horror and disgust, but also signify an awareness of remarkable possibility. All the analogies that insist on the similarities of minute and vast, of physical process and spiritual, of human and divine, reflect the same wonder. The rejection of earthly commitments for which Donne argues requires growing through the things of the world, not shoving them aside. The world must be known before it is left behind. The knowledge of objects and of happenings conveyed by physical perception and recorded in imagery is a stage in the progress toward more significant knowledge; without the world of objects and happenings, the world of spiritual understanding could not be discussed. Donne's imagery dramatizes a sense of human possibility and expresses the ineffable. Growth has almost infinite possibilities; its end is the union of the soul with God.

Pope's version of the possibilities of knowledge, in contrast, concentrates on the necessary limits of human achievement. The limitations of perception are as central a subject of the *Essay on Man* as is perception's power; the tension between power and limitation is a crucial form of the poem's "drama of man's refusal to accept his nature."[36] Reuben Brower has commented acutely on Pope's "belief that only by a fuller exercise of intelligence can mind be saved from itself."[37] In exploring "knowing" as theme and technique, Pope investigates the possibilities of intelligence as well as its inevitable shortcomings.

To know, in Pope's sense, is to "see" the past and the present in equivalent ways and to manipulate abstract and concrete, general and particular, in order to achieve understanding. Through imagery he exemplifies possibility. The voice of the poet is that of the ideal observer. Since comprehension, as the ultimate goal of observation, implies comprehensiveness, his concern is with the full physical and moral universe. Seeing the world, he sees its laws; seeing man, he sees his limits. Here is part of his version of history:

> 'Till then, by Nature crown'd, each Patriarch sate,
> King, priest, and parent of his growing state;
> On him, their second Providence, they hung,
> Their law his eye, their oracle his tongue.
> He from the wond'ring furrow call'd the food,
> Taught to command the fire, controul the flood,
> Draw forth the monsters of th'abyss profound,
> Or fetch th'aerial eagle to the ground.
> 'Till drooping, sick'ning, dying, they began
> Whom they rever'd as God to mourn as Man.
> (III, 215–224)

The visual material in these lines is concrete without being specific. The passage presents the king's relation to his people through vignette. Such occupations as planting grain, building fires, fishing, and hunting, evoked in exalted rhetoric, appear as magic feats. The effect depends on the simple irony in the conjunction of repeated images of awe-inspiring control and the vivid participles suggesting the inevitable human failure of control. The ambiguous reference of those participles hints the universality of the king's fate: his mourners too are subject to "drooping, sick'ning, dying." And the final line, with its definition of opposed emotional responses, reveals the paradox that the king's value to his subjects increases with the manifestation of his mortality; the monarch's loss of control implies a new power over the hearts of those he rules.

A series of tableaux here supplies emblems of hierarchical relationship: people and king; king and nature; king, people, and nature; people and dying king. Each sketches a scene; none provides scenic details. The passage's technique examplifies the poem's way of seeing. Mere assertion of the people's dependency, the king's power and his loss of power, would not serve the same purpose as its embodiment in emblematic scenes.

But Pope's imagery does not merely create pictures. Emotion derives, in such a passage as the one under consideration, from the communication of an intricate relation between abstract and concrete. Imagery is known to elucidate abstractions by providing concrete analogues for them, but Pope's subject as well as his method is the intertwining of abstract and concrete, so as to represent the furthest reach of knowledge. The lines about the king repeatedly pair the two. "Providence," "law," "oracle" are abstract terms given concrete embodiment in the person of the king. "Profound" and "aerial," terms of spatial definition, also connote the abstract concepts of depth and height, suggesting power as well as location. The startling expression "wond'ring furrow" implicitly questions established categories by jarringly modifying the securely inanimate with a term applicable only to the animate. The drama of the king's death is a drama of developing human awareness, in which a presumed abstraction ("rever'd as God") becomes finite and mortal—

and valuable partly as a result of that finiteness and mortality. Man's power to abstract exemplifies the limitless possibilities of intelligence; the ineluctable facts of the concrete embody his limitations. This view contrasts with Donne's suggestion that to come to terms with the concrete may be a means of mystical transcendence. The subject of the *Essay on Man* is the human condition, defined as the conjunction of what man can imagine, deduce, speculate, and what he can literally see or touch.

Even when he presents a series of metaphors, Pope is likely to use them as a way of dramatizing the meaningful conjunction of abstract and concrete:

> Mean-while Opinion gilds with varying rays
> Those painted clouds that beautify our days;
> Each want of happiness by Hope supply'd,
> And each vacuity of sense by Pride:
> These build as fast as knowledge can destroy;
> In Folly's cup still laughs the bubble, joy;
> One prospect lost, another still we gain;
> And not a vanity is giv'n in vain.
>
> (II, 283–290)

The movement here is toward increasing abstraction. Only the first metaphor has sensuous reality; the final couplet, although it may contain a metaphor (traveling through mountains), is essentially abstract. The idea of building to supply the vacuities of sense and the want of happiness, as well as to compensate for the destructions of knowledge, is not realized in physical terms, and "the bubble, joy" has more reality in the sense suggested by Maynard Mack ("The word takes on additional meaning from its common early sense—'deceptive show' and 'dupe' "[38]) than as an imagined bubble in an imagined cup. Pope's metaphor series reveals how tenuous is the line between abstract and concrete. Opinion, rather surprisingly symbolized by the sun, is the only abstraction in the first couplet, where the effect depends on the ambiguous emotional value of clouds: "painted clouds," which "beautify" but are nonetheless traditional symbols of negative forces. The identification of opinion with the sun generates a similar troublesome ambiguity. Such ambiguities persist through the entire passage, where hope seems equated with pride, knowledge appears a destructive force, joy is associated with folly, vanity becomes obscurely valuable. Yet one understands that these connections are false as well as true. After the opening couplet, succeeding lines contain increasing numbers of abstractions treated as though they were concrete: "want of happiness," "vacuity of sense," "knowledge can destroy." The lines lead toward the peroration of the second epistle, where what one is to "see" is the folly of man in the context of God's wisdom. Man's folly is his unwillingness to see things as they are, his inability to penetrate ambiguity. His equations of abstract and concrete, as Pope here demonstrates through the troubling sequence of metaphors, may mislead as well as illuminate. Proper seeing requires proper evaluation of abstractions and of concrete facts, as well as of the relation between them.

Not all sections of the poem deal so clearly with the relation of abstract and concrete, but it is not surprising that this should be a recurrent concern of a poem whose announced purpose is to examine abstractions. Pope examines most often by comparison. When, adopting the precise tone and method of his third moral epistle, he calls gold "yellow dirt" (IV, 279), he restores concreteness to and thus implies judgment of what has become a virtual abstraction, the idea of money. When he defines differences of fortune as the difference between rags and brocade (IV, 196), or observes that Reason should "instruct Mankind" by inviting man to study the works of ants and bees (III, 180–190), or draws out the implications of the metaphor of reason as a "weak queen" (II, 149–158), he does the same thing, using example, history, and metaphor as different kinds of images to test abstractions by concrete experience. The examples, history, and metaphors, however, often lack the vividness such points of reference have in Donne because the *Ding an sich* is not sufficiently interesting even for the moment: it is specifically important as a way of knowing. Pope is interested in the concrete universal, not in the streaks of the tulip. The concrete universal provides the only valid means of testing abstractions. The judgments that impart poetic texture to the *Essay on Man* derive from and depend on this testing. Poetically as well as philosophically, the poem is formed by them. It affirms, through technique and substance alike, the importance of "seeing" as a mode of knowing; it enlarges, by its way of using imagery, the reader's sense of what "seeing" means and implies; it both tells and shows that to "know" the universe is the only way to endure its necessities with full humanity. Further, the tension, stability, and energy of Pope's versification imitate the larger order of the universe; and the intellectual control of the perceptions recorded by the poet creates a dynamic complexity of meaning which mirrors that order in yet another way:

> Say, will the falcon, stooping from above,
> Smit with her varying plumage, spare the dove?
> Admires the jay the insect's gilded wings?
> Or hears the hawk when Philomela sings?
> Man cares for all . . .
>
> (III, 53–57)

The ostensible purpose of these lines is to contrast man's capacity for aesthetic appreciation with the lack of such a capacity in animals. The selectivity of "varying plumage" (vague yet suggestive) and "gilded wings" (not only visually evocative but hinting the relevance of different scales of value from man's) derives from philosophic as well as visual perception. Each image reminds the reader of the fullness and variety of the Great Chain of Being, and of the many modes of activity possible within it. "Philomela" juxtaposes man's mythologizing tradition with the simple brutality of the hawk; it also reminds one of man's capacity for brutality. In every line, simplicity opposes complexity; yet the passage preserves the poise between them, stressing the value and necessity of animal directness as well as of human elaboration, and illuminating the potential triviality as well as the possible grandeur of man's discriminations. To be "smit" with the dove's beauty seems evasive in comparison with the directness of the kind of "smiting" implied by the falcon; and the lines recognize the possibility for evasion in man's aesthetic capacities as well.

The cumulative effect of the poem's abundant imagery, which

forms and manipulates the reader's perspective, his way of "seeing" in philosophic and physical terms, is to create two contrasting concepts of man's nature. They are man seeing, exemplified by the poet in the poem, and man seen, regarded as an object of perception. This distinction corresponds significantly to that between God as *natura naturans* and *natura naturata*. In his seeing aspect, man partakes of the divine energy. He who sees also creates; the poet is seer first, then imaginer. In contrast, man as object of perception is part of the created universe, his stature technically superior but closely analogous to that of the lower animals. He resembles the weed rather than the oak (I, 35–40), the dull ox or at best the proud steed (I, 61–64), the lamb, the sparrow, the performing ape. Although Pope refers to "Man's imperial race" (I, 209), he never makes one feel man's imperial power. The distinction between the "poor Indian" of "untutor'd mind" (I, 99) and the sophisticated and learned Englishman is more apparent than real: both are alike unknowing—unseeing—about all that matters.

The different status and stature of man as perceiver is perhaps best exemplified by the opening passage of the *Essay*, with its tone of urbane distance and control. When the poet invites Bolingbroke to "beat this ample field" (I, 9), the entire "scene of Man" (5), to examine the ways "Of all who blindly creep, or sightless soar" (12), the difference between his own capacity for perception and the blindness of those who are its object is real and vivid. The nature of the persona as comprehender also emerges from the tone of succeeding passages: the absolute authority of his perceptions and judgments, the absolute scorn in his revelations of human incapacity and pretentiousness, the range of his "vision" in time and space. He represents man at his most godlike, but he sees man at his most bestial. Man seeing, man as recorder and poet of his perceptions, embodies the ideal balance of the human capacity to abstract and the ability to perceive concrete reality. He thus suggests the possibilities of salvation through intelligence, the human form of the ideal balance of tensions. Man seen, however, displays a ludicrous or horrifying imbalance. His capacity to abstract, and thus to abandon the immediate locus of reality, is his major mode of self-destruction. This is the typical operation of pride, which causes men to "quit their sphere, and rush into the skies" (124) instead of learning from direct observation. The poem's firm commitment to physical perception, its reliance on concrete imagery, dramatize the poet's opposition to the "philosophizing" that makes men wish to free themselves from the limitations which, the poet argues, they should accept and even glory in.

The relation and contrast between its two views of man is the central paradox of the poem. It reveals the complexities of the human position "on this isthmus of a middle state" (II, 3) more fully than could any explicit discussion; the imagery that enforces recognition of the paradox and its complexities thus forms the meaning of the poem. This double view of man has a universality and power greater than that of the more narrowly conceived doctrine which largely shapes the *Essay*'s prose argument. It involves and reflects the poet's emotional as well as his intellectual commitments. Although it receives memorable explicit statement at the opening of the second epistle, its pervasive force depends rather on the effect of the imagery: the insistent conjunction of man with the animals, the judgments enforced through such a conjunction, and the implications of the tone with which those images are presented.

The nature and abundance of imagery in the *Essay on Man* suggests that in this poem Pope may have experimented with perception as a principle of control—in much the same sense as he used wit as the controlling force of the *Essay on Criticism.* Both statements are largely figurative, since perception, wit, and judgment are so inextricably mixed in any act of poetic creation that their separation must be artificial and false. But in the *Essay on Criticism,* the poet's wit used his perceptions and expressed his judgments; in the *Essay on Man,* his perceptions seem to contain his judgments and to form his wit. The *Essay on Criticism* made frequent direct statements about the value of wit; the *Essay on Man* constantly implies and asserts the necessity for man to use his perceptions—most often, to "see"—as a way of achieving the understanding that alone leads to internal harmony and to a sense of harmony with the universe. Through perception, properly used, man discovers the principles of control inherent in the nature of things. The power of the imagery of the *Essay on Man,* like that of the *Anniversarie* poems, is metaphysical—but the metaphysics is different. The imagery's power derives from its dramatic revelation that what man can see shows him what he is, that his acceptance of the necessary limits of perception and expression may lead him to transcendence, that the disciplined seer—the poet in a new incarnation—is a symbol of human grandeur. The sources of poetic and philosophical coherence are here identical, as they are in Donne and in all truly metaphysical poetry. This fact defines the poem's achievement but also suggests a source of its difficulty for modern readers, to whom the poet who demonstrates the divine creative power of the word is likely to seem more compelling than one who insists that merely to see reality is an imitation of divinity.

Four

# Worlds of Unreason

## *The Dunciad* and *The Waste Land*

The divine creative power of the word is, as Aubrey Williams has brilliantly demonstrated, a central concern of *The Dunciad.*[1] Between the *Essay on Man* and the final version of *The Dunciad,* Pope wrote most of his greatest satiric verse. His apparent assumptions shifted: the implicit metaphysics of *The Dunciad* is closer to Donne than to the *Essay on Man.* Having experimented with wit and with perception as focuses of aesthetic control, the satirist committed himself at last to the crucial importance of judgment, the manifestation of that reasoning ability which makes man not merely *animal rationis capax,* but *animal rationale,* and which, at its best, makes him little lower than the angels. Again in this final long poem his aesthetic principles reflect the moral concerns that are his explicit subject. His verse demonstrates the devastating energy of the judgmental faculty, which the poet, almost alone, retains in a world dominated by forces of antireason. It shows that judgment can be a powerful poetic resource, organizing the brilliances of wit and commenting on the meanings of perception.

The nature of the commitment to reality in *The Dunciad* is difficult to discover and define. In the *Essay on Man,* concrete detail enforced a sense that comprehension might develop from perception. Looking at the physical world, man saw reality; the facts he perceived implied a cosmology. Perception led directly to judgment. Observation of human realities, individual and social, might generate some disturbance, but observation of nature helped to compensate for it. The poet, who embodied the proper way of seeing, asserted the possibility of a universal view in which apparent evil was ultimate good. The clarity of life's progression up the animal scale provided a comforting metaphor for the cosmic scale; perception of order in minute details led to assertion of larger forms of order. Although reflection on the place of the individual in the total order might lead to moments of pessimism, when man seemed only a lamb led to slaughter, the conclusion of the *Essay on Man* is that reality is perceptible or deducible, and ultimately benign.

*The Dunciad* depicts a state of affairs in which the observation of nature has become itself a form of perversion, leading men away from instead of toward God. Observation of society is unrelieved horror. Moreover, the possibility of false perception is more vivid than in the earlier poem, where the asserted blindness of men is readily counteracted by the poet's clear vision. The poet's vision provides the clarities of *The Dunciad*, too, but as in T. S. Eliot's *The Waste Land*, a poem significantly resembling Pope's, clarity reveals confusion. By the end of the poem, the poet can see nothing: there is no longer anything to see. The muse obeys the power of Dulness, the great anarch who lets the curtain fall, and universal darkness eliminates the possibility of perception. The darkness derives largely from the various forms of false perception that the poem's imagery has revealed. Men make it ever more difficult for themselves to distinguish between real and apparent; the lack of such distinction is damnation. Hope can survive only with clarity of moral, not physical, perception.

To see clearly the nature of moral reality is difficult not only because perception is by its nature private, but because the proper interpretation of perception is perplexing. George Berkeley spelled out the difficulty in physical terms. All men can perceive, he wrote, is "our own ideas or sensations. . . As for our senses, by them we have the knowledge only of our sensations, ideas, or those things that are immediately perceived by sense, call them what you will: but they do not inform us that things exist without the mind, or unperceived, like to those which are perceived." Yet reality remains, contained in the mind of God: "If any man thinks this detracts from the existence or reality of things, he is very far from understanding what hath been premised in the plainest terms I could think of."[2]

Although Berkeley saves himself from the difficulties of believing in nothing beyond his own mind, he is forced to recognize the degree to which men must depend on their own mental capacities for their knowledge of reality, as well as to confront the constant likelihood of error. A man who sees the moon at a distance may conclude, on the basis of physical perception alone, that it is "a plain lucid surface, about a foot in diameter." If he could proceed close enough to make more precise observations, he would come to a different conclusion. But the problem as Berkeley understands it is not in perception: the man's "mistake lies not in what he perceives immediately and at present . . . but in the wrong judgment he makes concerning the ideas he apprehends to be connected with those immediately perceived."[3]

*The Dunciad*, with its elaborate structure of physical images for moral conditions, translates Berkeley's insights into another realm (I am not suggesting the necessary influence of Berkeley, only an analogy). Despite the existence of received ideas about morality, every man must finally see for himself where good and evil lies. Men are likely to see wrong, but even more likely to judge wrong. Like the moon-watcher, Pope's dunces misinterpret their own perceptions. And their mistakes are more sinister than his because in the moral world, Pope suggests—going one step farther than Berkeley—perception alters reality. Those who see men as things help convert them to things; men who understand words as restrictive forces make them so; concentrators on insects become what they see. The relation between imagery and "reality" in *The Dunciad* is complicated by the fact that the prevalence of dunces alters the nature of reality. The extravagant imagery that condemns the disciples of dullness reflects not only the satirist's disgust but the victims' true nature and their self-perceptions. The proportions of each component are difficult to determine.

For example, Book IV presents as one of its central concerns the dangerous "segregation of words and things."[4] Like the rest of *The Dunciad*, it concentrates on a process of becoming rather than an achieved state of being. Its imagery describes how dunces destroy themselves and their world. Through verbal process and through action, the misguided turn themselves into equivalents for the things that obsess them: there is an essential, not merely a verbal, identity between men and the metaphors that describe them. Aristarchus, speaking directly of one sort of duncelike perception, exemplifies a version of the process. Observing that critics may concentrate on words in isolation, he resorts to a revealing metaphor: "The critic Eye, that microscope of Wit, / Sees hairs and pores, examines bit by bit" (233–234). Such an eye, he continues approvingly, never sees larger meanings, which the critic will only understand "When Man's whole frame is obvious to a *Flea*" (238). From his point of view, the microscope, with its suggestions of expanded human possibility, is a dignifying metaphor. The context, however, suggests other connotations. "Why has not Man a microscopic eye?" Pope had inquired in the *Essay on Man*, to reply immediately, "For this plain reason, Man is not a Fly" (I, 193–194). *The Dunciad*'s allusion to the earlier couplet reveals that the critic's intellectual concentration on parts to the exclusion of wholes is substantially identical to the scientist's physical concentration on the minute. Whether one devotes oneself to words or things, the result is the same: the wondrous complexity of the eye, literal or metaphoric, becomes the less wondrous complexity of the mechanical instrument, creation of man rather than God. The outcome, an apparent increase in perception, is in fact a diminishment in meaningful seeing. Aristarchus' choice of metaphor reveals his intellectual inadequacy which, failing in discrimination, finds mechanical operations superior to human ones. It is no coincidence that his concluding metaphor promises, "With the same Cement, ever sure to bind, / We bring to one dead level ev'ry mind" (267–268). Seeing man and experience as mechanistic and material, he demonstrates by mechanical speech and action the degree to which he has become what he perceives; and his speech threatens to have the effect that dullards have on those around them, turning men into fleas, bringing all minds to the same "dead level." This is a resounding and significant pun in the dunces' world of death-in-life.

The fourth book provides abundant examples of dehumanization: not just the satirist's conventional equations of men with insects or animals, but a systematic perception of men as becoming what they believe in. Teachers hang padlocks on the minds of their students (159–162). The "accomplished Son" of Dulness, whose education includes the grand tour, is wafted willessly over Europe until classic learning turns for him into "*Air*, the Echo of a Sound" (322), deprived of all substance. He returns triumphantly, equipped for life "With nothing but a Solo in his head" (324). The collector Annius goes one step farther toward subhumanity, "False as his Gems, and canker'd as his Coins" (349). The resemblance between devotees and the objects to which they devote themselves is shown by the tribe concerned with insects and flowers, which appear "thick as Locusts black'ning all the ground" (397). Silenus sums up the reductive process, which has been duplicated with various details throughout the book, when he describes "ev'ry finish'd Son" of Dulness (500). Here again, incidentally, is a significant pun, for Dulness' votaries are "finish'd" in that they are "perfected" in her mysteries but also destroyed as men. They are described as:

> Bounded by Nature, narrow'd still by Art,
> A trifling head, and a contracted heart . . .
> Mark'd out for Honours, honour'd for their Birth,
> To thee the most rebellious things on earth:
> Now to thy gentle shadow all are shrunk,
> All melted down, in Pension, or in Punk!
> (IV, 503–504, 507–510)

Pope describes intellectual regression in physical terms: men, objects to be bounded, narrowed, contracted, are only things at best, which can be reduced to shadows. The explicit identification of men with things is repeated toward the end of the book, in Dulness' final blessing to her children, which concludes with the vision of "some daring son" (599) who may be "nobly conscious, Princes are but things / Born for First Ministers, as Slaves for Kings" (601–602). The man with such consciousness can "MAKE ONE MIGHTY DUNCIAD OF THE LAND!" (604). To understand men as things is thus dullness' final achievement.

The entire poem provides examples of the ways in which the dunces' perception and understanding affect their activity and the world they inhabit. Bays's prayer, in Book I, provides a paradigm of the dullards' mental processes. He begs for the preservation of his native night, appealing to the goddess Dulness to:

> quite unravel all the reas'ning thread,
> And hang some curious cobweb in its stead!
> As, forc'd from wind-guns, lead itself can fly,
> And pond'rous slugs cut swiftly thro the sky;
> As clocks to weight their nimble motion owe,
> The wheels above urg'd by the load below:
> Me Emptiness, and Dulness could inspire,
> And were my Elasticity, and Fire.
>
> (I, 179–186)

Edwin Fussell has commented that this passage shows Cibber as a "congeries of machinery": "with the abdication of the will comes an inhuman stiffening of the mind and the person."[5] But the effect of the description depends partly on the speaker, who values precisely what the reader assumes to be "inhuman." For a poet to describe his satiric victims as insectlike or leaden is a purposeful and lucid technique, which is easy to understand. But to make the victims insist on their own desire to be empty, dull, insectlike, and inanimate has a more complicated effect. If a man prefers cobwebs to reason as the result of his own intellectual activity, to identify him as a spider is only an acceptance of things as they are. The character Bays, who represents Cibber, is aware of such concepts as reason, inspiration, elasticity, "fire," yet he prefers their opposites. The imagery of his self-description, which would be bitingly derogatory if presented in the voice of the poet, is from his point of view laudatory. His smug conviction of rightness, his rejection of alternatives belonging to established realms of value, make him a threat to the order of traditional moral assumption. His determined mediocrity makes him impervious to invective, which he can accept as praise—a fact that suggests how dunces in their inadequacy may destroy the very foundations of society.

Even the images in *The Dunciad* that seem particularly far-fetched, bizarre, and satiric may have disturbing, confusing affinities with literal fact. One cannot be hasty in coming to conclusions about what constitutes reality:

Yet by some object ev'ry brain is stirr'd;
The dull may waken to a Humming-bird;
The most recluse, discreetly open'd find
Congenial matter in the Cockle-kind;
The mind, in Metaphysics at a loss,
May wander in a wilderness of Moss;
The head that turns at super-lunar things,
Poiz'd with a tail, may steer on Wilkins' wings.
(IV, 445–452)

The "congenial matter" that dullards find creates natural metaphors for psychological conditions. Despite the pastoral sweetness and sympathetic tone of this account, it implies a serious indictment of excessive interest in things. In each case the object of interest, considered as a metaphor for the mind it engages, becomes an image of deflation. The connection between mind and deprecating image is not accidental, not merely asserted; it is essential, a part of reality. The dunces by the nature of their concentration create new forms of self-definition, subhuman self-images that illuminate the dangers of narrowing attention to physical objects.

Because the dunces reject the normal assumptions of value and fail to make distinctions in their moral perceptions, they create a world in which it is difficult to distinguish between metaphor and reality. Pope exploits the possibilities of verbal ambiguity to obscure the line between literal and metaphoric statement. Alvin Kernan has written, "The fantastic shapes which the dunces and the world assume in *The Dunciad* are, of course, to be taken quite seriously, for they express the monstrous metamorphoses of which dullness is capable."[6] They also express the simple facts of the world of Dulness, where distinctions between people and animals, even between human beings and inanimate objects, largely disappear: metamorphoses are unconscious and unnoticed. Dulness draws helplessly into her vortex all who knowingly or unknowingly acknowledge her power. "None need a guide, by sure Attraction led, / And strong impulsive gravity of Head" (IV, 75–76). The votaries of Dulness are at once human and inhuman. Their "gravity" suggests weight, the heaviness of lead, one of the symbolic metals of dullness. It also suggests the peculiar mindless seriousness of the dull, that "weightiness" which gives false importance to the trivial and signifies destruction of value. The "sure Attraction" that draws the dunces comes from without, being the power of inferior ideas over inferior minds, but also a magnetic force acting on the special metal of which they are morally composed. Their gravity is "impulsive," both in its lack of rational control and its power to generate action. Attraction and gravity combine to reduce the dullards to powerless, dehumanized victims of their devotion and to establish the fact that their leadenness of mind makes their true humanity impossible. Inner and outer states are inextricably involved in the function of the imagery; indeed, the power of the image lies in its performance of just such a bridging function.

For the romantic poets, the idea that "all that we behold / . . . all the mighty world / Of eye, and ear" is composed of what we "half create, / And what perceive" was a source of imaginative excitement.[7] For Pope, the same insight, applied to society rather than to nature, produced despair, because it suggested a situation of profound disorder, in which not even the traditional clarifying function of perception could be assumed. What Dulness, personifying the nature of contaminated minds, half-creates is a world of disturbing distortions. Perceiving a realm of geographical and logical impossibilities, where "gay Description Aegypt glads with show'rs, / Or gives to Zembla fruits, to Barca flow'rs" (I, 73–74), she views it with "self-applause" (82) as her own achievement. The phantasmagoric quality of the duncelike world reflects the chaos of duncelike minds. Action and setting sometimes even provide a loose allegory of what takes place in the corrupted mind. Hell is a state of mind: "Why this is Hell, nor am I out of it," explains Marlowe's Mephistopheles to Faustus. The dunces might say the same thing. In the visionary third book, Bays's guide, Elkanah Settle, shows him "a new world to Nature's laws unknown" (241), in which "The forests dance, the rivers upward rise, / Whales sport in woods, and dolphins in the skies" (244–245). The images depict the extravagances not only of contemporary stage representation, but also of Bays's mind. When he asks their source, Settle replies, "Son; what thou seek'st is in thee! Look, and find / Each Monster meets his likeness in thy mind" (251–252). A few lines later he reiterates the point: "And are these wonders, Son, to thee unknown? / Unknown to thee? These wonders are thy own" (273–274). Only the imagination of corruption can produce the fact.

In this respect too, Bays's mind exemplifies the intellects of his comrades. When Dulness encounters "momentary monsters" (I, 83), a suggestion is soon offered of their origin: Bays has a "monster-breeding breast" (I, 108). The goddess has already observed that London's citizens are made in her image and likeness, but she recognizes herself most vividly in Bays because of his emotional capacity to generate monstrosities. Uncontrolled emotion marks his early utterances in the poem, which display a hysteria of unrelated references and incoherent attitudes reminiscent of passages from Cibber's *Life* quoted in Pope's footnotes. Bays is, by his own account, "This arch Absurd, that wit and fool delights; / This Mess, toss'd up of Hockley-hole and White's" (I, 221–222). His world, also a mess of incompatibilities and absurdities, in this respect strikingly resembles him. The confusions, distortions, and impieties that dullness generates in the mind produce their external counterparts.

The operations of Dulness are first of all mental: within the individual mind phantoms are judged men; men are leveled by being covered with cement; concentration on the petty produces pettiness. The sinners in Dante's hell are blown by the winds of their lust, roll against one another the rocks of their anger, and freeze in the emptiness of their betrayals. The images of their damnation objectify their interior states. Similarly in *The Dunciad*, the satiric, degrading imagery, action, and setting of the dunces project interior states of dullness. Dullness is damnation, its crimes their own punishments, its world an image of hell.

This sort of stress on the psychological origins of external facts might suggest that Pope is concerned with the portrayal of individuals and their mental processes. Such is not the case. Pope concerns himself with the general, with the largest conceivable forms of truth. He sees the existence, indeed the necessity, of large unities. In a note to the fourth book of *The Dunciad*, Pope alerts his readers to the existence of several levels of reference in the poem. Explaining "To blot out Order, and extinguish Light" (IV, 14), he writes, "The two great Ends of her [Dulness'] Mission; the one in quality of Daughter of *Chaos,* the other as Daughter of *Night. Order* here is to be understood extensively, both as Civil and Moral, the distinctions between high and low in Society, and true and false in Individuals: *Light,* as Intellectual only, Wit, Science, Arts." Dullness operates on individuals and on societies; it concerns the moral and the intellectual as well as the "Civil"; everywhere it obviates distinctions. Its importance depends on the largeness of its relevance. Pope was disdurbed about the realities of a disordered society. "I can tell you of no one thing worth reading, or seeing," he wrote to Gay after the publication of the first version of *The Dunciad;* "the whole age seems resolv'd to justify the Dunciad, and it may stand for a publick Epitaph or monumental Inscription, like that at Thermopylae, on a *whole people perish'd!*"[8] But public destruction begins with private corruption. "I think the way to have a Publick Spirit, is first to have a Private one," the poet had explained to Swift, responding to his friend's famous assertion, "I hate and detest that animal called man, although I hartily love John, Peter, Thomas, and so forth."[9] Relations between individuals are the origin of social facts.

Martin Price has described the general nature of dullness as a psychological force: "Dulness is less a real being than a projection of the moral inertia of the man who prefers the ease of remaining what he is to the pain of becoming properly human. The sleep that she offers is not simply a relaxation of intellectual faculties, but a freedom from moral cognition and, most of all, from moral effort . . . She provides her sons with the comfort of being less conscious and therefore less anxious." And again "The psychological meaning of Dulness is, clearly, the surrender of thought to sensation."[10] Here is Pope in a note on the same subject: "Dulness here is not to be taken contractedly for mere Stupidity, but in the enlarged sense of the word, for all Slowness of Apprehension, Shortness of Sight, or imperfect Sense of things. It includes . . . Labour, Industry, and some degree of Activity and Boldness: a ruling principle not inert, but turning topsy-turvy the Understanding, and inducing an Anarchy or confused State of Mind."[11] The use of "Anarchy" as a synonym for "confused State of Mind" stresses the connection between private and public: the anarchy which at last destroys civilization originates in the individual mind, and it is fed by every form of intellectual confusion. Dullness is a psychological phenomenon, but its ultimate effects are social.

Not only is it true that individual weakness produces social weakness, but the reverse is also the case. In another note to *The Dunciad,* Pope emphasizes that he has described "the whole Course of Modern Education," all parts of which he finds "equally concurring to narrow the Understanding, and establish Slavery and Error in Literature, Philosophy, and Politics. The whole finished in modern Free-thinking: the completion of whatever is vain, wrong, and destructive to the happiness of mankind, as it establishes *Self-love for* the sole Principle of Action" (IV, 501n). Carol Johnson has written of *The Dunciad,* "Annihilating subjectivity is the prevailing note in the kingdom of Dulness."[12] Since for Pope the unity of intellectual, social, and philosophic or religious experience seems inescapable, the major theological error of "Free-thinking," which includes agnosticism, atheism, and deism, is identified with the psychological problem of solipsism. The unity of all aspects of human life, for good or evil, is the ineluctable intellectual foundation of *The Dunciad.* Self-love produces solipsism, which isolates man from his natural unities. That solipsism which is assumed by such later poets as Eliot to be a necessary condition of life seems to Pope a symbol of ultimate evil.

But although the individual mind is the source and goal of evil and destruction in the poem, Pope makes little apparent attempt to suggest individuality or even humanity in his victims. Their sense of their own specialness is part of their self-delusion, since from Pope's point of view they comprise an undifferentiated mass. The poet's insistence on their subhumanity is central to his argument, which defines them as deviating from the common human standard assumed to be available to all. Yet some aspects of this definition are upsettingly "realistic." Tony Tanner has written, "One of the more disturbing effects of the *Dunciad* is the fantastic unawareness of the participants: they tumble into pools of excrement, they compete in urinating competitions, they dive happily into deep mud, without ever giving any sign that they are aware of anything odd about their behaviour. This indeed has the effect of making them seem like automata . . . It is an estranged world; humans have become impersonal, alien and hostile, in a word, inhuman."[13] What is yet more disturbing is the degree to which these "automata" are in fact recognizably human—an aspect of their characterization hinted at by Tanner's use of such terms as "alien" and "hostile," familiar sociological language for the description of twentieth century man. The inhabitants of *The Dunciad* are indeed "unaware," yet they are full of effort and will, directed toward strange ends; they display human energy and commitment. Their diving into the mud is not only happy, but determined. In the games of Book II, they display a strong will to win, both because they wish to excel, and because they wish to possess the chamberpots, phantoms, and whores provided as prizes. If they were only subhuman and mechanical, they could be more readily dismissed; in fact, they are also characterized (although not individualized) by familiar human modes of will and action.

Individual figures in *The Dunciad* resemble one another in their obsessive search for power, victory, and personal gain, which demonstrates their self-obsession. Their solipsism, cutting them off from God as well as from other men, is the basis of Pope's ultimate indictment. But they are unaware of the meaninglessness of their lives; their ridiculous activities occupy them fully. They do not know that they suffer, for the poet conceives them, and they conceive themselves, largely in mechanical terms. Although these dullards, according to Pope's conception of human nature, must have potential power to reverse their downward course, they lack the developed capacity for moral perception that might save them. "By the blind man we generally understand the sinner," wrote a medieval commentator.[14] The dunces are from Pope's viewpoint sinners precisely because of their moral blindness. At the end of the poem, when Dulness triumphs through the elimination of light, this cosmic debacle is the logical fulfillment of Bays's original prayer: "And lest we err by Wit's wild dancing light, / Secure us kindly in our native night" (I, 175–176). Blindness is not the natural state even of dunces; it is the condition of security to which they aspire. The final demonstration of the way in which psychic phenomena can affect objective reality is Pope's inverted presentation of the traditional microcosm-macrocosm relation, in which the macrocosm—society and finally cosmos—reflects the obscurity and confusion of the microcosm, the individual mind. Bays, praying for the victory of darkness, does not understand the meaning of his prayer. He values his limitation of perception, even longs for an increase of restriction that will, by destroying choice, eliminate the burden of decision and the possibility of wrong choice. The dunces' limited perception is the origin of the darkened world, which the poet-seer perceives but is powerless to change.

So the relation between perception and reality, between imagery and fact, in *The Dunciad* implies a pseudometaphysics resembling Berkeley's, a questioning of assumptions about the relation between moral perception and moral actuality. What appears at first to be wild exaggeration, comes to seem like accurate embodiment of mental process. What seems to be metaphor may be fact. The "real" affinities between people and the images describing them are repeatedly suggested. On one level, the poem's imagistic extravagances are direct reflections of realities. It is usually assumed that a satirist's degrading imagery for deviants from the order he upholds creates an imaginative distance between the reader and the poem's subjects, removing the possibility of irrelevant human sympathy and forcing one to understand moral deviants as phenomena rather than as human beings. Pope, however, by raising questions about the relation between the way his victims see themselves and their world, and the way they appear to him, complicates the issue. Though it may be artificial to distinguish between the poet's perceptions and the perceptions of characters who exist only as his creations, this is a meaningful artifice, pointing to one way in which *The Dunciad* challenges social fact and suggesting a special justification for its most traditional satiric techniques.

"Where history appears so disordered, the poetic backward glance may give meaning to the present, which becomes significant through the realization of what has been destroyed or lost in it. In this sense, the mythical method is basically satirical. It provides the author with a point of view and a set of standards which give power to his invective and tragic weight to his criticism."[15] These remarks apply precisely to *The Dunciad*, but their subject is *The Waste Land*. Eliot, like Pope, confronted a culture in decay. Like Pope, he invoked the literature and standards of the past to comment on the present; more explicitly than Pope, he rendered the life around him as a version of hell. His fragmented version of epic, like Pope's more vividly satiric one, conveys a special relation between the perception of reality and its linguistic ordering.

Whereas *The Dunciad* testifies to the power of mind, *The Waste Land* affirms, at most, the existence of a particular mind. Eliot has brought together various material and placed it in precarious suspension, shoring insecure fragments against the ruins. The quotation from F. H. Bradley incorporated in his notes to the poem suggests how severely limited is Eliot's sense of the lasting power of intellect—a sense of limitation he shares, with most of his contemporaries. "My external sensations," wrote Bradley, "are no less private to myself than are my thoughts or my feelings. In either case my experience falls within my own circle, a circle closed on the outside; and, with all its elements alike, every sphere is opaque to the others which surround it . . . In brief, regarded as an existence which appears in a soul, the whole world for each is peculiar and private to that soul."[16] The implication is that one can make no dependable distinction between recorded sense impressions and fantasy, since there is no way to be sure of external reality. The reality of the individual mind is all that mind can know for certain. Everyone's world is "peculiar and private," which clearly describes the ambience of *The Waste Land*.

As a presentation of society, therefore, the poem makes no ultimate claim to "realism"; in fact, such a claim would be impossible, given the philosophic assumptions on which it rests. However, if it is not "documentary," neither can *The Waste Land* profess to be entirely a satire, since satire implies belief in a standard of what society should be—a manifest absurdity if it is impossible even to know what society *is*. If the poem claims only to be a record of perceptions, it never makes clear whose perceptions they are. Though literally they must be the poet's, his technique suggests the presence of various imagined consciousnesses as well. And the assumption that perception must be absolutely private creates further aesthetic and psychological problems. The possibilities for artistic organization seem limited; one must wonder to what extent, on what principles, with what meaning the artist can order the details that impinge on his consciousness.

Eliot inhabited a shrinking world. Bradley testified to its metaphysical shrinkage, which implied a corresponding social fragmentation. In a letter to a Harvard neurologist written in 1915, Freud discusses whether people who have been psychoanalyzed can be expected to be better human beings than those who have not. He concludes that analysis "makes for *unity*, but not necessarily for *goodness*."[17] The notion of psychic unity implied by *The Waste Land* is as limited, and in the same way, as that which Freud suggests. To separate the idea of unity from that of goodness is to narrow the imagination of what can be unified. The aim of the analyzed man is merely a self-sufficient integration of personality. The "well-adjusted" man is not necessarily "good." A small, self-contained unity is imaginable, for an individual can hope to achieve a sense of his own integrity. But he will find no necessarily meaningful relation among, for example, his intellectual, social, or religious experiences; and he does not necessarily share the professed or actual values of the society he inhabits.

It may seem that *The Waste Land* assumes the possibility of that larger cultural unity of human experience in different times and places which makes Hindu philosophy or a play of Kyd's relevant to the twentieth century. In fact, though, the pervasive literary allusions of the poem have a dislocating rather than a unifying effect, an effect comparable to that suggested for quotations by Walter Benjamin. Hannah Arendt, in her essay on Benjamin, has summarized his attitude: "He discovered that the transmissibility of the past had been replaced by its citability and that in place of its authority there had arisen a strange power to settle down, piecemeal, in the present and to deprive it of 'peace of mind,' the mindless peace of complacency . . . This discovery of the modern function of quotations, according to Benjamin . . . was born out of despair . . . out of the despair of the present and the desire to destroy it; hence their power is 'not the strength to preserve but to cleanse, to tear out of context, to destroy.' "[18]

The feeling about tradition here suggested is much like that implied by *The Waste Land,* where a sense of fragmentation extends to include the historical and literary past. Eliot's insistent citation of vanished literary splendors reflects despair, creating an impression not of permanence but only of bits and pieces contained by the poet's mind. Discussing Benjamin's use of quotations as "thought fragments," Arendt remarks that they "have the double task of interrupting the flow of the presentation with 'transcendent force' . . . and at the same time of concentrating within themselves that which is presented."[19] Similarly Eliot's reminders of the past both interrupt and concentrate his meaning. They repeatedly recall vanished values, but they affirm no present possibility. "Quotations . . . seem to float like alien bodies in the sentences of . . . *The Waste Land.*"[20] Their "alien" quality, the sense they convey of belonging to some other world while remaining obscurely relevant to the facts of the present, mirrors the alienation of individuals that the poem depicts. The artist, feeling his own isolation—and lacking the corresponding sense of power that informs *The Dunciad*—finds images for it in the isolation of others and in the music of disjointedness.

The poem's inhabitants function as individuals, outlining the symptomology of a corrupt civilization, but having no discernible effect beyond their immediate environment. They belong to no meaningful whole. Eliot's notes stress his dependence on the myth of the Holy Grail and on the even more ancient religious traditions recorded in *The Golden Bough*: traditions and rites of societies in which an individual's "quest" had social and religious as well as psychological functions, in which men could feel part of something greater than themselves. The vastly different quest in the foreground of *The Waste Land* is a search for individual salvation in almost Freudian terms. "I can connect / Nothing with nothing," says one of the Thames daughters (301–302), whose plight is representative. The chief source of desolation is the loss of self, exemplified by the woman who in the context of adult aimlessness recalls the joys of childhood sledding, the typist who allows herself to be casually seduced, lacking reason to resist, the neurotic lady who panics over the question of what to do tomorrow, and her equally tormented male companion who, knowing what they are likely to do, knows also how meaningless it will be. None of these characters has a coherent sense of identity or of relation to any larger reality. The people of *The Waste Land* are victims of the lives they lead, the world they live in; their responsibility for their own misery is never clear.

Although the focus on individuals is intense, the importance of the individual seems dubious: the perceiving consciousness is aware of its own insignificance. Individuals have little individuality. As George T. Wright has put it, "Personality is shadowy and tentative; the human, not the individual, occupies almost all the poet's attention. The characters are like unconscious immortals who, in the fashion of Tiresias, change shape, setting, culture from age to age and repeatedly perform the same ritualistic functions in Egypt, in Greece, in England, from behind masks that betray nothing of the distinctive face."[21] The Thames daughters, the women in the pub, "Marie" who reads and goes south—each embodies a social class and the problems peculiar to its representatives at specific times of life. They are presented as aware of their own suffering, as seeking solutions or as unable to imagine solutions. The corrupt society that surrounds them makes meaningful resolution almost inconceivable; the environment destroys its inhabitants.

Perception, a self-evident good from Pope's point of view, in Eliot's vision has more ambiguity of value. Many of his characters are afflicted with severely limited awareness, but limitation may be preferable to its alternative. Even the difference between life and death often seems a technicality in *The Waste Land*. The crowd that flows over London Bridge is a mass of the living dead, verbally associated with those in Dante's Limbo. As life approaches death, as people approach loss of consciousness, horror becomes more endurable. Unconsciousness is not itself damnation, as in *The Dunciad*, but it helps to make damnation tolerable; men come to feel that hell is their natural condition. The seduced typist is "Hardly aware of her departing lover; / Her brain allows one half-formed thought to pass" (250–251); she smoothes her hair with "automatic hand" (255), automatism suggesting her psychic state. Her limitation of awareness has allowed the seduction; it also enables her to endure it. Winter is the desired season, as the poem opens, because it provides "forgetful snow" (6), while the cruelty of April is its stirring of awareness. The poem's "clairvoyante," Madame Sosostris, seems not to see very clearly, although she "Is known to be the wisest woman in Europe" (43). She also has a bad cold, a suggestive image for the choked and stifled state characteristic of the poem's inhabitants. The wealthy neurotic woman asks her uncommunicative companion, "Are you alive, or not? Is there nothing in your head?" (126). Her question, more appropriate than she knows, echoes through the poem's empty world. In the young man's head, in all heads, are incoherence and despair. "Thinking of the key, each confirms a prison" (415). Images of limitation, restriction, lack, define the human condition. Loss of consciousness is a relief in a world that destroys meaning and possibility.

Tiresias, the voice of wisdom in the poem, bears the burden of heightened consciousness, that is, of heightened suffering. The poem as a whole manifests the agony of awareness. F. R. Leavis has written of Eliot: "We have . . . considered the poet as being at the conscious point of his age. There are ways in which it is possible to be too conscious; and to be so is . . . one of the troubles of the present age . . . We recognize in modern literature the accompanying sense of futility."[22] The author of *The Waste Land* seems at least as aware as Leavis of the sense of futility and its source in excessive consciousness, for it is one of his major themes. Embodying, as perceiver and spokesman, the possibility of awareness, he moves inevitably toward the chaos of allusion that concludes the poem, a version of the chaos always implicit in understanding too much. *The Waste Land* is, among other things, a cry of the misery of excessive perception familiar from much of the art and experience of the present time.

To see is to suffer, in Eliot's world; one avoids suffering only by death, literal or metaphorical. The possibility of religious salvation exists in the background, but in the foreground sterility dominates. Salvation, which comes by grace, has no connection with real life; rather it represents the possibility of escape from life's horror. Society has become a meaningless mass in which individuals lose their selfhood, and religion is a survival from the past that has virtually disappeared as a present reality. For example, the splendid church of St. Philip Magnus, which provides momentary comfort, is slated for destruction. Intellect and sensitivity intensify suffering, but even the mindless suffer, without full awareness.

Such ideas by implication deny the significance, perhaps even the possibility, of poetry. If the evil of society infects all lives, the poet can hardly be free. If awareness leads to perception of chaos, the individual poet, reflecting on what he perceives, can record only disorder, producing at best a "heap of broken images" (22). The dedication to Ezra Pound as "il miglior fabbro" (the better maker) recalls the great tradition of the poet as creator, duplicating on a small scale the divine Creator who by the power of the word formed order from chaos—the tradition that informed Donne's greatest work. But Pound as a maker is, like Eliot himself, a collector of quotations, a creator of verbal collage. The possibilities of "making," suggests *The Waste Land,* are now limited. Only a temporary, obscure, often private order is possible at best: the poem requires footnotes. Its very form, implying acceptance of severely limited resources, reflects the self-deprecation—perhaps even the self-pity—characteristic of the twentieth century. By its lyric power *The Waste Land* partly transfigures such unattractive emotions, but it also denies the lasting possibility of more dignified kinds of feeling.

To say that the possibilities of order are restricted is not to say that they are nonexistent. *The Waste Land* does, finally, make a kind of coherent statement with relevance outside itself, by demonstrating poetry's resources in a time of incoherence and despair. The fragmentation of images, like the fragmentation of personality they help to depict, preserves real perception. Despite the isolation of the perceiver, communication can be achieved. His recording of what he sees, through its verbal energy and exactness, demands response. Although there can be no assurance about the nature of external reality, it often appears that many people have seen the same thing. Samuel Johnson refuted Berkeley's skepticism by kicking a stone; Eliot, while accepting Bradley's skepticism, demonstrates its practical limitations by creating a recognizable world and thus implying human identity as well as human separation. The collocation of the grand and the trivial, here achieved by insistent literary reference, is a classic method of satire and has a necessary satiric effect; but the unrealities and grotesqueries of this wasteland are mostly perceived, not invented. Despite its fantastic elements, it is not understood as fantasy.

Jacob Korg has written of the poem, "By taking nonsymbolic elements borrowed from real life, such as the quotations from 'Mrs. Porter and her daughter' and 'London Bridge is falling down,' and examples of flat, objective realism like the aimless and trivial reminiscences of the character who identifies herself as 'Marie,' and the talk of the women in 'A Game of Chess,' and putting them side by side with imagined people and events, the poem insists upon both the distinction and the relationship between art and actuality. The quoted material and lines of mundane dialogue are concrete instances of the spiritual condition which is the theme of the poem."[23] Many of Korg's descriptive terms are questionable, which suggests how difficult it is to speak accurately of relations between art and reality. What he calls "nonsymbolic" and "borrowed from real life"—the references to popular lyric and nursery rhyme—have symbolic weight in their new context and are borrowed not from "life" but from popular literature. "Marie" and the women in "A Game of Chess" are as truly "imagined people" as anyone else in the poem. Yet the distinction between art and actuality is indeed an important subject of *The Waste Land,* if only because the poem raises the question of how a meaningful art can be made from what seems sordid and meaningless.

Eliot does not, like Pope, deal in labels or in explicit judgments. But he leads the reader to attach appropriate labels, to see the modern world with such clarity that he also sees its meaning. The individuals who inhabit the wasteland systematically make themselves unreal and, at their most anguished, half perceive their own unreality. "I read, much of the night, and go south in the winter," Marie remarks (18), describing activities equally automatic and meaningless in her experience. "My nerves are bad tonight. Yes, bad. Stay with me. / Speak to me. Why do you never speak. Speak," says another women (111–112). The nervous staccato defines the emphasis of self-obsession, implies the assumption that one's inadequacies should be reason enough for the concern of others.

In both quotations, the impression of incomplete humanity depends not on exaggeration or extravagance but on the poet's selectivity and precision in rendering the speech of modern time. He forces one to listen to what he often hears without listening. Forced to listen, and to see, the reader observes men and women "pinned and wriggling on the wall," lacking human stature, capacity, or will, incapable of love, reduced to animal couplings and abortions. Never told that these men and women are insects or animals, as he is constantly told by Pope, the reader is simply faced with the degradation of the twentieth century. Seeing it, finding it recognizable, he experiences the seeing as suffering. What is seen is horror—psychological, social, and finally metaphysical, despite the apparent disjunctiveness of experience.

The philosophic assumptions of *The Waste Land* dicate a particular kind of art. Even if the individual is rigidly confined by the limitations of his own perceptions, he can record those perceptions with exactitude and force. Limitation is not for Eliot, as it often is for Pope, a primary source of philosophic or aesthetic strength; but it is the necessary condition of art. The data of direct observation and of literary knowledge coexist in the poet's mind, which orders the poem. Technique as negation dominates *The Waste Land* and contradicts the cautious optimism of its ending. The disparity of rhetorical levels, sharp and unaccountable shifts of tone, frequent, sometimes opaque, literary allusions, have led critics to agree in general that the poem's unity is difficult to discern. Certainly the impression of randomness is stronger than that of organization. It is possible to find verbal connections between one section of the poem and another, to "understand" the application of the literary allusions, and to be excited by the suggestive power of the imagery, without feeling any inner sense of form. Yet Eliot does not merely imitate the chaos he perceives; what he imitates is the form given to chaos as a result of perception and understanding. In this sense *The Waste Land* testifies to and depends on the power of a mind, the only reality to which it is finally committed.

*The Dunciad* seems deliberately to multiply confusions about reality and the possibility of perceiving it. If the dunces' states of mind determine the nature of the realm they inhabit, it is equally true that in certain aspects the literal world of objective fact is as bizarre as anything dunces might imagine. It is on this level that Pope's elaborate structure of footnote documentation carries special weight, for the footnotes call attention to verifiable details of eighteenth century life so fantasic in themselves that they seem to justify the farthest reaches of satiric fantasy. In conjunction with the poetic text, the notes also insist on the poet's power of perception: he sees the facts of his world, available to any observer, but he also sees their meaning as metaphors for mental process and particularly for mental deterioration. The notes themselves often represent an artful selection from or heightening of reality; they intensify the impression created by the poem that the line between fact and metaphor is impossible to draw.

The interaction between psychic and physical reality as something continuous and complex, is an obsessive subject of *The Dunciad,* which not only creates images for dullness but also discovers them in the real world:

> Close to those walls where Folly holds her throne,
> And laughs to think Monroe would take her down,
> Where o'er the gates, by his fam'd father's hand
> Great Cibber's brazen, brainless brothers stand.
> (I, 29–32)

Folly's realm is Bedlam, presided over by Dr. John Monro; Cibber's father was a sculptor, on whom Pope's note comments, "The two Statues of the Lunatics over the gates of Bedlam-hospital were done by him, and (as the son justly says of them) are no ill monuments of his fame as an Artist." The physical facts of the setting are thus approximations of the truth, although the poet supplies their significance. But in one instance he has deviated from exactitude—presumably at first by inadvertence, later by deliberation. The statues over the gate to Bedlam were not of brass but of stone. In a postscript to a letter to the printer Bowyer, tentatively dated November 13, 1742, Pope writes, "Just now I receive yours about the *Brazen* Image. I would have it stand as it is, & no matter if the Criticks dispute about it."[24] But he adds a note to *The Dunciad,* "Mr. Cibber remonstrated that his Brothers at Bedlam, mentioned Book i. were not *Brazen*, but *Blocks;* yet our author let it pass unaltered, as a trifle, that no way lessened the Relationship (II,3).[25] The truth of Cibber's metaphorical brazenness transforms his "brothers' " literal stoniness, although the footnote also exploits the metaphoric possibilities of "blockhead." Such transformations raise yet another set of questions about the nature of reality, with their implication that the truth of metaphor transcends and alters the truth of fact.

The truth of metaphor often seems so nearly identical with the truth of fact that it becomes difficult to separate verbal from physical reality. Here is part of what purports to be Settle's self-description. The facts provided are facts indeed, as the explanatory footnotes attest, but their presentation transforms them into metaphors for the Grub Street author's career:

> Tho' long my Party built on me their hopes,
> For writing Pamphlets, and for roasting Popes;
> Yet lo! in me what authors have to brag on!
> Reduc'd at last to hiss in my own dragon.
> Avert it Heav'n! that thou, my Cibber, e'er
> Should'st wag a serpent-tail in Smithfield fair!
> Like the vile straw that's blown about the streets,
> The needy Poet sticks to all he meets.
>
> (III, 283–290)

A few lines earlier, speaking of theatrical effects, Settle tells Cibber, "On grinning dragons thou shalt mount the wind" (268). Pope's note comments, "In his letter to Mr. P. Mr. C. solemnly declares this not to be *literally true*. We hope therefore the reader will understand it *allegorically* only." He thus calls attention to the problem of how a poem relates literal and allegorical truth. The note to Settle's account of his own career, however, reveals that Settle's dragon is literal: "he acted in his old age in a Dragon of green leather of his own invention." Literal, but hardly real: a dragon of his own invention for a self-invented poet. Once more, a struggle is needed to reconcile various levels of reality: the allegorical dragon, which seems no less "real" than the literal dragon, becomes itself a disguise for the poverty-stricken poet but also, in its inability to harm, its propensity to hiss, and its imitation of ferocity, an emblem of that poet's "real" nature.

Similarly, Settle literally roasted a simulacrum of the Pope: "He had managed the Ceremony of a famous Pope-burning on *Nov.* 17, 1680." The fact that he really burned an unreal Pope becomes in presentation a metaphor for the operations of writers whose destructiveness, one degree removed from reality, is aimed, for purposes of self-advancement, at religious leaders or at the poet Pope. Its metaphorical significance transforms biographical accident into logical necessity; the metaphor makes more sense than the fact, which Pope associates with Settle's instability and randomness of political action and principle. The linguistic ordering of experience contrasts with the factual disorder of dullards' lives, and it represents the poet's heightened perception of reality. For the dunces, experience is haphazard, insecure, and often meaningless, while the poet perceives the meaningful pattern in their chaotic existences. The patterning of his couplets affirms the inherent logic he perceives, whereby accidents reveal essential truth.

The explicit questioning of established notions of reality and permanence is a subterranean theme of *The Dunciad*. The "vision" presented in the third book, for example, is offered with due attention to the question of its truth or falsity. The visual panorama of Dulness' reign, as it has operated in the past, dominates the present, and will control the future, is compelling and terrifying because convincing. It offers an interpretation of known history and a projection which, like the history itself, is idiosyncratic and exaggerated, but consistent with a considerable body of known fact. The book's last line, however, is, "And thro' the Iv'ry Gate the Vision flies." Its significance is explained by the Virgilian reference appended, as well as by Scriblerus' note to lines 5 and 6 of the same book: "Hereby is intimated that the following Vision is no more than the Chimera of the Dreamer's brain ["Then raptures high the seat of Sense o'erflow, / Which only heads refin'd from Reason know"], and not a real or intended satire on the Present Age . . . For fear of any such mistake of our Poet's honest meaning, he hath again at the end of this Vision, repeated this monition, saying that it all past thro' the *Ivory gate*, which (according to the Ancients) denoteth Falsity."

The disclaimer of satiric intent is a familiar device, easily discounted. But its form here presents difficulties, particularly in conjunction with the new sentence added to the note in 1742 and attributed to Bentley: "How much the good Scriblerus was mistaken [in believing the vision false], may be seen from the Fourth book, which, it is plain from hence, he had never seen." The simple irony of the original footnote is inadequate to deal with the poetic effect: if one tries to operate as the note implies, one is forced, by mere reversal, to feel that this "Chimera of the [stupid] Dreamer's brain" is penetrating truth, a possibility forbidden by the vision's frequent chaotic extravagances. However, neither can one dismiss the dream as altogether false—it is too often recognizable, and too compelling in its emotional demands. The addendum to the note confuses the issue further, by suggesting that the fourth book—more extravagant and contrived than any preceding section—represents a clear standard of truth; again, one can neither accept nor entirely reject such a claim. The reader is forced to attend to the problem of truth implicit throughout the poem: where does reality lie, how can it be determined, in what form is it available to dunces and, for that matter, to twentieth century readers of Pope?

Despite the poem's detailed demonstration of the power of duncelike minds to control the external world, it does not allow one to rest in the assumption that psychic facts are necessarily more "real" than their physical analogues. Here, too, there seems a deliberate attempt to create confusion. The lack of clarity about where description stops and metaphor begins encourages a sense of disorientation. In Book I, Bays is "Sinking from thought to thought, a vast profound! / Plung'd for his sense, but found no bottom there, / Yet wrote and flounder'd on, in mere despair" (118–120). In Book II, the goddess Cloacina recalls how Curll has "fish'd her nether realms for Wit" (101). This sort of "Wit," derived from the depths presided over by the goddess of sewers, is precisely equivalent to its scatological rhyme, which is more predictably associated with the sewer. Later in the same book, various contestants dive into the Thames, marked by "quaking mud, that clos'd, and op'd no more" (292). Bays's mental activity seems to take place in a physical setting and to be identical with the divers' physical activity. His minds' bottomless abyss is indistinguishable from the bottomless mud of the Thames, and both resemble Cloacina's domain, whose "Wit" also resembles that to be found in the unplumbed depths of Bays's mind. Once more, physical and psychic reality reflect one another so intricately that they seem interchangeable. The mud of Bays's mentality, of Cloacina's sewers, of the River Thames—all are equally real, equally fantastic.

Although Pope goes to some pains to suggest the substantiality of the dullards' fantasies as they project themselves into society, he is also at pains to hint that nothing here is at all real. The characters of *The Dunciad* are presented with such manifest artifice that the reader accepts their fictional nature as given. He does not feel involved in this world of dunces, because through many literary devices the poet suggests that it is not real. The coronation of a King of Dulness, the center of the poem's "plot," has many literary antecedents but few actual ones. The reader is kept at a distance from what is going on, which after all is only a joke—or so it seems at the beginning. There is no reason to take the characters as serious versions of real people, because even their names have by now lost reality; rather, they seem like creations of the comic (or satiric) imagination. "The *Poem was not made for these Authors, but these Authors for the Poem.*"[26]

"These Authors" themselves often prefer the unreal to the real. The "phantoms" that Dulness creates at the beginning of Book II are a case in point:

> She form'd this image of well-body'd air;
> With pert flat eyes she window'd well its head;
> A brain of feathers, and a heart of lead;
> And empty words she gave, and sounding strain,
> But senseless, lifeless! idol void and vain!
> Never was dash'd out, at one lucky hit,
> A fool, so just a copy of a wit.
>
> (42–47)

In its linguistic emptiness and lack of sense and life, this "image" is identical with the bad poet it imitates. The competing stationers, offered the false poet as prize, can hardly be blamed for valuing it, because of its "poet's name" (51) and its fashionable apparel, but "the tall Nothing" (110) melts into air before they can achieve possession of it, to be replaced by new false images contrived by decking out bad writers to look like good ones (121–130). Then Dulness suggests that what she has done resembles the activities of "the sage dame, experienc'd in her trade, / [who] By names of Toasts retails each batter'd jade" (133–134); thus the unfortunate Frenchman returning from London complains "of wrongs from Duchesses and Lady Maries" (136). Pope in an early letter had described the difficulty of "being a public author without, like a whore, being at everyone's disposal"; the metaphor of prostitutes for poets was a particularly compelling one.[27] But to suggest that they are prostitutes pretending to be fine ladies is a yet more biting indictment. Falsity is an important resource of Dulness, and one to which Pope insistently calls attention.

Like Swift in the *Tale of a Tub*, Pope here suggests that appearance is more important than reality in a corrupt world. The Frenchman's difficulty in distinguishing between a true and pretended Lady Mary implies that such a distinction would be difficult for anyone, since the noblewoman resembles a whore in the first place. The copy of a wit is as satisfactory as the original because false wit is universally confounded with true. False perception leads to false valuation. Society values shadows as highly as substance, and shadow images in individual minds yield shadows in the world, so that the distinction between true and false becomes ever harder to make. Pope's declared target in *The Dunciad* was the "impositions" of dunces on society. To Hugh Bethel he wrote, "I little thought 3 months ago to have drawn the whole polite world upon me, (as I formerly did the Dunces of a lower Species) as I certainly shall whenever I publish this poem [*The New Duncia*d] . . . But a Good Conscience a bold Spirit, & Zeal for Truth, at whatsoever Expence, of whatever Pretenders to Science, or of all Imposition either Literary, Moral, or Political; these animated me, & these will Support me."[28] "Zeal for Truth" leads the poet to attack pretenders and their impositions, but it leads him also to the realization that truth is often impenetrable.

The hair that perhaps divides the false from the true is difficult to discern. Poets are particularly apt to be victims of illusion, for when "raptures high" overflow "the seat of Sense" (III, 5), the result is:

> the Fools' Paradise, the Statesman's Scheme,
> The air-built Castle, and the golden Dream,
> The Maid's romantic wish, the Chemist's flame,
> And Poet's vision of eternal Fame.
>
> (9–12)

The poet, through his concern with language and reputation, through his very preoccupation with fancy, may be led away from substance. As Pope had written twenty years before, " 'Tis no figure, but a serious truth I tell you when I say that my Days & Nights are so much alike, so equally insensible of any Moving Power but Fancy, that I have sometimes spoke of things in our family as Truths & real accidents, which I only Dreamt of; & again when some things that actually happen'd came into my head, have thought (till I enquird) that I had only dream'd of them."[29] Given such a state of mind, the poet's capacity to discern may diminish; and in a society of dunces, fulfilling his responsibility to see clearly becomes even more difficult. But Pope's poetic commitment to the discernment of reality is apparent throughout *The Dunciad*; his emphasis, through technique and substance alike, on the problem of finding where reality lies attests the commitment's seriousness. If he claims implicitly or explicitly that his satire is only fiction, such a claim is ultimately a device for demonstrating his focus on truth. Although he explores more fully than Eliot the possibilities for confusion and error in perception, the obscurities involved in attempting to find the real, he also demonstrates, as Eliot cannot, the firmness of his belief that reality does exist and can be discovered. To believe that there are shadows, one must have faith in substance; to condemn falsity, one has to know truth. Pope is aware of both sides—shadow and substance, falsity and truth—and of the necessity to distinguish between them. The solidity of the poet's stance in *The Dunciad* contrasts with the fluidity of the speaker's position in *The Waste*

*Land*; the solidity of the literary tradition Pope evokes has a reassuring effect in contrast with the dislocating force of the literary references in *The Waste Land*. Both poems convey impressions of social chaos by stressing the tenuousness of reality and the difficulty and complexity of proper perception. But *The Waste Land* goes farther, to question the possibility of accurate perception, the existence of anything external to the perceiver. In *The Dunciad*, the poet's authority is final; the poet-perceiver can achieve and render a complex understanding of truth.

The poet, however, is not only a perceiver. As *The Dunciad* demonstrates, in a decaying society perception alone is not a sufficient guide to truth, though confidence in the existence of a truth pervades the poem. Whereas *The Waste Land* ends with a note of affirmation in the concluding Sanskrit invocation, *The Dunciad* ends by asserting the final disappearance of intelligence and culture. Yet *The Waste Land* leaves an impression of despair; and the darkness, literal and metaphoric, of *The Dunciad's* ending is not enough to destroy its frequent exuberance of tone or the sense of triumphant intelligence generated by the author's lucidity and dexterity. If *The Waste Land* displays technique as negation, *The Dunciad* demonstrates the possibility of technique as affirmation. The rich inventiveness that describes and condemns the dunces and their activities, the ingenuity and complexity of reference to the past, the skill with which Pope intermingles fact and fantasy—all provide irrefutable evidence of the power of mind. Mind and antimind, or dullness, are the contending powers of the poem. The contest's implicit metaphysic is that of the *Essay on Criticism*: light and darkness in opposition reflect the eternal opposition of good and evil.[30] Intellect and its manifestation, wit, derive from light or good, and hence from God. Pope's capacity to create comedy out of chaos, to understand the dunces as both menacing and ridiculous, testifies to the exactitude of his judgment. The energy and authority of judgment ordering the poem account for the power of the packed couplets, the patterns of imagery, and the structure of allusion. Judgment insists on the possibility and the necessity of order. When the sleep of dullness destroys all consciousness in the world, even overpowering the muse, the triumphant fact of the poet's ordering consciousness, his dominant judgment, remains. The poem remains, as a testament of faith.

Looking at *The Dunciad* as an achievement of judgment, one can understand it in new ways. One realizes, for example, that it is not enough to speak of the way in which the dunces see themselves and one another, for Pope's presentation of their curious modes of seeing adds another dimension, controls the reader's evaluation of the dunces and of duncery. The gap between Bays's understanding of his prayer to Dulness and the reader's, or between Aristarchus' judgment and the reader's of the value of bringing to one dead level every mind, is a gap created by Pope, and created largely by his mastery of imagery. The images that reflect the reality of the dunces' minds and of the ways in which they alter and finally dominate the world simultaneously judge the process they describe. Satire begins by presenting reality distorted, and ends by showing reality judged.

By making his readers aware of complexity, Pope involves them in the process by which accurate judgment is attained. He convinces one that his characters may be more accurately described as bugs and blockheads than as men, since their "real" nature is embodied in such images; but he makes one aware that the opposite is also true. In fact, these particular bugs and blockheads really are men, and cannot be understood without awareness of their humanity. Two different versions of reality, two levels of understanding, come into conflict. To reconcile them, or to accept the impossibility of reconciling them, is to begin to come to terms with the problems of value that *The Dunciad* raises.

To some extent it supplies the standards by which chaos is to be judged, even while describing chaotic actuality. The fact of mock epic itself implies this paradox, but it also operates outside the epic connections. "It is not every Knave, nor (let me add) Fool, that is a fit subject for a Dunciad," William Warburton pointed out, comparing Pope's version of epic with the variety it parodies. "There must still exist some Analogy, if not Resemblance of Qualities, between the Heroes of the two Poems; and this in order to admit what Neoteric critics call the *Parody*, one of the liveliest graces of the little Epic. Thus it being agreed that the constituent qualities of the greater Epic Hero, are *Wisdom, Bravery,* and *Love,* from whence springeth *heroic Virtue*; it followeth that those of the lesser Epic Hero, should be *Vanity, Impudence,* and *Debauchery.*"[31] Each quality of the mock hero recalls, by grotesque similarity as well as by contrast, a virtue of the true hero. Urinating, diving, and tickling parody activities recorded in genuine epic; each image implies a grander counterpart of itself, so that description contains judgment.

Traditions broader and more immediate than those of epic are employed in similar ways. As the mock epic parodies the real and thus reveals the decadence of the world it reflects, so the dunces' glorification of "virtue" points to their abandonment of established principle. In 1724, Pope had commented, "Instead of the four Cardinal Virtues, now reign four Princely ones: We have Cunning for Prudence, Rapine for Justice, Time-serving for Fortitude, and Luxury for Temperance."[32] By the time he used a similar idea in *The Dunciad,* he had found visual images to suggest the perversion involved in the dunces' pageantry of virtue. He describes a parody of the representation of the cardinal virtues in the spectacles associated with the Lord Mayor's Day, defining the "virtues" in action while presenting them in static poses.

> Four guardian Virtues, round, support her [Dulness'] throne:
> Fierce champion Fortitude, that knows no fears
> Of hisses, blows, or want, or loss of ears;
> Calm Temperance, whose blessings those partake
> Who hunger, and who thirst for scribling sake:
> Prudence, whose glass presents th' approaching jayl:
> Poetic Justice, with her lifted scale,
> Where, in nice balance, truth with gold she weighs,
> And solid pudding against empty praise.
>
> (I, 46–54)

The traditional names of value remain, given new content by the actualities of the dunces' experience. Hisses, blows, poverty, the pillory, and jail are the realities with which such men must contend; they redefine old ideals in terms of new pragmatic demands implied by such realities.[33] In this society the solidity of gold and pudding overbalances the lightness of truth and reputation; justice must function accordingly. But because the pageant and the virtues it celebrates recall the forms and values of the past, a time when abstract terms of good and evil had more moral substance, the group of posed personifications implies its own condemnation, containing within itself clear allusions to established standards of judgment. The scene implies a confrontation of appearance (the symbolic representations of virtue) with reality (the recalled moral essence of virtue); it invokes the power of tradition to judge a corrupt present.

Judgment resides also in images that do not so obviously draw on literary or moral tradition. Though the recording of disorder is a temptation to artistic disorder, Pope through imagery creates order even while providing sensuous impressions of its opposite. An example is the passage early in the first book where Dulness surveys her realms:

> Here she beholds the Chaos dark and deep,
> Where nameless Somethings in their causes sleep,
> 'Till genial Jacob, or a warm Third day,
> Call forth each mass, a Poem, or a Play:
> How hints, like spawn, scarce quick in embryo lie,
> How new-born nonsense first is taught to cry,
> Maggots half-form'd in rhyme exactly meet,
> And learn to crawl upon poetic feet.
> Here one poor word an hundred clenches makes,
> And ductile dulness new meanders takes;
> There motley Images her fancy strike,
> Figures ill pair'd, and Similies unlike.
> She sees a Mob of Metaphors advance,
> Pleas'd with the madness of the mazy dance:
> How Tragedy and Comedy embrace;
> How Farce and Epic get a jumbled race;
> How Time himself stands still at her command,
> Realms shift their place, and Ocean turns to land.
> (55–72)

The power of dullness, through the goddess herself or through her instruments, can turn "nameless Somethings" into specific realities, create and control action, or manipulate time and space. Such creation, control, and manipulation produce grotesqueness, madness, and horror, suggested in particular by the sexual image of miscegenation and by the description of nonsense as a newborn infant who must be taught to cry. The images unite with one another to evoke a pattern of response because of their unity of emotional suggestion. Formlessness and randomness are the theme.[34] Images of infantilism, human and animal, of vigorous but meaningless nonhuman activity ("an hundred clenches," the "new meanders" of dullness, which foretell the "running Lead" of nonsense that slips "thro' Cracks and Zig-zags of [Bays's] Head," I, 123–124), and of equivalent human activity, turning finally into the distorted sexuality that produces unions of Tragedy and Comedy and generates children from Farce and Epic—this sequence forms a coherent emotional pattern from an incoherent series of phenomena. Thus, wittily, false wit is described. Ordinary experience reveals little necessary connection between literary dependence on puns, the use of inaccurate similes, the popularity of bad drama, and lack of faithfulness to genre. Each may be a sign of artistic decay, but beyond that they have nothing in common. Pope, making concrete and specific the meaning of such an abstraction as artistic decay, demonstrates how disparate phenomena may be unified by a discerning intellect that opposes the force of dullness.

Judgment discriminates, wit unites, in the eighteenth century view. Both function in this passage to select the evidence of literary decadence, to create images that dramatize the nature of decadence, to reveal how the merely whimsical ("maggots") shares sinister implications with the more serious, and to show the likeness of the various forces, trivial and significant, that move literary and social consciousness toward disorder. The order of intellect opposes the chaos of dullness in the act of representing it.

The judgmental function of imagery is particularly important in a satire where the positive norms, although named and on occasion identified with real people, are far less clear and forceful than the powers opposing them—or at any rate, their force is less obvious than that of evil and stupidity. By careful manipulation of imagery, Pope evokes the disgust and revulsion that are appropriate responses to the corruptions of dullness, and he repeatedly suggests the existence of positive alternatives to lazy or evil behavior. Rebecca Parkin has defined the characteristics of the *Dunciad's* metaphor as "richness and complexity . . . the use of ambiguity and paradox to convey ironical meanings in metaphor; the constant interlocking and interplay of the metaphors; and the tendency of them all to converge toward the central theme or to stand for it in little."[35] The interlocking patterns and their tendency to converge are vital in conveying the poem's central meanings.

Two characteristic image-sequences may shed light on the technique of judgment by image. They concern eating or drinking and sexuality—two forms of the debauchery that characterizes the hero of mock epic.[36] Pope uses the word *debauchery* to refer specifically to sexual excess, but its implications extend to other forms of physical self-indulgence. A dominant theme of the references to eating is established by the first food image contrasting solid pudding with empty praise early in the first book. Though both pudding and praise are conceivable rewards for the poet, the literary man dedicated to dullness is likely to choose the first, because of its apparent solidity and because of his own necessities. It is typical of dunces to be hungry and thirsty, and *The Dunciad* supplies an explanation. The most obvious reason is that they are literally poor, a fact that for Pope reflects and symbolizes their intellectual poverty. Those who hunger and thirst after righteousness are blessed, the Bible says, because they shall be filled. The dull, whose hunger and thirst is part of their unrighteousness and their dedication to endless and meaningless "scribling," can never be filled; their desire is insatiable. Bays, in his first appearance, is seen "Swearing and supperless" (I, 115), a conjunction that suggests his nature. Poverty of mind and of pocket deprives men of nutriment. Such poverty displays itself in blasphemy as well as in the inflated self-valuation and perverse longings of the next speech. The "bards of these degen'rate days" are "starv'ling" (II, 40); in contrast, the "image of well-body'd air" formed by Dulness is "All as a partridge plump, full-fed, and fair" (41–42). The booksellers' avid competition for possession of the prize seems itself a form of hunger: their goal in life is to eat up poets.

The implication of destructiveness in such hunger is borne out by other metaphoric references to eating. Bays, "an industrious Bug," sips and sucks the work of others; his eating and drinking, as the language of the passage makes apparent, are forms of plunder (I, 129–130). Around him lie "poor Fletcher's half-eat scenes" (131). His nourishment, like that of the bedbug he resembles, depends on violation. The sources of creativity have vanished in him: for invention he substitutes theft, and the metaphor of destructive eating suggests the use he makes of what he steals. At higher levels of intellectual endeavor, similar activities dominate. Aristarchus proclaims:

> In ancient Sense if any needs will deal,
> Be sure I give them Fragments not a Meal;
> What Gellius or Stobaeus hash'd before,
> Or chew'd by blind old Scholiasts o'er and o'er.
> (IV, 229–232)

Pope's notes gloss Stobaeus as "an author, who gave his Commonplace book to the public, where we happen to find much Mincemeat of old books," and explain the last line quoted as describing "These taking the same things eternally from the mouth of one another." The alimentary performances here described are more specific and more disgusting than Bays's; they confirm the idea that dullards nourish themselves by destroying value. "Sense" disappears through fragmentation, significant writings turn to hash, and inadequate scholars pass half-chewed food from one mouth to another, unable even to derive benefit from what they ingest. The perversion of natural physical process symbolizes the perversion of mental process. The ordinary procedures of eating and digestion are so normal as hardly to seem normative; Pope indicates the horror of such procedures distorted and suggests that the ordinary, in its very ordinariness, may be a standard of value.

When natural process comes to natural conclusion, it is for Pope another image of the distastefulness of duncery. Curll, racing, slips on a pile of excrement, described as the "evening cates" of his mistress, which she was "wont, at early dawn to drop / . . . before his neighbour's shop" (II, 71–72). Nourishment, for all human beings, produces filth; for the dunces, this fact supplies a crucial comic metaphor. Its more striking use is in the fourth book, in which appears the collector who swallows "Grecian gold" medals: "Receiv'd each Demi-God, with pious care, / Deep in his Entrails" (383–384). When in the natural course of events they issue as excrement, in an ugly "second birth" (386), they become the possession of another connoisseur. The repulsiveness of this procedure and their lack of awareness of that repulsiveness define the dunces' "taste." They use the language of religion ("I rever'd them there, / I bought them, shrouded in that living shrine" [384–385]) for the transaction, as well as the language of finance ("that thus I eat, / Is to refund the Medals with the meat" [389–390]). Their notions of value, spiritual and material, are grossly inappropriate. Once more, Pope invokes the discriminations of ordinary common sense—gold is not to be eaten, defecation is not birth, finance is not religion—to judge his victims through metaphorical descriptions of what they do.

The largest number of references to eating and drinking suggest that for dullards what should be a simple matter of nourishment becomes perverse and destructive self-indulgence. Drunkenness is the natural condition of dunces, whose "inspiration" is likely to be physical intoxication (II, 425–426; III, 169–170). The dead laureate Eusden "thirsts no more for sack or praise" (I, 293), though while alive, he longed for intoxicants physical and psychological. Liquor may, however, destroy the limited capacities of dull poets: Ward is told that he may aspire to become "Another Durfey" if he can free himself "From the strong fate of drams" (III, 145–146). Alcohol may provide the dunce with inspiration or with its reverse, the approach to unconsciousness that is the deep desire of the dull. The final detail of Dulness' triumph in Book III is the image of "Alma mater . . . dissolv'd in Port" (338), an image echoed in the next book by the suggestion that Bentley "now sleeps in Port" (IV, 202). A "clam'rous crowd is hush'd with mugs of Mum" (II, 385) suggests that as a device to lessen awareness and activity, liquor is a valuable resource of dullness.

So is food. Dulness surveys the London scene to find that "May'rs and Shrieves all hush'd and satiate lay, / Yet eat, in dreams, the custard of the day" (I, 91–92). Satiate, they remain insatiable; food is their fulfillment and—dunces that they are—therefore their soporific. Dulness' vision of a perfect society includes her suggestion that she will "Fatten the Courtier, starve the learned band, / And suckle Armies, and dry-nurse the land" (I, 315–316). Cramming is as useful as starvation to reduce men to subjection. "Full-fed Heroes" (III, 281) are the tools of Dulness: a man "cramm'd with capon" (IV, 350) is sure to be a villain, and his villainy is amplified by a metaphor of animal longing for further food, or prey: "Soft, as the wily Fox is seen to creep, / Where bask on sunny banks the simple sheep." (351–352).

The extended image of the sacrilegious priest (IV, 549–564) amplifies the horror of concentration on food. To choose particular objects of concern involves the exclusion of others. Dunces, involved with the achievement and maintenance of their individual well-being, too limited to imagine well-being in other than physical terms, neglect and pervert their own spiritual states. Their misapplied devotion makes the worse appear the better, elevates the low and eliminates the high, so that it becomes equivalent to an active force of evil. Obsessed with the physical, unable to comprehend abstractions, these men denude abstractions of meaningful content.
Their world shrinks to its physical dimensions, as they shrink to eaters and drinkers. Yet they continue to see themselves as priests and bishops, although their highest concern is how to stow "an hundred Souls of Turkeys in a pye" (IV, 594).

The imagery of eating and drinking judges and orders what it describes, not by providing meaningful organization of disparate details, nor by literary allusion or reference to traditional verities, but by invoking the most common-sense standards of normality and sanity. Men use eating for destruction, deprive themselves of meaningful nourishment, value excrement, long for stupefaction, dream only of custard, and confuse the achievement of an elaborate dish of partridge with commitment to the Holy Trinity. For such achievements, "Contending Princes mount them in their Coach" (IV, 564), indicating that the civilization which surrounds them shares their values. Yet the ridiculousness, distortion, and ultimate impiety of their actions and assumptions are obvious. Their inability to deal sensibly with fundamental human processes suggests their inadequacy of comprehension and the ways in which inadequacy becomes evil.

The sexual allusions operate in a similar way. No single allusion to sexual activity is so highly developed or emphatic as the account of cookery's priest, yet the cumulative effect of the sexual references is more striking because more concentrated than that of the imagery of eating and drinking. The technique of sexual allusion in *The Dunciad* depends almost entirely on suggestions of guilt by association. Through metaphor and through direct accounts of their activities, the dunces are associated with sexual corruption and with its ugly results. Such an association is itself an indictment. One is not inclined to consider overeating or even overdrinking as a serious sin, but Pope creates harsh judgments of such an indulgence by indicating its larger significance. In contrast, the very mention of whores and venereal disease, illegitimate children, lust, and abortion contains a built-in negative judgment. The imagery suggests that such details are appropriate metaphors for the mental as well as the physical activity of duncery.

Several examples of one kind of allusion to sexual material have already been mentioned: the spawn, abortions, and miscegenation associated with the confusion of creative endeavor inspired by Dulness; the monster-breeding breast of Bays; and the embryos and abortions that surround him at work ("Round him much Embryo, much Abortion lay," I, 121), all of which add potential horror to the comic chaos in which Dulness and her disciples flourish. Suggesting the distortion of natural process, they concentrate on the perversion of generativity. When Settle offers his triumphant vision of the supremacy of Dulness, he prophesies:

> Another Aeschylus appears! prepare
> For new abortions, all ye pregnant fair!
> In flames, like Semele's, be brought to bed,
> While op'ning Hell spouts wild-fire at your head.
> (III, 313–316)

Birth becomes associated with the spectacular stage effects characteristic of theatrical corruption; parturition is itself a potential spectacle. Abortions are appropriate emblems for the inadequacies and grotesqueries of duncelike literary production. When one dunce accuses another of "vile . . . insect lust" which "Lay'd this gay daughter of the Spring [a prize carnation] in dust" (IV, 415–416), his indictment seems accurate. The predator's lust is "insect" by association with the object of his devotion, a butterfly, but also by its pettiness, subhumanity, and destructive effect. And the concentration of men on objects displayed in Book IV may be seen as misplaced sexuality as well as misplaced religious devotion: it is not the first time that Pope anticipates Freud. The processes of sex and fertility are themselves ugly in Dulness' realm, and the ugly perversions of normal physical fruitfulness accurately define the perversions of literary fruitfulness.

Yet even sexual purity can represent dullness' inadequacies. Bays, sacrificing his manuscripts as he prays to his goddess, commands:

> Go, purify'd by flames ascend the sky,
> My better and more christian progeny!
> Unstain'd, untouch'd, and yet in maiden sheets;
> While all your smutty sisters walk the streets.
> (I, 227–230)

Pope's note quotes from Cibber's *Life*: "my muse and my spouse were equally prolific." The playwright elaborates his metaphor in terms different from Pope's, and the elaboration suggests, like much of his self-description, how witty he finds his own literary inventiveness. Pope demonstrates how Bays's metaphors can turn against him. The king of the dunces prefers his literary to his human children because they more fully feed his vanity. Their "purity" consists in being unread and unacted, facts which their author manages to use to his own advantage. But the metaphor cuts in two directions. It exemplifies Bays's vanity and the distortions it causes, while also suggesting that, for such work as his, the fate of dying unread really is preferable to the likely alternatives of being read only in "the plantations" or used to light fires or to wrap oranges to pelt bad actors (I, 232–236). Bad literature is a form of whoring, like bad opera, "a Harlot form soft sliding by, / With mincing step, small voice, and languid eye" (IV, 45–46). Imagery of prostitution underlines the associations of private and public vice, social and literary corruption, and condemns by implication not only those who corrupt art by prostituting their work but also those who accept whorish literature.

Thus, "pious Needham" (II, 324), a famous madam, plays an important role in the progression of Dulness' reign throughout London; Curll's mistress, Corinna, is the source of excrement; the sluttish Eliza Haywood with her "Two babes of love" (II, 158) is an appropriate prize for the urinating contest; the traveling youth who "The Stews and Palace equally explor'd, / Intrigu'd with glory, and with spirit whor'd" (IV, 315–316), thereby reveals the quality of his education; a whorish "Venus" is adored by all "the sons of sons of sons of whores" (IV, 332) who comprise a corrupt nobility; and the "finish'd Sons" of Dulness are "All melted down, in Pension, or in Punk!" (IV, 510). The allusions stress the decay of social and sexual values, the acceptance of sexual looseness as worth, and the connection of weakened standards in all spheres of activity. The point becomes more emphatic in the simile that compares the trickery of Dulness in making false poets appear true ones with the trickery of "the sage dame" who labels her whores with the names of noble ladies (II, 131–134). Curll's venereal disease, stressed in Pope's note, exemplifies his moral disorder. The collector who is urged to "postpone" his bride for a "headless Phoebe," a statue (IV, 367), represents a yet more shocking form of sexual perversion: his lust, like that of the collector of butterflies, has not even the merit of being properly human.

The most important and extended sexual reference is the portrait of the "youth unknown to Phoebus, in despair" (II, 213), who lacking all literary gifts but still desirous of patronage, finds the efficient way to success by pimping for a nobleman, to whom he offers his sister and consequently "marches off, his Grace's Secretary" (220). The next line contains the goddess' injunction, "Now turn to diff'rent sports"; but almost all the "sports" of Book II have obvious or concealed sexual significance. Triumph in the mud-diving contest involves being "suck'd . . . in" (332) and titillated by mud nymphs; triumph in urinating wins a whore; triumph in the contest for a patron seems likely to go to a tickler whose "gentle touches wanton o'er" the duke's face (201), until it is awarded to the pimp. Scriblerus' note points out that "a creature unlettered, who serveth the passions, or pimpeth to the pleasures of such vain, braggart, puft Nobility, shall with those patrons be much more inward, and of them much higher rewarded" than those who try to win wealth by literary means. The indictment, once more, involves not only artistic prostitution but the enthusiasm with which a decadent society rewards it. A worthy aristocracy might check the evil of worthless writers, but where dullness triumphs, no meaningful distinction exists between nobility and Grub Street. For general decay of standards, sexual imagery is appropriate, since it alludes to a universal passion. Pope depicts a culture in which almost everyone concerns himself, on one level or another, with serving the passions and pimping to the pleasures of those with money and power. Sex is disgusting in such a culture, and becomes a fitting metaphor for other disgusting aspects of intellectual and social endeavor.

The dual function of *The Dunciad*'s imagery—to represent the reality of dullness and simultaneously to judge it—is crucial in generating the poem's extraordinary tonal complexity, unequaled, so far as I know, by any other satiric work. Not even Swift has created such multileveled implication. Swift, withdrawn behind one distorting mask or another, works by the quick succession of conflicting demands on the reader, revealing the inadequacy of each attitude he has previously seemed to require of the sensitive audience. The "proper" attitude toward the phenomena he describes or implies is difficult to ascertain, since he never commits himself to it directly. Pope, however, makes his standards clear. He supplies not only concrete examples but abstract labels for them, such as "Dulness," "true wisdom," and "folly." He states his standards: "Learn, ye DUNCES! not to scorn your God" (III, 224), and he supplies names of real people who embody value: Bacon, Locke, Newton, Christopher Wren, Burlington, Swift, and Gay. But the force and clarity of his indictment depend heavily on his complex use of imagery to reveal the facts of the world as he sees it and to force the reader's negative response to them.

Acceptance of perception as a controlling aesthetic principle in the *Essay on Man* implied the poet's belief in the reality of the observable world. Committing himself to judgment as ordering force in *The Dunciad* argues faith rather in the reality of standards, ethical and intellectual. Since such standards survive meaningfully, if at all, only in the human mind, mental facts are here more significant than physical ones. The technique of the poem, a demonstration of the resources of intellect, affirms the values implicitly defended by the satire's direct attack on intellectual irresponsibility. Although the deity of the *Essay on Man* was God the creator of the existent, observable universe, the act of divine creation was imagined as having already taken place, producing a system of the greatest possible fullness and order. The God implicit in the metaphysics of *The Dunciad* is endlessly active, manifest in the creative process of the poet, that imitation of the ordering of the divine word, which opposes the endless activity of Dullness, the anti-Christ of wit, which narrows and destroys linguistic possibility.[37] The poet committed to the intellectual power of judgment achieves through it, for himself and his readers, the light of clarity, a light that survives the asserted destruction of the poem's ending.

Such considerations are relevant also to *The Waste Land*. To say that it simply depicts reality, or even reality as contained in the poet's mind, fails to account for the way in which the poem forms its response. Nor does it traffic in judgments, provide immediately viable standards, or make a virtue of clarity. However, it does limit the possible reactions to what it presents, partly by complexity rather than lucidity of vision. "Nowhere better than in Eliot," Delmore Schwartz has written, "can we see the difference between being merely literary and making the knowledge of literature an element in vision, that is to say, an essential part of the process of seeing anything and everything,"[38] Because Eliot's mode of seeing the present includes seeing the past, he forces at least a reaction to modern reality in contrast with ancient—a response sometimes sentimental, often colored by simple romanticism, but almost inevitable given the conjunctions he offers. And he limits the possible reactions to his vision of the present itself.

To see clearly, or even complexly, does not necessarily imply the capacity to judge. To judge requires awareness of alternative courses of conduct, and no clear alternatives exist in the wasteland. Judgment rests on standards, but standards in *The Waste Land* survive only in the past. The poet's technique and the response demanded from the reader depend not on judgment but on sensibility, on the capacity to feel, not to evaluate. "Right feeling" is as important to Eliot as to the romantic poets a century before; his sensibility is his most important resource. Delmore Schwartz has commented on this aspect of the poem, too: "In one way, the subject of *The Waste Land* is the sensibility of the protagonist, a sensibility which is literary, philosophical, cosmopolitan and expatriated. But this sensibility is concerned not with itself as such, but with the common things of modern life."[39] To describe Eliot's sensibility in these terms rescues the word from its old-fashioned associations, but the old-fashioned meaning—sensitivity of emotional response, capacity to understand through feeling rather than intellect, a quality opposed to "sense"—is as relevant to Eliot as to Jane Austen. Sensibility is more useful than judgment for dealing with the dilemmas of the modern world. "The common things of modern life" can be fully comprehended only by emotional means. Living in a time when an intellectual response to experience seems often either impossible or inadequate, when faith in the absolute standards that once made judgment viable has eroded, modern man is forced toward faith in his immediate feelings, which seem to come more from what he is than from what he has learned. Believing that security lies only in himself—even if precariously—he must believe in the importance of personal feelings. Judgment—involved with cause and effect, with necessity—is modestly passed over. Eliot's world in this respect resembles today's. The poet's sensibility is more vital to the effect of the poem than is his learning. Learning, in the form of literary, philosophic, and anthropological allusion, contributes to the expression of sensibility. So it is that he can make beauty out of sordid material, conscious of the terrible gap, literary and experiential, between past and present, and conscious of the emotional as well as intellectual import of the gap. And so it is that he demands certain responses, of feeling rather than of judgment, to the material he presents. His own feeling shapes his selectivity, his imagery, his collocations; thus it shapes the reader's feeling, in a way that substitutes for judgment. Pope's imagery convinces first that it portrays reality; then it conveys vital distinctions between the real and the apparent, and offers a version of reality judged. Eliot's purports, on the whole, to be merely descriptive; but its deeper truth is that of emotional response.

A case in point is the famous seduction scene, representative of the complexity of response Eliot achieves. Its introductory section suggests its method:

> I Tiresias, though blind, throbbing between two lives,
> Old man with wrinkled female breasts, can see
> At the violet hour, the evening hour that strives
> Homeward, and brings the sailor home from sea,
> The typist home at teatime, clears her breakfast, lights
> Her stove, and lays out food in tins.
> Out of the window perilously spread
> Her drying combinations touched by the sun's last rays,
> On the divan are piled (at night her bed)
> Stockings, slipper, camisoles, and stays . . .
>    the young man carbuncular, arrives,
> A small house agent's clerk, with one bold stare,
> One of the low on whom assurance sits
> As a silk hat on a Bradford millionaire.
> The time is now propitious, as he guesses,
> The meal is ended, she is bored and tired.
>
> (218–227, 231–236)

Echoes of Tennyson and Keats and associations from classical mythology contribute to the effect of this scene, but the melody of the lines does not entirely depend on them. Using traditional rhythms, almost doggerel verse, and largely commonplace diction, Eliot in the first section (218–227) writes a passage strangely pleasing both to ear and inner eye. The "violet hour" touches with its magic the drying underwear, dirty dishes, and canned food. Although the stage properties hover on the verge of the comic, in presentation they escape comedy, to generate nostalgia and pathos. Nostalgia, a wistful looking backward, and the sense of pathos in lives devoid of tragic dignity, dominate much of *The Waste Land.* This is one way for the poet's sensibility, and the reader's, to respond to the emptiness of a life nonetheless rich in detail. The pathetic minutiae of the typist's existence generate nostalgia for more aesthetically satisfying ways of life. Eliot makes a melody of the sordid, but he also reminds one of earlier melodies. Creating beauty from trivia, he wins a limited victory in the struggle against decay.

However, this presentation of the typist and her clerk also arouses negative feelings: a fastidious distaste at times approaching disgust. The rhetorical splendor of "carbuncular" makes pimples into an index of human negligibility. The snobbish self-assurance with which Eliot characterizes the young man's assurance invites the reader's participation in the easy drawing of negative conclusions on social grounds. The meticulous rendering of sordid details calls for a response to sordidness as well as to pathos. Even the doggerel quality of the verse expresses the poet's sense of the trivial and meaningless atmosphere of the experience he records. This sense coexists with the recognition of universal patterns and meanings articulated by and implicit in the figure of Tiresias; it does not contradict, although it counteracts, the perception of pathos and even of limited beauty in the typist's life.

Sensibility substitutes for judgment as a guide to value and a controlling principle. It organizes what might otherwise seem a random assemblage of perceptions into a revealing sequence. When the violet light that illuminated the typist recurs, it shines on a weird scene, rendered with a different sort of quatrain music:

> A woman drew her long black hair out tight
> And fiddled whisper music on those strings
> And bats with baby faces in the violet light
> Whistled, and beat their wings.
>
> (378–381)

The surrealistic quality of the description reflects the exacerbated sensibility of a man too long deprived of water, to use one of the poem's controlling metaphors. Such perceptual distortion implies no judgment, no comparison to a norm, no isolatable meaning. Critics have found specific symbolic significance here, as everywhere in the poem. One is told that "hair has been immemorially a symbol of fertility" and that the violet light "indicates the twilight of civilization," but that the color itself also "symbolizes repentance and . . . is the color of baptism" and that the baby faces of the bats carry forward the theme of baptism.[40] Yet the effort to attach specific meanings to such details contradicts the most important implications of the technique here used. The "meaning" of such a scene is the state of feeling it reflects, the response it evokes: a response, once more, to the inextricable intermingling of beauty and horror. It is also a reminder that the strangeness of the world may derive from the strangeness of man's perceptions, that emotions both create and destroy meaning, and that phantasmagoria can for these reasons be as "true" a rendition of actuality as simple realism.

More exactly, the poem suggests that, since reality is largely private, "realism" in the modern world is as impossible as judgment. Because sensibility is less dependable than judgment, surrealism offers less security than realism. Both reflect the limitation of modern possibility—although both seem at first to be enlargements of possibility, like the expansions of Pope's "microscope of Wit," which, seeming to enlarge, actually diminishes. Sensibility and surrealism provide only the enlargement of accepted instability. Yvor Winters has defined the artistic process as "one of moral evaluation of human experience, by means of a technique which renders possible an evaluation more precise than any other." And again, "The poem is more valuable than the event [it records, or upon which it comments] by virtue of its being an act of meditation: it is the event plus the understanding of the event."[41] Winters' standards reflect a notion of poetry close to traditional ones: Samuel Johnson, with his constant search for proper moral evaluation, and William Wordsworth, who believed that poetry originated in emotion recollected in tranquility, might both have approved. But Winters' statements cast a cold light on Eliot's achievement as compared with Pope's. The implicit evaluation and understanding recorded by *The Waste Land* may be profound, but they are not precise, depending as they do on ideas of universal instability and individual privacy. Judgment rests on recognizable and discussable standards. Sensibility is by definition personal, and thus is hardly a subject for argument. Poetry based on it must abandon the larger claims of poetic significance. The poet can no longer function as unacknowledged legislator of mankind, for he has come to see that legislation is impossible.

Yet the poetry of sensibility has peculiar power to involve the reader and make him reflect on his own experience. The process of dehumanization which *The Waste Land* reveals takes place from within and without, from the way the characters live and the way in which they see one another and are seen by the poet. And the reader is involved in the same dilemma as the poem's inhabitants, for he too destroys meaning in his life and finds value destroyed all around him. The distance between the poet, or the reader, and the world of the poem is minimal, created almost entirely by the elaborate pattern of literary allusion, which recalls bygone standards of judgment, aesthetic and moral; reveals their irrelevance to the plights of the twentieth century; conveys the poet's nostalgia for a world that made judgment possible; and intensifies perception of the amorality of the world revealed. *The Waste Land* calls upon knowledge as a way toward feeling and perception. It implies the existence and significance of a hierarchy of awareness, and the ambiguous but real importance of heightened perception and heightened feeling as the only conceivable guides to meaning and value.

The technique of the poem, in short, like that of *The Dunciad*, reflects as well as depicts cultural reality. The poet describes the diminishment of full human consciousness as a consequence of modern life. His mode of description makes one aware of the anguish of the alternative, how terrible it is to open one's eyes to horror. He shows a process of dehumanization through action and through perception. His technique of literary allusion recalls earlier lives of dignity and meaning, earlier literature of beauty. By subject and technique alike, then, he reveals the degree to which sensibility has become a substitute for judgment as a mode of organizing and understanding experience: his fragmentary images derive from a particular kind of emotional capacity. If the horror he shows cannot be judged, can only be felt, the reader is invited to feel, to realize that feeling may be his only resource, and that to retain the capacity for emotion is itself a bitter triumph. The nature of the poem represents in little the nature of the world from which it derives.

The distinction between *The Waste Land* as a poem of sensibility and *The Dunciad* as a poem of judgment may seem to perpetuate the myth that the early eighteenth century was an age of reason, that the difference between eighteenth and twentieth century poetry is the difference between poetry of intellect and poetry of feeling. Nothing could be further from the truth. The logic of *The Dunciad* is a logic of feeling as well as of idea and event. The poem's passion is inescapable, particularly in the fourth book, where genuine terror invests the account of the final total triumph of dullness and the total destruction of art, learning, and potentiality. It is passion, not reason, that creates imagery of excrement and insects, passion that forms the damning characterizations of the fourth book, and passion that supplies the energy of such lines as:

> Happier thy fortunes! like a rolling stone,
> Thy giddy dulness still shall lumber on,
> Safe in its heaviness, shall never stray,
> But lick up ev'ry blockhead in the way.
> (III, 293–296)

Much of *The Waste Land's* power depends on its rendering of an immediate grasp of experience, the grasp of personal perception and intuition. Eliot has argued, in prose, that a poem can be appreciated without being understood; *The Waste Land* supports his case. In sections of the poem where rationality provides little help, one reacts with a direct intuitive response. Literary allusions that do not invoke the reader's knowledge often move him nonetheless directly. "Reality" may be only private, but the honest presentation of one man's experience of it calls forth an immediate, forceful reaction from the reader.

In Pope's poem, the intuition and sense perception that enable one to absorb and describe data from without are suppressed in favor of intellectual and emotional reactions to actuality. *The Waste Land,* recording one man's perceptions, evokes equivalent perceptions from the reader. Despite the fact that it assumes the instability of actuality, it seems to tell what the world is like. *The Dunciad* concentrates more on what the world means. The poem's power comes from its fusion of thought and feeling to provide clear and passionate judgment, to make one feel and believe in the necessity of such judgment, and in the possibility that judgment can provide aesthetic as well as moral control.

*Five*

# Forms of the Human and Superhuman

To simplify human beings into images instead of attempting to render the complexities of character and personality, a poet deliberately accepts severe restrictions, suggesting character through a few isolated and often apparently superficial traits. He thus may achieve, paradoxically, both concentration and penetration. His aesthetic focus provides a clarified perspective implying the possibility of moral judgment and revealing essence through appearance. Such people are Pope's most meaningful images: real people, transformed by poetry; imagined exemplary figures; and abstractions, or even objects, given the rich life of personification. They suggest the wide aesthetic and moral range of the imagery of limits.

Until the late eighteenth century, the personification was considered a rhetorical figure of special emotional power. Lord Kames wrote, in 1762, "Abstract and general terms, as well as particular objects, are often necessary in poetry. Such terms however are not well adapted to poetry, because they suggest not any image to the mind: I can readily form an image of Alexander or Achilles in wrath; but I cannot form an image of wrath in the abstract, or of wrath independent of a person. Upon that account, in works addressed to the imagination, abstract terms are frequently personified."[1] Two decades earlier, William Melmoth had observed, "To represent natural, moral, or intellectual qualities and affections as persons, and appropriate to them those general emblems by which their powers and properties are usually typified in pagan theology, may be allowed as one of the most pleasing and graceful figures of poetical rhetorick."[2] And about the time Pope was writing *Windsor-*

*Forest*, his friend Thomas Parnell, in *An Essay on the Different Stiles of Poetry*, specified a particular purpose for personifications:

> There stand the new *Creations* of the *Muse*,
> *Poetick Persons*, whom the *Writers* use
> Whene'er a Cause magnificently great,
> Wou'd fix Attention with peculiar weight.[3]

To "fix Attention with peculiar weight" was the special function of the personification, which was assumed to appeal directly to the emotions and the imagination. The reasons for its emotional power were variously specified. Perhaps the most touching account, and one particularly relevant to Pope's practice, was Hugh Blair's, late in the century: "One of the greatest pleasures we receive from poetry, is, to find ourselves always in the midst of our fellows; and to see every thing thinking, feeling, and acting, as we ourselves do. This is, perhaps, the principal charm of this sort of figured style [personification], that it introduces us into society with all nature, and interests us, even in inanimate objects, by forming a connection between them and us, through that sensibility which it ascribes to them."[4]

When Pope chose to conclude the expanded version of *Windsor-Forest* with a pageant of personified rivers, one of whom gives a long speech containing a further series of personifications, he may have wished to establish some such "connection between them and us," to stress the humanistic aspects of the natural world, suggested before in the poem by the comparison between patterns of shade and a nymph's coyness and by the myth of Lodona. He certainly wished to "fix Attention"; and he concentrated on the creating of images. Indeed, so intense is this last purpose that to some degree it overpowers the others. In Pope's later verse, image is always subordinated to idea; here it partly creates, partly suppresses idea.

To see how these early personifications work, it is necessary to quote at length from what is for many no longer very appealing poetry:

> In that blest Moment, from his Oozy Bed
> Old Father *Thames* advanc'd his rev'rend Head.

His Tresses dropt with Dews, and o'er the Stream
His shining Horns diffus'd a golden Gleam:
Grav'd on his Urn appear'd the Moon, that guides
His swelling Waters, and alternate Tydes;
The figur'd Streams in Waves of Silver roll'd,
And on their Banks *Augusta* rose in Gold.
Around his Throne the Sea-born Brothers stood,
Who swell with Tributary Urns his Flood.
First the fam'd Authors of his ancient Name,
The winding *Isis*, and the fruitful *Tame*:
The *Kennet* swift, for silver Eels renown'd;
The *Loddon* slow, with verdant Alders crown'd:
*Cole*, whose dark Streams his flow'ry Islands lave;
And chalky *Wey*, that rolls a milky Wave:
The blue, transparent *Vandalis* appears;
The gulphy *Lee* his sedgy Tresses rears:
And sullen *Mole*, that hides his diving Flood;
And silent *Darent*, stain'd with *Danish* Blood.
High in the midst, upon his Urn reclin'd,
(His Sea-green Mantle waving with the Wind)
The God appear'd; he turn'd his azure Eyes
Where *Windsor*-Domes and pompous Turrets rise.
(329–352)

The stress on visual detail creates three kinds of image: those rendered in gold and silver on Father Thames's urn, the different sorts of river, and the mythological personages. In some instances the kinds seem barely compatible: it is difficult to think of the "Oozy Bed" and the "rev'rend Head" of Father Thames together, or to imagine something at once "gulphy" and possessed of "Tresses." But Pope demands of his readers simultaneous perception of two levels of reality, for the personifications are not intended to obscure the facts they render.

The scene engraved on the urn orders the rather chaotic impressionism of the river description, creating a static and hierarchical version of active reality: the moon presiding and controlling the movement of waters, the rivers themselves made permanent in silver, the city that commands the river rendered in gold, as a measure of its value. Marshall McLuhan has referred to the "visual slickness and pomp and opulence made possible by the new wealth and applied knowledge of the middle class" when the Middle Ages moved into the Renaissance.[5] The scene on the urn and the setting in which the urn exists display an equivalent stress on just such visual qualities as slickness, pomp, and opulence, which magnifies the importance of the new wealth and power of the commercial middle class. The splendor of Father Thames is largely iconographic: his shining horns, dew-dropping tresses, the urn itself, the sea-green mantle and azure eyes, all point to significant aspects of the river. But the heightened language of the presentation—such phrases as "blest Moment" and "rev'rend Head," or the depiction of the god as "High in the midst, upon his Urn reclin'd"—lends the scene a majesty justified not by its immediate reference but by the vision it precedes, of England as dominating the world through her commercial power:

> There Kings shall sue, and suppliant States be seen
> Once more to bend before a *British* QUEEN . . .
> The Time shall come, when free as Seas or Wind
> Unbounded *Thames* shall flow for all Mankind,
> Whole Nations enter with each swelling Tyde,
> And Seas but join the Regions they divide.
> (383–384, 397–400)

The role of Father Thames is more important for what it may become than for what it is.

The general effect of the grouping of personifications is clear and forceful: Father Thames vividly described in the center, with "Sea-born Brothers" standing round his throne. The brothers, however, lack clarity of rendition because of Pope's double focus on geographic and personalized imagery. The large panorama of different kinds of river—slow and swift, dark and chalky, transparent and obscure—reinforces the poem's stress on "order in variety," and an imagination accustomed to such iconography might evoke from clues like "sullen" and "silent" different sorts of people whose variety of personality also supports the theme. But for modern readers the actual rivers are so much more real than the beings who represent them that it comes as a shock to return to Father Thames on his urn. The river personifications are imaginative visual constructs inadequately integrated with their emotional or ideational meanings. They display the poet's verbal and pictorial wit through puns and the visual contrasts of their presentation, but the richness of the presentation, unlike that of the allegorical presiding figure, derives from what they really are and how the poet can play with their names and appearances, not from the larger meanings they imply.

Personification of yet another kind appears in the long speech of Father Thames, in which embodied abstractions are given appropriate attitudes and appurtenances. These personifications create equivalents for psychic states rather than interpretations of physical facts:

> Exil'd by Thee from Earth to deepest Hell,
> In Brazen Bonds shall barb'rous *Discord* dwell:
> Gigantick *Pride*, pale *Terror*, gloomy *Care*,
> And mad *Ambition* shall attend her there.
> There purple *Vengeance* bath'd in Gore retires,
> Her Weapons blunted, and extinct her Fires.
> (413–418)

Although the individual figures are vague, they have suggestive reality deriving partly from a long literary and pictorial tradition. E. R. Dodds has written, "When Theognis calls hope and fear 'dangerous daemons,' or when Sophocles speaks of Eros as a power that 'warps to wrong the righteous mind, for its destruction,' we should not dismiss this as 'personification': behind it lies the old Homeric feeling that these things are not truly part of the self, since they are not within man's conscious control; they are endowed with a life and energy of their own, and so can force a man, as it were from the outside, into conduct foreign to him." And again, "The Greek had always felt the experience of passion as something mysterious and frightening, the experience of a force that was in him, possessing him, rather than possessed by him."[6] To call Pope's rendition of similar feelings "personification" is by no means to "dismiss" it. On the contrary, personification provides a means to convey the exact kind and weight of importance he feels in the passions, whose monstrous nature, in their imagined semidemonic roles, reveals their sinister power. These are almost supernatural forces, supernaturally dangerous, yet subject to rational control, which reduces them to powerless captives. Pope's pageant reveals his belief that irrational energies need not only be endured. The hell he imagines confines and disarms the powers that may distort men's minds. It is sinister because of their presence, but the imagination of their presence in such circumstances projects the optimism of belief in discipline's possibilities on the social as well as the individual level.

For the modern reader, to whom the separation of poetry and painting—for Pope real "Sister-arts"—is more apparent than their inherent similarity, abstract terminology dominates this passage, and its few details are not sufficient to create physical reality. In today's era poetry and painting alike often subordinate image to idea (although they are also capable of abandoning "idea" entirely). The relation of image to idea in Pope's time was more balanced: personifications might be self-sufficient pictorial facts, interesting for their emotional and evocative power and their visual complexity, but certainly they were as "real," for the poet and for his readers, as what they represented. Their physicality might depend, as in Pope's description of hell, on precise epithets, from which a sympathetic reader could extrapolate a scene that had compelling power in its imagined concreteness as well as in its meaning.

Yet despite the exactness of epithet in this passage, its personifications are wooden in comparison with a version of the same scene written almost thirty years later. The later example, from Book IV of *The Dunciad,* belongs to a satiric context; this fact alone energizes the presentation. But the underlying conception of the resources and limitations of personification has undergone a significant change.

The new version of hell bears a closer resemblance to the actual world, but its inhabitants are intellectual and moral qualities:

> Beneath her [Dulness'] foot-stool, *Science* groans in Chains,
> And *Wit* dreads Exile, Penalties and Pains.

There foam'd rebellious *Logic*, gagg'd and bound,
There, stript, fair *Rhet'ric* languish'd on the ground;
His blunted Arms by *Sophistry* are born,
And shameless *Billingsgate* her Robes adorn.
*Morality*, by her false Guardians drawn,
*Chicane* in Furs, and *Casuistry* in Lawn,
Gasps, as they straiten at each end the cord,
And dies, when Dulness gives her Page the word . . .
There to her heart sad Tragedy addrest
The dagger wont to pierce the Tyrant's breast;
But sober History restrain'd her rage,
And promis'd Vengeance on a barb'rous age.
There sunk Thalia, nerveless, cold, and dead,
Had not her Sister Satyr held her head.

(21–30, 37–42)

Characters and technique seem fresher and less predictable than in the earlier passage. No longer do adjective-noun combinations define personages and control the reader's response; definition and response now depend more on action than on descriptive evocation. "Shameless," "sad," and "sober" are adjectives of the old defining sort, although, unlike most of the epithets in the *Windsor-Forest* sequence, their weight is more emotional than descriptive. The reader's knowledge of the characters' essential nature is assumed, so that the poet makes little effort to suggest his beings' physicality, concentrating instead on the miniature drama of their relationships. Logic's bonds, unlike Discord's, generate dramatic action. The personifications act, suffer, resist; their emotional force depends less on what they are than on what happens to them, which acquires meaning as a result of the reader's automatic responses to the idea of wit or logic or science.

Although the cast of characters here comprises intellectual rather than emotional forces, they are imagined with greater passion than their earlier counterparts. It is still true that the pictorial reality of the presentation makes its own demands on the reader, but the "picture" now is a drama rather than a set of attitudes. Ethos and pathos, action and suffering, fuse in this group of personifications, as they do not in the earlier one, where the physical postures of suffering substitute for the tensions of action producing anguish.

The personifications of *The Dunciad* function like real people, whose actions create and reveal meaning. Indeed, a real person appears, without differentiation, in this sequence: Dulness' "Page" is, as Pope's note makes clear, the hanging judge Sir Francis Page. The double pun pronounces a judgment on his stature and depersonalizes him. Although his inclusion in this company emphasizes that the forms of evil find human agents, the fact that he and the personifications exist on the same level suggests that these abstractions are characters as real as any other in the strange world of *The Dunciad.*

The tendency to de-emphasize the merely pictorial aspects of personification and to stress the human is marked in Pope's development. An instance of detailed descriptive personification in Book IV of *The Dunciad,* the account of Italian opera, contrasts with the presentation of Father Thames in *Windsor-Forest:*

> lo! a Harlot form soft sliding by,
> With mincing step, small voice, and languid eye;
> Foreign her air, her robe's discordant pride
> In patch-work flutt'ring, and her head aside.
> By singing Peers up-held on either hand,
> She tripp'd and laugh'd, too pretty much to stand;
> Cast on the prostrate Nine a scornful look,
> Then thus in quaint Recitativo spoke.
>
> (45–52)

The details of her appearance, like those of Father Thames's, have iconographic significance: the foreign air, languid eye, patchwork robe suggest relevant qualities of Italian opera and create a descriptive reality at least as vivid as that of Father Thames. The harlot, like Father Thames, delivers a speech, but her significant function is very different from the earlier figure's. Father Thames is presented in ways that emphasize his distance from the ordinary. His splendor and strangeness, his air as of a figure in an allegorical painting, even his role as deity, have an alienating effect: the reader may "look at" him but has nothing in common with him. "Opera," in contrast, is in effect a human being, given a specific social role, a feminine personality, and a pair of human attendants. Hugh Blair's comment on the pleasure felt in discovering everything "thinking, feeling, and acting, as we ourselves do" is more relevant here than for the earlier personification: the response to this figure depends on what the reader recognizes and understands. She clarifies the meaning of a large phenomenon and directs one's feelings toward it by triggering an emotional response: revulsion at the idea of prostitution, and comic delight at the ingenuity of the poet's manipulation, which create a complex satiric effect. The difference between the two personifications is like that between Wordsworth's and Coleridge's contributions to *Lyrical Ballads:* Father Thames makes the familiar strange, the "Harlot form" makes the strange familiar.

Pope's stress on the human aspects of personification occasionally removes his figures almost entirely from the realm of imagery. Here is an account of Reason and her relation to man from the *Essay on Man:*

> We, wretched subjects tho' to lawful sway,
> In this weak queen, some fav'rite still obey.
> Ah! if she lend not arms, as well as rules,
> What can she more than tell us we are fools?
> Teach us to mourn our Nature, not to mend,
> A sharp accuser, but a helpless friend!
> Or from a judge turn pleader, to persuade
> The choice we make, or justify it made;
> Proud of an easy conquest all along,
> She but removes weak passions for the strong:
> So, when small humors gather to a gout,
> The doctor fancies he has driv'n them out.
>
> (II, 149–160)

This personification is an argumentative device. Lacking visual reality, it has a vague personality and character and a well-defined function. As an objectification of a psychological force, it resembles the Homeric gods, from which it differs in its concern with general rather than with particular truth—not the forces operating on an individual man, but those that govern mankind. The figure of the queen does not disappear altogether after its initial introduction: she lends arms and is proud of her conquest. However, her alternate roles as accuser and friend, judge and pleader, belong to a vague conception of her as human, not to imagining her as queen. The passage's most vivid moment is the final simile, which also concerns the psychological more than the physical. The personification here is a temporary means of creating immediacy. It resembles other instances of Pope's usage: the presentation of Superstition (*Essay on Man,* III, 246–260) as a "she" who teaches, sees, feels, and "fixes" but has no physical being, not even a vague definition of a role; or the portrayal of Gluttony (*Imitations of Horace, Epistle* I, vi, 112–114), who utters a command without having any embodiment. Such presentations are clear attempts to bring *"home to Men's Business and Bosoms"* the nature of forces operating in the world, but they do not create sensuous reality.[7]

Concern with the psychological does not necessarily eliminate interest in the physical. The personified playing cards in *The Rape of the Lock,* like the personified inhabitants of the Cave of Spleen, although more indirectly, call the reader's attention to an important realm of psychological reality. Yet their rendition is emphatically and at times exclusively physical:

> Behold, four *Kings* in Majesty rever'd,
> With hoary Whiskers and a forky Beard;
> And four fair *Queens* whose hands sustain a Flow'r,
> Th' expressive Emblem of their softer Pow'r;
> Four *Knaves* in Garbs succinct, a trusty Band,
> Caps on their heads, and Halberds in their hand;
> And Particolour'd Troops, a shining Train,
> Draw forth to Combat on the Velvet Plain.
>
> (III, 37–44)

This is an unusual sort of personification, in that it requires no imagination of physical detail: the description merely depicts the faces of cards. Yet its function is similar to that of the personified abstractions Pope more commonly employs. In comic-satiric fashion, the humanized cards heighten the importance of what is going on: their situation, parodying a "Cause magnificently great" on which the poet "Wou'd fix Attention with peculiar weight," conveys an ambivalence of value that echoes the poem's other ambivalences. The mock heroic attribution of importance to pieces of pasteboard reflects the significance attached to their combat in Belinda's social world, where success or failure at cards symbolizes larger triumphs and defeats. The card evoke the psychological reality of social preoccupation with power. Toward the end of the game, the King of Hearts "springs to Vengeance with an eager pace, / And falls like Thunder on the prostrate *Ace*" (97–98). Belinda's reaction is specified in the next couplet: "The Nymph exulting fills with Shouts the Sky, / The Walls, the Woods, and long Canals reply." The extravagance with which the movements of cards are humanized and dramatized corresponds to the extravagance with which the players respond to their manipulations of the cards. The cards have approximately the same degree and kind of humanity as the players.

The inhabitants of the Cave of Spleen belong to a more conventional descriptive mode. Their designations are predictable—Pain, Megrim, Ill-nature, Affectation—but their delineation demonstrates once more Pope's primary concern with psychology. Here, for instance, is Affectation:

> There *Affectation* with a sickly Mien
> Shows in her Cheek the Roses of Eighteen,
> Practis'd to Lisp, and hang the Head aside,
> Faints into Airs, and languishes with Pride;
> On the rich Quilt sinks with becoming Woe,
> Wrapt in a Gown, for Sickness, and for Show.
> The Fair-ones feel such Maladies as these,
> When each new Night-Dress gives a new Disease.
> (IV, 31–38)

Characterization proceeds by successive evocations of appearance, symbolic activity, and dress. The concluding analogy, however, suggests the true focus of the entire presentation, being a depiction of a "Fair-one" more than of an abstraction. Affectation could be labeled Flavia and described in the same way. Pope uses his satiric observation of women to provide the details to isolate and objectify a single trait. The reality of the personification is human, not pictorial, and it suggests the satiric perception that a large class of women could in fact be summarized under the label of an abstraction.

The fine line between Pope's personification and his characterization is also suggested by his fondness for collective personification, the figure that uses the language of personification to designate a group or class of people: "Behold yon Alms-house, neat, but void of state, / Where Age and Want sit smiling at the gate" (*Epistle to Bathurst,* 265–266). Humility, Justice, and Truth appear in this fashion in the *Essay on Man,* where the poet plays against the conventional technique of providing personified figures with appropriate symbolic appurtenances:

> The soul's calm sun-shine, and the heart-felt joy,
> Is Virtue's prize: A better would you fix?
> Then give Humility a coach and six,
> Justice a Conq'ror's sword, or Truth a gown,
> Or Public Spirit its great cure, a Crown.
>
> (IV, 168–172)

To reward the humble man is to destroy his humility. The satiric animus of these lines suggests that possessions create character. Personification is here a technique of economy and emphasis, giving general weight to the poet's assertions. When he addresses "Impudence of wealth" as a person (*Imitations of Horace, Satire* II, ii, 117–118) or includes "Avarice" and "Profusion" among the victims of a world in which trade in kind suddenly replaces currency (*Epistle to Bathurst,* 47–48), he achieves the weight of generalization with the force of particularity, and conveys with precision his awareness of various kinds of humanity.

Even more extreme, and more revealing, is the use of the techniques of personification to refer to a single human being. A relatively minor instance is in *Epistle to a Lady,* where the feminine portraits include "Sin in State, majestically drunk" (69). This woman is described in much the same way as Narcissa, whose description precedes hers, and Philomedé, who comes next and may in fact designate the same person. To call her "Sin" emphasizes with striking effect the fact that such portrayals are in fact generalizations, although disguised as accounts of individuals; the label suggests how seriously Pope takes the moral deviations he describes. The character is unchaste, fickle, aimless in activity and thought; in short, frivolous—and frivolity is sin. The line between individual and type has disappeared; everyone, the technique indicates, is both.

The most striking and complex use of this technique is the account of Vice at the end of *Epilogue to the Satires* (I). The woman here vividly described is at once an image of Vice and a representation of Walpole's mistress Molly Skerret—with underlying allusions to the Empress Theodora.[8] She appears with the splendor, dignity, and deliberation of the most traditional sort of personification, is accompanied, like Father Thames, with her attendants, and displays limited but meaningful activity:

> In golden Chains the willing World she draws,
> And hers the Gospel is, and hers the Laws:
> Mounts the Tribunal, lifts her scarlet head,
> And sees pale Virtue carted in her stead!
>
> (147–150)

The pageantry of her presentation belongs again to the world of the allegorical tableau:

> Lo! at the Wheels of her Triumphal Car,
> Old *England*'s Genius, rough with many a Scar,
> Dragg'd in the Dust! his Arms hang idly round,
> His Flag inverted trails along the ground!
> Our Youth, all liv'ry'd o'er with foreign Gold,
> Before her dance; behind her crawl the Old!
>
> (151–156)

As James Osborn has pointed out, no "contemporary reader was so literal-minded as to believe that the second Lady Walpole played a black trumpet [an activity which occurs two lines later] or rode in a chariot."[9] The description of Vice is entirely allegorical; it has the power of the pictorial as well as of moral imagination. The details of scene and action suggest the nature and effect of Vice's influence on society. But the fact that this depiction also has a personal dimension gives it added vibrancy. This particular solution to the problem of whether satire should be personal or general is more than the achievement of "elegant and satiric ambiguity" that Warburton thought it.[10] It involves a refinement and darkening of the central technique of *The Rape of the Lock*. Molly Skerret is both enlarged and diminished by becoming an image of Vice. Deprived of human reality and made into a symbol, she is revealed as ultimately corrupt, but also as possessing great symbolic importance, since her power of evil is made possible by the nature of society, which is also exposed by the personification and its accompanying pageantry. The symbolic presentation, general and particular at once, simultaneously illuminates and condemns what it depicts.

Personification is a form of imagery, but so can be direct characterization, which may create sharply defined physical images. The dehumanizing technique so characteristic of satire often reduces people to inanimate objects that may themselves be vividly imagined. *The Dunciad* offers abundant examples, as do the other satiric poems. As early as the *Essay on Criticism* one encounters: "The Bookful Blockhead, ignorantly read, With *Loads* of *Learned Lumber* in his Head" (612–613). Hardly a man at all, he is more distinctly a wooden structure containing wood. A more refined version of the technique appears in *Epistle To Bathurst*:

> Who sees pale Mammon pine amidst his store,
> Sees but a backward steward for the Poor;
> This year a Reservoir, to keep and spare,
> The next a Fountain, spouting thro' his Heir,
> In lavish streams to quench a Country's thirst,
> And men and dogs shall drink him 'till they burst.
> (173–178)

The special effect of the lines depends on the conjunction of language appropriate to the human and the nonhuman. "Mammon"—an abstraction imagined as human figure—has some existence as a man: he is pale, he pines, he is a sort of steward. One is invited to "see" him in terms of contemptuous nonhuman images (contemptuous only because nonhuman, inasmuch as fountains and reservoirs are pleasant objects, but men should not be merely objects), and then is recalled with shock by the personal pronoun in the last line to the fact that he remains a man as well. "By combining the metaphor with the tradition that the avaricious man is hydropic, [Pope] has dehumanized such fathers and sons by freezing them ludicrously into features of a formal garden, just as, later in the poem, inhuman Hopkins will transform himself into a statue."[11] The "inhumanity" implicit in the misuse of wealth is dramatized when the bad gardening of *Epistle to Burlington* goes one degree farther: men not only plan their gardens poorly but so plan their lives that they reduce themselves to features of the environment, to be misused by others.

In such instances "character" and "image" are identical because the metaphorical presentation of psychological or spiritual reality deliberately converts the unseeable to the visible. These "people" become images because they are seen as something other than people. A more problematical area is the nonmetaphoric evocation of character or personality. Here, too, there are some clear cases: mostly glancing references, which suggest essence by appearance:

> Boastful and rough, your first son is a 'Squire;
> The next a Tradesman, meek, and much a lyar;
> Tom struts a Soldier, open, bold, and brave;
> Will sneaks a Scriv'ner, an exceeding knave.
> (*Epistle to Cobham*, 103–106)

These lines deal directly with the degree to which assumptions about "image," in the modern public relations usage of the word, determine reality or control perception. The stereotypes through which society operates affect individuals' understanding of themselves and of others. The accepted social image of a squire is self-preserving: it moves people to become what their manner suggests they are, and influences their behavior once a way of life has been chosen.

Glimpses of action and setting may convey moral essence:

> The rest, some farm the Poor-box, some the Pews;
> Some keep Assemblies, and wou'd keep the Stews;
> Some with fat Bucks on childless Dotards fawn;
> Some win rich Widows by their Chine and Brawn;
> While with the silent growth of ten per Cent,
> In Dirt and darkness hundreds stink content.
> (*Imitations of Horace, Epistle* I,i, 128–133)

Pope here communicates his contempt for socially acceptable corruption, most clearly in the verb of the last line, but also through the ironic conjunctions and puns of the preceding couplets. The juxtaposition of Beau Nash's elegant assemblies with brothels; the pun in "fawn," with its hint that dotards accept deer as substitute children, although the deer are in fact food; the innuendo in "Brawn' that rich widows may be won by the physical powers of a man as well as by his gifts—these display the poet's judgment and expose the world he inhabits and condemns. The comedy in such conjunctions and puns suggests the reconciliation of the perceiver who accepts the value of his perception without liking what he sees.

Because of a wit that unifies the disparate, these capsule characterizations approach the function of metaphor. The accounts of profitable activity embody distortions of natural harmony between man and his environment. Farming and hunting, which in *Windsor-Forest* signify the good possibilities of human life, turn now to corrupt ends, and the growth of money in metaphorical dirt and darkness parodies the fruitful development of bulbs and seeds. The range of exploitative occupations evoked symbolizes the entire spectrum of social possibility; the "stink" of those who live by unearned income permeates society. Pope's tiny vignettes suggest far more than they assert.

The characteristically satiric device of depicting people as images of themselves involves a deliberate commitment to the importance of the superficial, an uncharitable assumption that idiosyncrasy and appearance reveal true character. Perhaps Pope's most vivid example of the technique is one in which laughter transcends real anger:

> (*Sir Plume*, of *Amber Snuff-box* justly vain,
> And the nice Conduct of a *clouded Cane*)
> With earnest Eyes, and round unthinking Face,
> He first the Snuff-box open'd, then the case,
> And thus broke out—'My Lord, why, what the Devil?
> Z—ds! damn the Lock! 'fore Gad, you must be civil!
> Plague on't! 'tis past a Jest—nay prithee, Pox!
> Give her the Hair'—he spoke, and rapp'd his Box.
> (*Rape of the Lock*, IV, 123–130)

Sir Plume's accessories are metaphors for his nature. The impoverishment of his language emphasizes the point implied by his appearance and action: his speech is a verbal equivalent for his "round unthinking Face"; and his obsessive preoccupation with snuffbox and cane account for his inability to deal with more abstract concerns. To depict a man in this way, the poet must preserve a distance from his subject, presenting him merely as a manifestation of one aspect of the common humanity and insisting that he is nothing more. As an image of human inconsequentiality, Sir Plume too has metaphoric richness: he sums up the severe limitations of cultivated superficiality and typifies social impotence.

It is possible, however, to use the technique in such a way that the object of satire includes the perceiver as well as the person perceived:

> The Man, who stretch'd in Isis' calm Retreat
> To Books and Study gives sev'n years compleat,
> See! strow'd with learned dust, his Night-cap on,
> He walks, an Object new beneath the Sun!
> The Boys flock round him, and the People stare:
> So stiff, so mute! some Statue, you would swear,
> Stept from its Pedestal to take the Air.
> (*Imitations of Horace, Epistle* II, ii, 116–122)

The scholar who has made himself a mindless "Object" by excessive concentration on things of the mind—more statue than man, a ludicrous appearance in an urban context—is an object of ridicule because of his incomplete humanity, the result of his own choice. But he inhabits London, a locality alien to artistic and intellectual achievement: "How shall I rhime in this eternal Roar?" (114). The "Boys" and "People" who find him ridiculous reveal in their limited perception the city's superficiality. City people, lacking time to discriminate, judge men by appearances because their lives consist in sequences of appearance. The scholar may in fact be as appropriate a subject for mockery as they think him; but his presentation as a mere "Object" comments on those who see, or fail to see, as well as on what is seen.

The proper place of appearance as a basis for judgment becomes almost an explicit subject at the end of *Imitations of Horace, Epistle* I, i:

> You laugh, half Beau half Sloven if I stand,
> My Wig all powder, and all snuff my Band;
> You laugh, if Coat and Breeches strangely vary,
> White Gloves, and Linnen worthy Lady Mary!
> But when no Prelate's Lawn with Hair-shirt lin'd,
> Is half so incoherent as my Mind . . .
> You never change one muscle of your face,
> You think this Madness but a common case,
> Nor once to Chanc'ry, nor to Hales apply;
> Yet hang your lip, to see a Seam awry!
> Careless how ill I with myself agree;
> Kind to my dress, my figure, not to Me.
> (161–166, 171–176)

The "kindness" of Bolingbroke (as of the interlocutor in Horace) consists in his willingness to rebuke—through laughter—a friend whose appearance is "incoherent." Taking appearances seriously, he yet fails to recognize that they may reflect a more important inner reality. The poem's speaker creates vivid images of his own confused attire and a self-describing generalization ("half Beau half Sloven").

His analogy between clothes and the mind reveals that what seems superficial may in fact be profound. Though one should take inner reality more seriously than appearances, he argues, appearances may be an index to truth. This is a crucial perception for the satirist, implying a philosophic justification for his tendency to dwell on damaging details. Pope's satiric use of people as images, which depends on the maintenance of a distance for judging and on the perception that recognizes the significance of appearances while penetrating them, is one of his most vital techniques.

A nonsatiric technique can be equally clear in its concentration on creating vivid appearances as a focus for meaning. The satiric uses of people turned to images, like Pope's personifications, direct attention to significant gesture, attire, appurtenances, action. The typical nonsatiric version of the same device resembles personification in its concentration on meaning. In the simplest cases, the statement of meaning is almost equivalent to personification:

> See, FALKLAND dies, the virtuous and the just!
> See god-like TURENNE prostrate on the dust!
> See SIDNEY bleeds amid the martial strife!
> Was this their Virtue, or Contempt of Life?
> (*Essay on Man*, IV, 99–102)

These figures in attitudes of gallant death are counterparts of the image of Vice at the end of the *Epilogue to the Satires* (I). Labeled as an abstraction, Vice also possesses the authenticity of historical fact; these men, labeled as historical figures, also represent virtue.

In generalizations about the nature of man, or about kinds of men, the poet often allows his characters fuller human reality, but they still display the simplifications of personification. The "poor Indian" of the *Essay on Man* (I, 99–112) is a case in point. Described in terms of his hopes and desires, with his dog for company, he is an illustration, a momentary creation, rather than a realized character. The hunters and fishermen of *Windsor-Forest* are analogous:

> In genial Spring, beneath the quiv'ring Shade
> Where cooling Vapours breathe along the Mead,

The patient Fisher takes his silent Stand
Intent, his Angle trembling in his Hand;
With Looks unmov'd, he hopes the Scaly Breed,
And eyes the dancing Cork and bending Reed . . .
Now *Cancer* glows with *Phoebus'* fiery Car;
The Youth rush eager to the Sylvan War;
Swarm o'er the Lawns, the Forest Walks surround,
Rowze the fleet Hart, and chear the opening Hound.
(135–140, 147–150)

As one would expect in a poem descriptive as well as political, these men have more specific physical reality than has the Indian. Like many personifications, they resemble figures in a painting, created by the poet, placed in appropriate settings, given activities that define, for purposes of the poem, their nature. But like the Indian, they exist for the meanings that their appearances illustrate. In the ideal relation of man to nature, every season has its appropriate activity, uniting man with the natural world yet declaring his dominance over it. To specify the ideal is an important part of the poet's argument; men as images help to make this possible without slowing the sequence because of the complexities of realism.

This technique of presenting human beings is altogether opposed to realism. It is a particular and important mode of artifice, whose essence is generalization. The typical satiric mode of depicting men as images concentrates on particulars as a way of suggesting larger implications. The nonsatiric method converts men to pictures or personifications by concentrating on their meanings. Pope's satire, when it works through appearances, is ostensibly concerned with the superficial; his generalized nonsatiric presentations are clear in their concentration on the profound. One final example, again from the *Essay on Man,* suggests the peculiar economy and point that characterize the method at its best:

Behold the child, by Nature's kindly law,
Pleas'd with a rattle, tickled with a straw:
Some livelier play-thing gives his youth delight,
A little louder, but as empty quite:

Scarfs, garters, gold, amuse his riper stage;
And beads and pray'r-books are the toys of age:
Pleas'd with this bauble still, as that before;
'Till tir'd he sleeps, and Life's poor play is o'er!
(II, 275–282)

This passage has moments of satiric observation, but its tone is on the whole compassionate. It illustrates the generalization that precedes it: "See some fit Passion ev'ry age supply, / Hope travels thro', nor quits us when we die" (273–274). What seems obvious and a bit flaccid in general statement becomes more compelling when converted into imagery. The assumption behind the entire sequence, too universally accepted to need explicit statement, is that it is better to be an adult than a child. In light of that assumption, the account of man's career acquires pathos. Pope makes a significant pun in the final line: what one has learned to think of as possessing the dignity of drama, perhaps even of tragedy, is also only the play of a child; and the aspiration toward adulthood can be at best illusorily fulfilled. Although every stage of life demonstrates the operation of "Nature's kindly law," the adjective "kindly" possesses ironic force: Nature's "kindness" is ambiguous. Generalizing through sharp images of man (which are explicitly metaphorical, unlike those in preceding examples), Pope demonstrates once more the value of perspective. To "see" men as images may be to see what they really are. The simplifications of imagery convey complexity.

Images, Milton Rugoff has written, "introduce material by way of analogy or illustration to clarify, embellish, heighten, or add to a given statement of meaning; and if we need an explicit definition of an image this may well serve."[12] If image is thus defined by function, Pope's characterizations almost exemplify the definition. They also fit a definition based on form: "a literal and concrete representation of a sensory experience or of an object that can be known by one or more of the senses."[13] Alvin Kernan has written, "the satirist is never interested in deep explorations of human nature. His characters are merely personifications of the particular form of dullness he wishes to give visible shape."[14] This extreme statement suggests the importance to Pope's methodology of "visible shape" as a mode of presentation, and the significance of "superficiality" in even extended depictions of character. Pope is in fact capable of interest in "deep explorations of human nature," but external presentation is crucial to his satiric effects and to the kind of psychic action typical of his work.

Poetry, like drama, is the imitation of an action. Pope agrees with Aristotle, to whom he appeals for authority on this point: "It is in Poetry, as *Aristotle* observes, as in Painting; a Painter puts many actions into one piece, but they all conspire to form one entire and perfect Action: A Poet likewise uses many Episodes, but all those Episodes taken separately finish nothing, they are but imperfect members, which all together make one and the same action, like the parts of a human body, they all conspire to constitute the whole man."[15] This comment belongs to Pope's discussion of Homer, and its immediate application is to epic poetry. Pope's own characteristic form is not narrative, but the loose assemblages of exempla that compose the verse epistles and the Horatian imitations. The "looseness," however, is illusory: such poems create and contain a unifying psychic action, to which individual images contribute. Character images in such a context often define an "action" that has no clear existence independently of them.

The kind of "action" characteristic of eighteenth century satiric verse demands formulation in abstract intellectual terms—which is not to deny, however, its capacity to generate emotion. Pope's versions are particularly complex in their working out. More typical of the century is the pattern represented by Samuel Johnson's *Vanity of Human Wishes,* whose "action," suggested by its title, is one of revelation rather than discovery.[16] The poem exists to illustrate and enlarge a pre-existent concept; its psychic movement is toward expanded understanding of the title's abstraction. Johnson is as adept as Pope at using slight visual suggestions to convey essential meaning:

> Low skulks the hind beneath the rage of pow'r,
> And leaves the wealthy traytor in the Tow'r,

Untouch'd his cottage, and his slumbers sound,
Tho' confiscation's vulturs hover round.[17]
(33–36)

The hind and the traitor, both generalizations of social roles, function symbolically as extremes of possibility. The "lowness" of the hind seems to imply a derogatory moral as well as social judgment, furthered by the implications of underhandedness in "skulks." But the untouched cottage and sound (i.e., guiltless) slumbers counteract such implications, as the negative "traytor" counteracts the positive possibilities of "wealthy," and the function of the Tower opposes its physical suggestion of eminence. The image of law enforcers as "vulturs" conveys an absolute moral judgment of political inequity, which complicates understanding of the peasants' happy state. This is far from resembling a romantic vision of blissful poverty. The immediate advantages of being inconspicuous depend on the corruptions of social and political conditions; "the vanity of human wishes" is not directly ordained by God, but depends on what man has made of man.

This group of images—low peasant, elevated traitor, human vultures—represents an early stage in the poem's progression toward an enlarged understanding. Its patterns repeatedly duplicate themselves:

From every room descends the painted face,
That hung the bright Palladium of the place,
And smoak'd in kitchens, or in auctions sold,
To better features yields the frame of gold;
For now no more we trace in ev'ry line
Heroic worth, benevolence divine:
The form distorted justifies the fall,
And detestation rids th' indignant wall.
(83–90)

The alternation of rising and falling, ubiquitous in the poem, is less ambiguous here than in the earlier example. Yet the stress on ways that a single physical object can embody opposed meanings emphasizes the ambiguity of all images. "The form distorted" is distorted only in the mind's eye, but the mind's distortions create conspicuous effects in the real world. Part of human vanity is the capacity to trust the stability of appearance. Everyone alike shares a propensity to "trace" in what he sees what he expects to find; man's wishes must be vain when he is incapable of understanding what he truly is.

The poem's insistence on reiterated patterns of imagery—its repeated examples of painful rising, catastrophic fall, and determined but fruitless battle—emphasizes the fact that the images clarify and expand existent meanings rather than create new ones. Repetition with variation is Johnson's crucial method. The famous description of Wolsey, elaborately developed, repeats the sequence of rise and fall but discovers new implications in it:

> Thro' him the rays of regal bounty shine,
> Turn'd by his nod the stream of honour flows,
> His smile alone security bestows:
> Still to new heights his restless wishes tow'r. . .
> For why did Wolsey near the steeps of fate,
> On weak foundations raise th' enormous weight?
> Why but to sink beneath misfortune's blow,
> With louder ruin to the gulphs below?
> (102–105, 125–128)

Enlargement of reference is itself enlargement of meaning. The metaphoric suggestions that human triumph must be hubristic, because it attempts to imitate the divine dominion of nature, prepare for an inevitable nemesis, in a form recalling that associated with the piling of Ossa on Pelion, an emblem of presumption. Man is "unnatural" in believing himself able to control natural forces, for the natural law dictating that whatever rises must fall is sure to defeat him. Human wishes are vain because based on inadequate or incomplete perception.

The poem's development of increasingly complex meanings and implications for the phrase "the vanity of human wishes" creates a rising dramatic tension, resolved but not eliminated by the final assertion of divine benevolence, which establishes new emotional as well as intellectual possibilities. To reveal the vanity of human wishes—a description of the "action" and the purpose of the poem—involves revealing also how the horror of reality can be humanly acceptable. The revelation is both rational and emotional; the presentations of character as image, involving the reader's thoughts and feelings, move him through an expanding sequence of implication.

The "action" of Pope's formal verse satires, although characteristically dependent, like Johnson's, on intellectual conception, usually involves more sense of discovery. It is often a version of argument—a nonlogical version, in which imagery largely creates meaning. A persistent twentieth century misconception about Pope has it that all process in his poems is only an imitation of some process previously completed. Thus Carol Johnson has written: "If in Pope we discern the results of reason reasoned, we experience in Donne the process of reason reasoning: in the former as a distillation, in the latter an appetitive force; in one a version of the mind made up, and in the other a state of mind."[18] Or more generally, C. Day Lewis has stated: "The Augustans were interested in ideas and in the versification of ideas: for them, the function of metaphor and simile was to illustrate ideas, not to create them."[19] Such accounts falsify the actual effect of much of Pope's best verse. Though reason is not quite "an appetitive force" in his satires, it is an immediate energy; the poems record an evolving mental state.

The action of *Epistle to a Lady*, for instance, is to define the nature and limits of feminine possibility, and the individual portraits that compose most of the poem are means of achieving this definition. The nature of Pope's intellectual energy is suggested by the fact that action for him may imply definition, achieved by a complexity of qualifications in which images generate ideas.

But Pope's kind of definition is too complex for any obvious orderly sequence; its discoveries derive partly from its reflection of social incoherencies. The repetitions of image patterns in *The Vanity of Human Wishes* contribute to the effect of enlarging understanding, because each successive appearance of a metaphor deepens its implications. But in *Epistle to a Lady*, the metaphor of a trip through a portrait gallery seems to justify random glances in all directions. The coherence of Pope's randomness depends on the orderly psychic movement that the poem reflects, a movement toward understanding which can absorb all incoherences into their meanings. Here, too, the notion of "meaning" is emotional as well as intellectual. The progression toward understanding is also toward love, involving compassion for the feminine frailties that the poem sharply defines. Though some of its early victims are seen without mercy, an expansion of emotional capacity parallels the epistle's developing insight.

The early sketches of the epistle proceed through a sequence of gathering intensity. Pope concentrates first on typical female schemes of self-presentation, the bases on which women seem to invite judgment. The first group of two-line characterizations concern obvious modes of appearance—the self-conscious shaping of appearances and what they reveal, which is not necessarily what their manipulator intends: "Here Fannia, leering on her own good man, / Is there, a naked Leda with a Swan" (9–10). The leering image of propriety and the self-conscious pose of Leda capture an identity of character more important than the apparent contrast of role: women, this sequence of images suggests, put their trust consistently in appearance as disguise. The next pair of portraits—Rufa flirting and studying Locke; Sappho "at her toilet's greazy task" (25) or dancing at a masque—use feminine activity to suggest essence, summing up Sappho's incongruities with the striking metaphor of busy insects in muck and in sun. Then come two portraits based on feminine forms of emotional display: Silia, alternately "soft" and raving because of the absence or presence of a pimple on her nose; Papillia, who pines for a park, then pines because she has it.

The first forty lines of the poem thus begin the process of definition by conveying a view of woman as dependent on either simple physical appearance, including dress and pose, or on the extended physicality of appearance based on activity or emotional display. With the generalizations beginning at line 41 ("Ladies, like variegated Tulips, show, / 'Tis to their Changes that their charms we owe") the poem develops a deeper level of perception, concerning itself not with how women intend to present themselves but with their actual effects on others. At this point, too, begins a series of sexual allusions, at first veiled and oblique, gradually becoming more explicit and forceful. Calypso, who "once each heart alarm'd" (45), also "charm'd" without beauty (46), "bewitch'd" by the power of her tongue and eyes (47), and was sure to create passion in her victims (51–52). Narcissa, next in the sequence, is "A fool to Pleasure" (61); "Passion burns" in her (65); she is "A very Heathen in the carnal part" (67). "Sin" displays a gamut of sexual looseness (70–78). Philomedé "makes her hearty meal upon a Dunce" (87), and the precise sense in which she devours men is ambiguous. Flavia, who toasts "our wants and wishes" (88), devotes herself to pleasure. Simo's mate divides her life between passion and prayer (106). Atossa, who completes the group, indulges passion without pleasure but with resultant scandal; her passions turn to hate when she yields in love (126–134).

In the same way that each of these women creates a kind of metaphor for some aspect of the feminine condition, the sexual conduct hinted or described in each life becomes a synecdoche for the woman's relationships. Although not every woman in the sequence represents an increase of evil over her predecessor, there is a general movement toward deepening sinister implications. Calypso generates passion "when she touch[es] the brink of all we hate" (52); her relationships are askew because she depends on her weaknesses as forms of strength. Narcissa, more dangerous, operates without feeling, exploiting the good nature of others (60) and placing self-indulgence on the same level as piety:

> Now Conscience chills her, and now Passion burns;
> And Atheism and Religion take their turns;
> A very Heathen in the carnal part,
> Yet still a sad, good Christian at her heart.
>
> (65–68)

The opening couplet establishes the horror of her nature: "Narcissa's nature, tolerably mild, / To make a wash, would hardly stew a child" (53–54). No one, it is assumed, would sacrifice a child to manufacture a cosmetic wash, so that the judicious appraisal implicit in "hardly" has a chilling effect. The woman's acts are so arbitrary that they challenge the most commonplace assumptions about humanity. Her sexual nature and her religious commitment are equally undependable, and she is unable to make real human connections. The same is true of "Sin," whose "Head's untouch'd" (74) since she is interested only in the life of the body; and of Philomedé, whose lectures "On the soft Passion, and the Taste refin'd" (84) do not prevent her from indulging a ravenous version of "Taste," destructive in purpose and in effect. Flavia's "impotence of mind" (93) derives from over-refinement, and the stress is more on her resultant misery than on her inability to give pleasure. Simo's mate, an object for contempt rather than pity, provokes the poet to a comparison of "Woman" and "Fool," with the conclusion that "true No-meaning puzzles more than Wit" (114).

The corruption involved in misguided relationships derives from interior corruption. Inasmuch as Pope concerns himself here with the inner life of the women he portrays, he dwells on lack of commitment: first as an idiosyncrasy, a mode of female charm, and gradually as a serious deviation from moral norms. The conclusions about Flavia, summing up the lack of integrity implicit in the entire gallery, suggest the poet's judgment on it and his awareness of the pathos as well as the evil implicit in feminine failures of commitment:

> Say, what can cause such impotence of mind?
> A Spark too fickle, or a Spouse too kind.
> Wise Wretch! with Pleasures too refin'd to please,
> With too much Spirit to be e'er at ease,
> With too much Quickness ever to be taught,
> With too much Thinking to have common Thought:
> Who purchase Pain with all that Joy can give,
> And die of nothing but a Rage to live.
>
> (93–100)

Each quality from which Flavia has separated herself represents the ideal of a life pleasing to others, marked by "ease"—that state in which one is in tune with oneself and one's world—capable of intellectual and moral development, and kept from error by acceptance of the universal, ordinary modes of thought. The final paradox is implicit in all the characterizations: women who proceed wrongly toward their goals discover—like men in analogous situations—that they gain the opposite of what they wish.

The portrait of Atossa, longer than any of the others, sums up the implications of all, as suggested by the poet's observation that she is "Scarce once herself, by turns all Womankind!" (116). Her constant state of conflict, within herself and with others; her intellectual and moral superficiality; her incapacity to commit herself emotionally or to receive nonperverse emotional gratification—all these traits echo qualities depicted in isolation in one or another of the poem's earlier characters. The nature of Atossa's relationships is more fully specified than those of her predecessors:

> Superiors? death! and Equals? what a curse!
> But an Inferior not dependant? worse.
> Offend her, and she knows not to forgive;
> Oblige her, and she'll hate you while you live:
> But die, and she'll adore you—Then the Bust
> And Temple rise—then fall again to dust.
> Last night, her Lord was all that's good and great,
> A Knave this morning, and his Will a Cheat.
> Strange! by the Means defeated of the Ends,
> By spirit robb'd of Pow'r, by Warmth of Friends,
> By Wealth of Follow'rs! without one distress
> Sick of herself thro' very selfishness!
>
> (135–146)

Language and detail enlarge the implications of Atossa's character: although she represents the sins of "Womankind," she embodies errors common to men as well. Her attitude toward superiors, equals, and dependents suggests that the result of individual moral and emotional weakness may be the destruction of social hierarchy. The introduction of the second person pronoun stresses the reader's necessary involvement in the issues raised by this woman's character. The bust and temple in their rapid rise and fall epitomize the transience of all human endeavor as well as of Atossa's emotional states. The concluding couplets, like those about Flavia, display the pathos within the horror of Atossa's condition, which exemplifies moral weakness and its emotional and social consequences. Just as the result of Timon's pride in the *Epistle to Burlington* is that "the Poor are cloath'd, the Hungry fed" (169), so the result of Atossa's perversity, which causes her to lack an heir despite all her children, may be that her wealth "wanders, Heav'n-directed, to the Poor" (150). Individual perversity cannot destroy cosmic order, nor is Atossa's moral deviance the exclusive characteristic of women.

This is not to say that Atossa's womanhood is unimportant. The process of definition comes to a preliminary climax in her presentation, exactly halfway through the poem. If her flaws are human rather than feminine (Pope concludes finally that woman, heaven's "last best work," is but "a softer Man," 272), their manifestations nevertheless specify possible areas of feminine endeavor. Unlike her counterparts in *Epistle to Bathurst* or *Epistle to Burlington,* Atossa does not have available to her accomplishment in the world of finance, architecture, or politics. The line "Full sixty years the World has been her Trade" (123) suggests the superficiality of her attitudes, but also the limitation of her possibilities: no other trade is open to her. Like other women, she is almost completely defined by her relationships, as wife, mistress, mother, friend, or social tyrant. Pope's concentration in the poem's first half on women's effects on others implies an important aspect of his total view of women, whose spheres of activity, more limited than those of men, are correspondingly more intense. The series of portraits add up to a preliminary judgmental definition of women as extensively involved in human relationships and thus as dangerous in their moral weakness, because this is necessarily expressed in their relationships, and because their "charm" relates directly to their weakness. Volatility bears a close similarity to lack of commitment, which culminates in the horror of an Atossa.

The last two portraits before the poet turns to a more general view of women return to the problem of appearances from a new perspective. Earlier depiction of appearance has been a way of suggesting inner reality. Now, with Cloe and the Queen, Pope considers the case in which appearance suggests something sharply divergent from the truth of character:

> 'With ev'ry pleasing, ev'ry prudent part,
> Say, what can Cloe want?'—she wants a Heart,
> She speaks, behaves, and acts just as she ought;
> But never, never, reach'd one gen'rous Thought.
> Virtue she finds too painful an endeavour,
> Content to dwell in Decencies for ever.
>
> (157–164)

Speech, behavior, and action, which have previously been modes of characterization, may display shocking divergence from "Thought." This disparity between form and content justifies the poet's final devastating dismissal: "Cloe is prudent—would you too be Wise? / Then never break your heart when Cloe dies" (179–180). The decorous treatment of Queen Caroline hints a similar disparity in her:

> The same for ever! and describ'd by all
> With Truth and Goodness, as with Crown and Ball:
> Poets heap Virtues, Painters Gems at will.
>
> (183–185)

Whereas Cloe substitutes decencies for virtue, the queen needs do nothing at all: an appearance of the appropriate virtues is provided her from without. But the aim of the true artist is "To draw the Naked" (188), the motive that informs the poem's effort to penetrate beneath feminine appearance.

For the final third of the epistle, Pope's own note offers a valuable gloss. He appends the note to yet another generalization:

> In Men, we various Ruling Passions find,
> In Women, two almost divide the kind . . .
> The Love of Pleasure, and the Love of Sway."
>
> (207–208, 210)

The note explains, "The former part having shewn, that the *particular Characters* of Women are more various than those of

Men, it is nevertheless observ'd, that the *general* Characteristic of the sex, as to the *ruling Passion*, is more uniform."[20] The distinction between the early concentration on "*particular Characters*" and the later stress on "*general* Characteristic" is illuminating. At this point the poem becomes, and continues, dependent on explicit and emphatic metaphors, which give particularity to a structure of generalizations. "The Love of Sway" as an aspect of femininity inspires the first extended metaphor, concerning "a whole Sex of Queens" (219), engaged in battle, alternately triumphant and defeated, doomed to the fate of loveless tyrants at last. More remarkable is the next metaphorical sequence, which explores the feminine desire for pleasure by comparing women first to children, then to witches and ghosts, finally to veterans:

> Pleasures the sex, as children Birds, pursue,
> Still out of reach, yet never out of view,
> Sure, if they catch, to spoil the Toy at most,
> To covet flying, and regret when lost:
> At last, to follies Youth could scarce defend,
> 'Tis half their Age's prudence to pretend;
> Asham'd to own they gave delight before,
> Reduc'd to feign it, when they give no more:
> As Hags hold Sabbaths, less for joy than spight,
> So these their merry, miserable Night;
> Still round and round the Ghosts of Beauty glide,
> And haunt the places where their Honour dy'd.
>
> (231–242)

The definition of women thus continues to proceed with reference to their human relationships: now the giving of sexual pleasure signifies the feminine sense both of possibility and of limitation. The "prudence" of youth makes women deny their sexuality, while that of age makes them assert a sexuality which has in fact vanished (as does Lady Wishfort in *The Way of the World*). The death of honor seems in retrospect a triumph. Sexual references imply the intimate relation between pleasure and power, while the metaphors also suggest the falseness of most feminine pleasure. It is the pleasure of children at best, dependent on false assessments of reality, and at worst, it is a mode of merry misery, in which spite replaces joy and the witch's perversity dominates the woman's desires. Women can neither receive nor give properly. Always they wish for more than they can get. When they are able to give, they are ashamed. Finally, giving reduces itself to pretence. When the poet sums up "how the World its Veterans rewards!" (243), he stresses the lack of reciprocity in feminine experience: "Young without Lovers, old without a Friend, / A Fop their Passion, but their Prize a Sot" (246–247). The six-line summary contains no verbs, except the opening imperative "See" (a verb that recurs frequently in this poem of images); this syntactical omission suggests in mimetic terms the purposelessness, the lack of meaningful activity ("Fair to no purpose, artful to no end," 245), characteristic of these women.

Such a passage does not provide "characterization" in any ordinary sense, since it purports to deal with "the sex" rather than with individuals or even types. In fact, however, like the evocations of Flavia or of Simo's mate, it concerns a subspecies rather than a species: the immediately succeeding panegyric on Martha Blount makes it clear that women of quite another sort do exist. The collective characterization, given sharpness through the use of illustrative imagery, creates pictures as vivid as any in the earlier part of the poem, although achieved by a different method. Benjamin Boyce, writing of the more conventional character sketches in Pope's poems, has remarked, "One is tempted to propose the neat generalization that in Pope's depictions the type tends to become more individual and the individual more typical. In the large I believe this is true."[21] It is a perceptive observation on the poet's technique, which applies even to so inclusive a description as the one just considered, where the emotional fluctuation, conflict, and anguish of "the sex" are so exactly specified that they are responded to as if to the emotions of an individual.

The main argument of the poem ends at this point, with the remaining forty-four lines creating the image of a "good" woman to set against the exempla of deviation. Through his animated images, Pope has revealed that the changeability of women, which can be taken as either a joke or a mode of feminine charm, makes adherence to a norm impossible and may produce serious moral deviance and emotional misery. The exemplification of this fairly simple idea in concrete terms gives it new dimensions of seriousness and complexity. The passion that informs many of the characterizations generates authority; the concentration on how women affect others provides immediacy. By the time one reaches the account of Martha Blount herself, who appeared at the poem's start with the provocative remark that "Most Women have no Characters at all" (2), but who at the end turns out to be a paragon, this final objectification of feminine possibility resolves an issue both relevant and difficult, namely, to define the possibilities for feminine accomplishment, given the contradictory nature of women.

To begin with, the poet elaborates a metaphor of the good woman as the moon:

> That Charm shall grow, while what fatigues the Ring
> Flaunts and goes down, an unregarded thing.
> So when the Sun's broad beam has tir'd the sight,
> All mild ascends the Moon's more sober light,
> Serene in Virgin Modesty she shines,
> And unobserv'd the glaring Orb declines.
> (251–256)

Just after the introductory section of the poem, as he playfully expanded his metaphor of himself as portrait painter, he had recommended, "Chuse a firm Cloud, before it fall, and in it / Catch, ere she change, the Cynthia of this minute" (19–20), and thereby introduced the series of pictures that compose most of the poem. Cynthia, goddess of the moon, was at that point an image for feminine changefulness. When Pope returns to the moon image, it has been transformed. The moon is still changeable, but also "mild," "sober," and "modest." Within the context of change, serenity remains possible. Martha Blount, as full of contradictions as any of her sisters, still has the power of self-control, which in women comes from that "Temper, whose unclouded ray / Can make to morrow chearful as to day" (257–258). Full of paradoxes though the good woman may be, they are paradoxes that create balance rather than conflict ("Reserve with Frankness, Art with Truth ally'd, / Courage with Softness, Modesty with Pride," 277–278). Accepting the logic of his own imagery, the poet finally transforms it, demonstrating that feminine inconsistency, concern with relationships, and relative helplessness in the organization of society can all turn to good as well as evil—a good that can be more forcibly described because of the established awareness of its negative counterparts. Martha Blount's "Fame," like Belinda's, depends on her being immortalized in poetry (see 281–292), which provides the controlling power to preserve her as a pattern, or image, of virtue. Although in reality she possesses the good qualities Pope claims for her, reality cannot be so pure as poetry, and the unalloyed quality of her goodness is the result of a poet's affection—and of the patronage of Apollo, god of poetry:

> The gen'rous God, who Wit and Gold refines,
> And ripens Spirits as he ripens Mines,
> Kept Dross for Duchesses, the world shall know it,
> To you gave Sense, Good-humour, and a Poet.
> (289–292)

Not only has the poet the climactic position in this list of blessings, but the poet's power to organize and reveal meanings in experience, as in women, has been demonstrated by the entire epistle. Martha Blount, like others of her sex, has become an image for meanings larger than herself—for the whole range of positive being and action open to women. Irvin Ehrenpreis has argued forcefully that the power of the *Epistle to a Lady* depends largely on the depth and cogency of its allusions to reality. He demonstrates that the poem ascends through various degrees of reality to the portrait of Martha Blount at the end.[22] But it might also be argued that the peculiar power of Pope's use of "reality" comes from his tranformation, simplification, and symbolic representation of it. His intimacy and playfulness of tone at the poem's end may derive from the emotional realities of an actual relationship, but he has also created a pattern of meanings and symbols having the power and significance of general truths. The "action" of definition is necessarily one of generalization. Images of character substantially create that generalization, and even the most personalized of them must participate in its larger meanings, making possible the complex manipulation through which the poet conveys an understanding of woman, including both an ethical norm and her deviations from it.

*An Epistle from Mr. Pope, to Dr. Arbuthnot* is another poem that proceeds through an argument of images. The action of this poem is vindication, for as the "Advertisement" states directly, this is an answer to a personal attack, its purpose being to justify the poet and his occupation, the writing of satire. But Pope's kind of vindication in fact includes and depends on a process of definition: both self-definition and clarification of what his opponents embody. Consequently, images of character (based on himself, his family, his friends, and his enemies) are crucial in creating the "action" of self-justification through understanding, which is once more a process of discovery, and once more a process revealing the crucial importance of control as an ethical ideal.

"The purpose of Imagery," wrote Daniel Webb in 1762, "is either to illustrate, or aggrandize our ideas."[23] It is a simple statement of what can be a complex function. The imagery of the *Epistle to Dr. Arbuthnot* "aggrandizes" ideas through development of intricate patterns of association. Self-defense becomes a mode of satiric attack as the speaker of the poem points up the contrasts between himself and his literary and personal enemies. Those enemies, as they appear en masse at the beginning, are characterized by meaningless or destructive energy. They rave, recite, and "madden" round the land, pierce thickets, glide through grottoes, renew the charge; they stop chariots, board barges; confined to madhouses, they scrawl with desperate charcoal; all "fly" to Pope at Twickenham. Collectively, they comprise a plague (29). Mental disease marks their conduct and their literary productions. They are asses, spiders, mad dogs, puppies, and toads; they glide like snakes or roar like lions. Sporus, the worst of them, is a butterfly, bug, spaniel, toad, and reptile. Pope justifies his contempt through such images, for they suggest not only negative judgment but the reasons for it: he believes his enemies perverse, meaninglessly active, undignified, subhuman. The three extended characterizations of individual enemies—Atticus, Bufo, and Sporus—focus on specific aspects of character for which the gathering self-portrayal supplies counterpoint.

Pope defines his personal ideal just before the portrait of Sporus:

> Oh let me live my own! and die so too!
> ('To live and die is all I have to do':)
> Maintain a Poet's Dignity and Ease,
> And see what friends, and read what books I please . . .
> I was not born for Courts or great Affairs,
> I pay my Debts, believe, and say my Pray'rs.
> (261–264, 267–268)

This is the classic ideal of moderation, integrity, and retirement, but with special focus on the dignity and ease of the poet, not the ordinary man. Earlier in the poem, the speaker had observed, "The Muse but serv'd to ease some Friends, not Wife, / To help me thro' this long Disease, my Life" (131–132). "Disease," previously personified in the plague of poetasters, is the opposite of "ease," of which the muse of poetry may be the source. But neither ease nor dignity is readily achieved, as both positive and negative characterizations make clear.

Atticus, "born to write, converse, and live with ease" (196), displays in his life a parody of ease. Each of his characteristics cancels another. For example, his apparent ease derives from lack of commitment—the same lack that defines Flavia's "impotence of mind" in *Epistle to a Lady*, and which deprives such characters as her and Atossa of even the appearance of ease. Never declaring himself, the literary dictator retains the reputation of being obliging without doing anything to oblige. His illusion of dignity depends on self-obsession; his irresponsible ease is both ludicrous and pathetic. The grotesque Bufo, in contrast, parodies dignity, like "Sin" who is "Proud as a Peeress, prouder as a Punk"(*Epistle to a Lady*, 70). He exemplifies the appearance of dignity without substance or discernment ("puff'd by ev'ry quill," 232). Sporus has not even false dignity and ease. Pope stresses his lack of either quality by the sequence of nonhuman metaphors, including not only animals, but a shallow stream, a puppet, and a "vile Antithesis" (325). Like the worst of the woman in *Epistle to a Lady* (and the connection, given his homosexuality, is perhaps not accidental), he is capable of various roles: "Amphibious Thing!: . . . acting either Part, / The trifling Head, or the corrupted Heart!" (326–327). Like them, too, his appearance bears little necessary relation to reality: he seems a butterfly but is only a bug, a "painted Child of Dirt that stinks and stings" (310). Sexual and moral ambiguity, ambiguity of role, appearance, and personality—these characterize Sporus. Whereas Atticus lacked commitment to any real substance, Sporus commits himself not even to his own appearances; he shifts from fop to flatterer, arrogance to baseness, froth to venom. Bufo, despite his lack of standards, at least recognizes the possibility of artistic value, but Sporus does not believe that value can exist. His pleasantries have no more motive than his malignance; he simply acts by whim. Refusing to use his proper human capacities, he becomes a devil, tempting others to similar rejection of their humanity. The defining nonhuman images justify Pope's horror of him.

The speaker feels himself the exemplar of opposition to such as Atticus, Bufo, Sporus, and the nameless horde of literary hangers-on. He strives for dignity and ease in his own life and work, recognizing that they can come only from commitment:

> Out with it, *Dunciad*! let the secret pass,
> The Secret to each Fool, that he's an Ass:
> The truth once told, (and wherefore should we lie?)
> The Queen of *Midas* slept, and so may I.
> (79–82)

After the portrait of Bufo, which challenges the standard of dignity, the speaker's tone heightens, and he gathers full rhetorical authority. As "defender of the faith," he fulfills the moral imperative to lash Sporus.[24] Then he defines personal and literary integrity, speaking of himself not as an individual ego but as a symbol of the poet—"more type than man, more passion than type," to use Yeats's phrase.[25] Declaring the importance of dignity, he also defines its internal enemies: the temptation to seek fortune, fashion, and position. By striving for such goals, one becomes, as structure and diction stress (334–336), a worshipper of false idols, a fool, a madman, or a mere tool. The pride of Bufo, the servility of Sporus, oppose the poet's proper poise ("Not proud, nor servile, be one Poet's praise / That, if he pleas'd, he pleas'd by manly ways," 336–337). If heroism seems necessary in the defense of the "Virtue" to which Pope commits himself ("Welcome for thee, fair Virtue! all the past," 358), ease is correspondingly difficult. In the Homeric world that the poet had inhabited for so long, to "perform the most difficult feats with ease" was "a traditional mark of divine power."[26] The epistle's redefinition of the virtues Pope admires follows the Homeric pattern: the possibility of ease depends not on the absence of difficulties, but on the capacity to accept all difficulty ("Full ten years slander'd, did he once reply?" 374) in the clear consciousness of a devotion to virtue.

The images of Pope's mother and father at the end of the poem represent nonliterary versions of this kind of devotion, along with the dignity and ease it produces, but the power of poetry is as important as that of virtue—probably more important—in preserving their "Unspotted Names! and memorable long, / If there be Force in Virtue, or in Song," (386–387). As poetry gives power to the image of Martha Blount, so it transforms the human reality of Pope's father, whose embodiment of alternatives to the evils that surround and threaten the speaker emerges through a long sequence of negative statements:

> Born to no Pride, inheriting no Strife,
> Nor marrying Discord in a Noble Wife,
> Stranger to Civil and Religious Rage,
> The good Man walk'd innoxious thro' his Age.
> No Courts he saw, no Suits would ever try,
> Nor dar'd an Oath, nor hazarded a Lye:
> Un-learn'd, he knew no Schoolman's subtle Art,
> No Language, but the Language of the Heart.
> By Nature honest, by Experience wise,
> Healthy by Temp'rance and by Exercise:

His Life, tho' long, to sickness past unknown,
His Death was instant, and without a groan.
Oh grant me thus to live, and thus to die!
Who sprung from Kings shall know less joy than I.
(392–405)

No mere exercise in filial piety, this segment is highly functional in the poem's argument. The epistle's previous human images give content to the sequence's abstract nouns. Pride, discord, civil and religious rage are the realities against which the speaker contends. The capacity of the good man to walk "innoxious thro' his Age"—through his own old age as well as through his era of corruption—is a triumph, because the world is so largely inhabited, as the poem has demonstrated, by noxious creatures. Lack of learning, lack of sophisticated language, become further indices of virtue, corollaries of the directly attributed virtues of honesty, wisdom, and health. The speaker's expressed wish to identify himself with his father's moral achievement is another exemplification of the solidity of character—the dignity and ease—being opposed to his evanescent but destructive enemies.

The epistle ends with reference to the poet's care for his mother and his desire that his friend Arbuthnot be preserved "social, chearful, and serene" (416). Arbuthnot, too, embodies the virtues the poet claims for himself and admires; and, as Peter Dixon has pointed out, the speaker's possession of such a friend is itself evidence of his virtue. "Nature, temper, and habit, from my youth made me have but one strong desire," Pope wrote to Gay; "all other ambitions, my person, education, constitution, religion, &c. conspir'd to remove far from me. That desire was to fix and preserve a few lasting, dependable friendships."[27] Joseph Spence has reported his saying, "There is nothing that is meritorious but virtue and friendship, and indeed friendship itself is only a part of virtue."[28] Dixon has added: "the mere fact that the friendship between Pope and Arbuthnot appears to have continued undiminished throughout the long disease of the poet's life provides valuable indirect testimony to their moral characters. Since they are old friends, it follows that they must also be good men."[29]

The structure of the poem's argument—the action of self-justification—is more intricate than that of *Epistle to a Lady,* to which it bears many thematic resemblances. Following the same large pattern of movement through a series of negative examples to an embodiment of positive alternatives, Pope also interweaves images of the good life throughout the poem: the first direct statement of his own rectitude begins as early as line 125. The consistent alternation of positive and negative examples dramatizes the poem's implicit contention that attack and defense are both aspects of a single heroic activity. In its sense of life as battle, this poem resembles *The Vanity of Human Wishes,* which also proceeds from negative examples to a positive image of conduct, although its positive exemplum is both generalized and tentative. For Pope, the poet is the exemplary warrior; for Johnson, the great fighter is the Christian. This difference of theme helps to account for the difference between the kinds of action created by the imagery of the two poems. What the Christian must do and must confront is known already, although it must be rediscovered and reconfirmed. But to claim that the poet embodies an ethical standard, although this idea has abundant classical sanctions, is in every individual case an individual affirmation. The right to make it must be won. And its winning is the drama of the *Epistle to Dr. Arbuthnot.*

Most of Pope's satiric works, even when they are not in any sense personal, contain comparable dramas. Although they depend on intellectual conceptions, they generate emotional force; and their characteristic movement of discovery helps to create the special atmosphere of Pope's poetry. Though *The Vanity of Human Wishes* is a very great poem, it is not exciting in the way that Pope's satires almost always are.[30]

Yeat's description of the poet as "more type than man, more passion than type" summarizes the self-presentation of many poets far less conscious than he of the ubiquity of masks. The persona Pope adopts in his late satires displays the kind of simplification characteristic of his presentations of other people as images; also, the same kind of circumstantiality and detail. John Aden has remarked, "Pope is not merely interested in the ethical proof of his moral and literary worth, the *ethos* which is partly a convention, partly a necessity, of the satirist; he is alive to himself as a personality, and his satires breathe the charm and force alike of his real presence." Aden concludes that it is misleading to emphasize the persona as satiric spokesman; although some such mechanism plays its part, "in the last analysis the voice we hear in a Popeian satire is that, not of a mask, but of a real personality, and that is a conspicuous factor in its appeal and impact."[31]

A more sophisticated version of the same argument has it that the "persona" is at once "real personality" and mask. The artifice that created the poet-hero of the late satires also operated in Pope's private life.[32] In life and in poetry, it is an artifice designed to reveal truth. "The 'mask' in Pope's satires is not a false face but an identity quite as real as any of the poet's other identities; it is fashioned not so that critics may admire its workmanship but so that readers may better understand the motives that made the poems necessary."[33] In this respect Pope follows Horace's practice for Horace's purposes, in avowed imitations and original poems alike. It is true that some of his evocations of himself have extraordinary immediacy and vividness. As early as the *Essay on Criticism* he had begun to use a version of himself as a symbolic character in a poetic argument. In the *Epistle to Miss Blount, on her leaving the Town, after the Coronation,* written in 1714, he uses self-description to resolve an argument never directly stated:

So when your slave, at some dear, idle time,
(Not plagu'd with headachs, or the want of rhime)
Stands in the streets, abstracted from the crew,
And while he seems to study, thinks of you:
Just when his fancy paints your sprightly eyes,
Or sees the blush of soft *Parthenia* rise,
*Gay* pats my shoulder, and you vanish quite;
Streets, chairs, and coxcombs rush upon my sight;
Vext to be still in town, I knit my brow,
Look sow'r, and hum a tune—as you may now.
(41–50)

The reference to headaches and to problems of rhyming, like the allusion to Gay, invites the reader to take this as a literal account of Pope the man. But it is also Pope the created character. The rest of the poem delicately evokes the language and values of a frivolous young woman, who dreams of "triumphs" in a double sense: in public festivities and in her personal battle of the sexes. Her distaste for the country rests on her acceptance of the superficial world of "sceptres, coronets, and balls" (39) as being preferable to "lone woods, or empty walls" (40): she lacks the resources to endure solitude. But such a summary makes the poem's criticism of her sound far too serious. In fact, its condemnation of Teresa Blount is hardly more serious than the self-criticism in the lines quoted above: the speaker recognizes, and the poem conveys, the parallels between his dissatisfaction with the city and hers with the country. The sense of human intimacy in his self-description pervades the entire epistle; its "criticism" is only a recognition of universal human failings. It is true that the woman's values seem more superficial than the man's, if only because he has, in writing poetry, a significant occupation. The picture of himself, as poet and as man, here represents no ideal, but it embodies a significant alternative to the frivolities of mere social life. The poet can perceive "coxcombs," where the woman imagines "Lords, and Earls, and Dukes, and garter'd Knights" (36). She dreams of a world in which the splendors of the coronation are everyday reality; the poet dreams of real human contact. His moral superiority, though slight, is real.

The conversion of this image of poet-man into the ideal figure of the late poems involves little change in the personality suggested, although much in the role. In the *Essay on Man* the speaker, although he had a real intellectual position, had no reality of character or personality; his interlocutor, Bolingbroke, had little more. The moral epistles have a distinctive voice, but it is not attached to a specific character. The *Epistle to Dr. Arbuthnot* and *Imitations of Horace, Satire* II, i, are the first of the late poems to use the persona to satiric purpose. The personality the poet establishes for himself in the epistle is heroic, but it is also very human: "I read / With honest anguish, and an aking head"; "I cough like *Horace,* and tho' lean, am short"; "Heav'ns! was I born for nothing but to write?"

(37–38, 116, 272). The satire, having the same theme as the epistle, rests on the same conception of character: the heroic fighter, "arm'd for *Virtue*" (105), who threatens law-breakers and brags of being "Un-plac'd, un-pension'd, no Man's Heir, or Slave" (116), but who also has trouble sleeping ("I nod in Company, I wake at Night," 13), who loves to pour himself out, and who lives happily outside the corrupt world, even though he may be plagued by it: "Know, all the distant Din that World can keep / Rolls o'er my *Grotto*, and but sooths my Sleep" (123–124). In *Satire* II, ii, the poet describes his humble existence on broccoli and mutton, but brags that "Fortune not much of humbling me can boast" (151); his humility comes from choice, not necessity. In *Epistle* I, i, he claims identification with virtue but also describes his figure in ludicrous terms, "My Wig all powder, and all snuff my Band" (162).

Examples could be multiplied, from all the Horatian poems and from the *Epilogue to the Satires*, but the point is already apparent: the ideal figure, the created poet-persona, who exemplifies the power of virtue in an age of corruption, belongs to the same conception as the figure of the eccentric private man with physical infirmities, personal idiosyncrasies, and "real personality." Personality is part of ideality. The figure of the poet, in his heroic aspect, is indeed more type than man, more passion than type: "Ask you what Provocation I have had? / The strong Antipathy of Good to Bad" (*Epilogue to the Satires*, II, 197–198). Yet his heroic role derives from his human reality—and not merely from his Horatian retirement, but from the fact that in retirement he eats broccoli, has feelings, and suffers from headaches. The importance of the heroism he asserts depends partly on the fact that it involves a transcendence of individual human limitations—limitations that Pope does not deny, in his creation of the persona, but which he claims to surmount. The poet-speaker has vivid physical and psychic reality. He is, in short, another of Pope's human images; and like the rest, he therefore combines the universal, the simplified, and the generalized with the particular.

The point may become clearer in the light of two quotations from Pope's letters. One concerns the figure of the Man of Ross from the *Epistle to Bathurst*, a characteristic nonsatiric example of Pope's conversion of people into images. He is writing to Jacob

Tonson, Sr., thanking him for sending particulars about the real Man of Ross:

> A small exaggeration you must allow me as a poet; yet I was determined the ground work at least should be *Truth,* which made me so scrupulous in my enquiries; and sure, considering that the world is bad enough to be always extenuating and lessening what virtue is among us, it is but reasonable to pay it sometimes a little over measure, to balance that injustice, especially when it is done for example and encouragement to others. If any man shall ever happen to endeavour to emulate the Man of Ross, 'twill be no manner of harm if I make him think he was something more charitable and more beneficent than really he was, for so much more good it would put the imitator upon doing. And farther I am satisfy'd in my conscience . . . that it was in his will, and in his heart, to have done every good a poet can imagine.[34]

This piece of self-justification makes it clear that Pope did not believe himself to be offering a realistic portrait of a real man. He has exaggerated, he claims, for the sake of virtue; the portrait is to create an example. In a later letter, he establishes the connection between "example" and "picture," which seems crucial to his mode of dealing with people in poetry. This is from a letter to Arbuthnot, which was probably not sent in the form in which Pope printed it. George Sherburn has suggested that it is "an expanded and able rewriting of the letter of 2 Aug. It is most probably a 'forgery,' but it is certainly Pope's best defence in prose of his satire, and as such is invaluable":[35]

> To attack Vices in the abstract, without touching Persons, may be safe fighting indeed, but it is fighting with Shadows. General propositions are obscure, misty, and uncertain, compar'd with plain, full, and home examples: Precepts only apply to our Reason, which in most men is but weak: Examples are pictures, and strike the Senses, nay raise the Passions, and call in those (the strongest and most general of all motives) to the aid of reformation.[36]

Examples are pictures. The satirist must always depend on examples, whether he wishes to label them particular persons or to call them embodiments of types. Not all satirists, however, are as conscious of Pope of the connection between example and picture, between moral perception and image. Wishing to appeal not only to reason but to the senses and the passions, Pope consistently converts general propositions into specific images, which yet retain generalizing power. He recognizes that his portraits are not renditions of reality, but he claims for them a groundwork of truth, and the justification for his technique is the effect he hopes it will have. Whether satire ever reformed anyone remains dubious; but in poetic if not in moral terms, the effect of using people as images is compelling.

The technique also represents an extension to the moral universe of the same principle of perception that controlled the presentation of the physical universe in the *Essay on Man*. Perception of physical reality was in that poem only a means to the comprehension that is man's proper goal, representing the full use of human capacities. Comprehension implies inclusiveness, and a fusion of judgment with perception. The observation of people manifest in Pope's satires displays the same approach. Precision of delineation is the necessary first step: to see what is there and to record it exactly. But the power of the poet is to make such precision reveal meaning. Pope wrote to his friend John Caryll, with reference to Caryll's grandson, "I would rather see him a good man than a good poet; and yet a good poet is no small thing, and (I believe) no small earnest of his being a good man."[37] One connection between good man and good poet is in this principle of comprehension. The good poet is obliged to use perception as the basis for judgment; writing thus becomes a moral act. Each of Pope's delineations of character uses the rendition of particularity to imply truths beyond the particular. Apprehension is the beginning of comprehension, and in his human images as in his nonhuman ones, Pope demonstrates both qualities.

*Six*

# Freedom Through Bounds

To think of wit, perception, and judgment entirely as principles of aesthetic control is to ignore one set of implications contained in the idea of each of these faculties. Wit is a source of exuberance in the *Essay on Criticism*; perception is as much an expansive as a restrictive principle in the *Essay on Man;* and judgment in *The Dunciad* generates the poetic authority that justifies the poem's extravagances. For Pope, it seems, ideas of control and of release are closely linked. It is a truism of Christian philosophy that real freedom can exist only in the context of proper discipline; for the eighteenth century poet, it is as obvious an aesthetic truism.

When Pope discusses or directly alludes to limits and boundaries, as literal fact or as metaphor, he is likely to display his awareness of the ambiguities implicit in the idea of control. Imagery of restriction recurs often in his verse, reflecting his ethical concern with the proper bounds of conduct, difficult to determine but vital to maintain. "God, in the nature of each being, founds / Its proper bliss, and sets its proper bounds," the *Essay on Man* declares (III, 109–110). The idea that the appropriate limitations for every being are implicit in its nature may war with the notion that society enforces limits necessary for public well-being but perhaps at odds with private needs. Moreover, the boundaries set by law and custom may not even serve the general good—a possibility that makes the appropriate attitude for individuals yet more problematic. However, the complex possibilities of the relation between "bliss" and "bounds" themselves provide rich ground for poetic investigation.

The *Epistle to Miss Blount, with the Works of Voiture* provides an early and representative example of Pope's use of the imagery of limits. It establishes two subjects that are to be of central relevance in the poet's treatment of proper boundaries: the restrictions appropriate to women and to artists. Erwin Panofsky, discussing various levels of interpretation appropriate to visual images, has commented on "the *intrinsic meaning* or *content*" contained in every work of art. "It may be defined as a unifying principle which underlies and explains both the visible event and its intelligible significance, and which determines even the form in which the visible event takes shape." This level of meaning may be apprehended, Panofsky continues, "by ascertaining those underlying principles which reveal the basic attitude of a nation, a period, a class, a religious or philosophical persuasion—unconsciously qualified by one personality and condensed into one work."[1] Such principles are particularly vivid in the ambiguous allusions to limitation contained in the *Epistle to Miss Blount*—a poem accurately described by Reuben Brower as offering Miss Blount an "image of freedom in contrast with the formal restraint of custom and a 'successful' marriage," but equally testifying to the value of restraints.[2]

The drama metaphor in the *Epistle to Miss Blount* immediately suggests the poet's complexities of attitude:

> Let the strict Life of graver Mortals be
> A long, exact, and serious Comedy . . .
> Let mine, an innocent gay Farce appear,
> And more Diverting still than Regular,
> Have Humour, Wit, a native Ease and Grace;
> Tho' not too strictly bound to Time and Place:
> Criticks in Wit, or Life, are hard to please,
> Few write to those, and none can live to these.
> (21–22, 25–30)

To use drama as a metaphor for life implies a vision of life formally controlled, whose shape gives it meaning. The "gay Farce" as well as the "exact, and serious Comedy" operate by rules and within formal restrictions, although the poet wishes life to be more diverting than regular, and "not too strictly bound." The most restrictive bounds, in any case, are not those implicit in form, but those created by the demands of others: in the immediate instance the hard-to-please critics of wit and of life, whose standards are rarely—

if ever—met. The rest of the poem emphasizes the degree of control implicit in various specific forms of social or sexual contract. Women, Pope suggests, are more restricted than men—by critics, "Severe to all, but most to Womankind" (32), and by custom (33). Their yielding nature (35) makes them easy victims; marriage releases them from the tyranny of honor and custom, but subjects them to a single, greater tyrant: "Still in constraint your suff'ring Sex remains, / Or bound in formal, or in real Chains" (41–42). The vignette of "Pamela" (49–56) illustrates the restriction women suffer even when they think themselves released to freedom through wealth. Pamela gains the symbols of riches she has sought, but only by accepting "a Fool for Mate" (52); the consequence is such a limitation of human capacity that she, like the dullards of *The Dunciad,* is reduced to a "Thing": "vain, unquiet, glitt'ring, wretched" (54). As in *The Dunciad,* inner and outer forces cooperate to alter substance.

The chains that symbolize the restriction of women can also be a symbol of their reciprocal power over man. It seems to be a deliberate technique of the poem to suggest various kinds of "intelligible significance" for a single visible phenomenon:

> Love, rais'd on Beauty, will like That decay,
> Our Hearts may bear its slender Chain a Day . . .
> *This* [good humor] binds in Ties more easie, yet more strong,
> The willing Heart, and only holds it long.
>
> (63–64, 67–68)

The willing heart gladly accepts ties easy and strong, as the poet accepts the formal restrictions of comedy and farce. Restriction implying discipline, order, and harmony is a positive value. Yet restriction can also be arbitrary and destructive. The problem peculiarly relevant to artists and to women—whose similarities to one another are the poem's subject—is how to utilize the positive and evade the negative values of life's necessary bonds. The solution is implicit in the words "ease" and "charm," which, with their cognates, recur several times in the poem's eighty lines.

As Pope's Belinda would make clear, women are artists whose great achievement is their selves. The woman's goal in life should be ease: "Aim not at Joy, but rest content with Ease" (48). Ease is also one of the qualities the poet-speaker desires in his own life-as-farce, along with humor, wit, and grace; and he demonstrates this quality in his poem, expressing himself "with a lightness and sureness of rhythm that beautifully symbolize an easy inner poise."[3] It is also conspicuous in the work of Voiture, whose "easie Art may happy Nature seem" (3), and in the "Ties" that bind men to good women (67). Charm is characteristic of Martha Blount, whose "now resistless Charms" (54) derive from her beauty, but who also has available to her the power of good humor, which "only teaches Charms to last" (61). Voiture displays the same kind of grace: "Sure to charm all was his peculiar Fate" (5); "And dead as living, 'tis our Author's Pride, / Still to charm those who charm the World beside" (79–80). And through the power of art, charm survives in women as well as in literature: "By this [Voiture's letters], ev'n now they live, ev'n now they charm" (71).

Charm is a source—or a variety—of power over others. Its reciprocal relation to ease is apparent: the lasting charm of good humor creates those "easie" ties that hold men; conversely, the "easie Art" of Voiture's lines generates the charm that preserves his fame. Charm conveyed by art has more longevity even than the charm of good humor. As in *The Rape of the Lock*, the beauty of poetry alone gives permanence to the beauty of physicality, and the artistry of women yields to that of writers—a point hinted in the final couplet quoted above (79–80), which stresses Voiture's power over women, hence the implicit superiority of his charm to theirs.

Images of three kinds give richness to the abstractions of ease and charm. The familiar metaphor of life as a play, here given great specificity, details the speaker's high regard for ease and charm by amplifying his conception of his own life as farce—a metaphor charmingly self-deprecating but, as elaborated, self-flattering as well. Like the notion of charm, the idea of farce may seem in itself trivial and irresponsible. But it is a function of the poem to attack such preconceptions. The innocence, wit, and grace of farce can redeem it; and natural feminine charm belongs to "the full Innocence of Life" (45), bound by the formal chains that govern all existence, but not by the real chain of marriage. The image of the poet's life as farce, specific though not concrete, defines and enriches the concept of a specific choice of life and deepens the significance of such values as ease and charm.

A detailed image of personality and social milieu emerges from the sketch of Pamela, which hints the possible dangers of feminine charm and dramatizes the absence of ease in vanity, "unquiet," and wretched glitter. The poem's most elaborate negative image, the portrait emphasizes the human importance of the issues at stake: the woman who fails to use her charm properly or who values ease insufficiently runs horrible dangers. Pamela is a warning for Martha Blount and for the reader—a warning most immediately against marriages of calculation ("Ah quit not the free Innocence of Life! / For the dull Glory of a virtuous Wife!" 45–46), but in a larger sense, against a social structure of false values: "Nor let false Shows, or empty Titles please" (47). The description of Pamela's career contains visual detail: "the gilt Coach and dappled *Flanders* Mares, / The shining Robes, rich Jewels, Beds of State" (50–51). But the image it establishes is hardly more visual than the one of life as farce. The glimpses of the accoutrements of wealth help to specify the meaning of "false Shows," but their reality is less powerful than that of the emotional adjectives—"vain," "unquiet," "wretched"—or the generalizing nouns—"Pride, Pomp, and State" (55). More exactly, they exist to give substance to the language of emotion and of generalization. Pamela's impact depends on her meaning, not her appearance. The suggestions about her appearance enlarge one's sense of her meaning; she functions as a defining image because she is vividly defined in conceptual terms.

The imagery of chains and bonds that represent various sorts of restriction is a more simple and conventional kind of metaphor. The strong verb "bound," associated with the formal or real chains that restrict woman; the simile describing the "slender Chain" of love ("As flow'ry Bands in Wantonness are worn; / A Morning's Pleasure, and at Evening torn," 65–66); the measured exactness of "more easie, yet more strong" for the chains of good humor—such details give the metaphor physicality. It is kinesthetic rather than visual. Its function is to define, specifying in physical terms the precise degree and weight of restriction. At one extreme is the "suffering" and "constraint" of being bound in chains; at the other, the mere "wantonness" of "flow'ry Bands," which only seem to offer control. At the midpoint—where, as usual, virtue lies—are the ties, easy and strong, which bind and hold the willing heart. The process of definition through image enlarges the concept of ease, which initially seems the opposite of existence in chains, but finally emerges as a state consequent on being held in appropriate ties.

Three different kinds of image thus convey the poem's serious meaning without interfering with its delicate surface and almost playful tone. The concept of ease finally opposes that of social falsity. Ease implies, one gradually realizes, personal integrity; it is associated with good humor and with self-knowledge; it coexists with and is partly the product of useful control—the formal control of the good life or the good work of art, the mutually accepted psychic control of love founded on respect; it defies the artificial and painful restraints of superficial marriages, superficial social values. Charm, which can be a device for achieving the false shows and empty titles that some believe they want, can also coexist with, derive from, and even produce true ease. The poem, which seems an occasional *jeu d'esprit,* is itself conspicuously a product of the artist's ease and charm. Its serious weight affirms the fact that values which may seem feminine and frivolous are relevant also to the artist and ultimately to every human being.

In *The Rape of the Lock,* concerned with almost identical issues but creating a larger panorama of social reality, the imagery of control has negative connotations, being consistently associated with ideas of torture and deprivation. The difference in emphasis reflects an important difference in point of view. The speaker in the *Epistle to Miss Blount* preserves an urbane distance from the social facts he observes; in *The Rape of the Lock,* much that is perceived reflects the special and limited mode of feminine perception that is a subject of the poem. From the feminine viewpoint, the immediate discomforts of restriction are far more real than any long-range value that restriction may have. Imagery of slavery and bondage describes women's cosmetic manipulations:

> Was it for this you took such constant Care . . .
> For this your Locks in Paper-Durance bound,

For this with tort'ring Irons wreath'd around?
For this with Fillets strain'd your tender Head,
And bravely bore the double Loads of Lead?
(IV, 97, 99–102)

The speaker is Thalestris, and the answer to her rhetorical questions is of course no. The goal of women's self-torture is to captivate men without capitulating to them, to create charm while preserving at least the appearance of honor, "at whose unrival'd Shrine / Ease, Pleasure, Virtue, All, our Sex resign" (IV, 105–106). But the arrangement seems less benign than in the *Epistle to Miss Blount.* "Captivate" here has its root meaning: "Love in these Labyrinths [of hair] his Slaves detains, / And mighty Hearts are held in slender Chains" (II, 23–24). The power of beauty to draw men by a hair is explicitly compared with the power of hair to trap birds and catch fish. It is a form of mastery, and the battle of the sexes, for Belinda as for the Wife of Bath, is a struggle for mastery. Women accept rigid limitations, symbolized by "that sev'nfold Fence," the petticoat (I, 119), whose "Silver Bound" (121) guards chastity while creating allurement; they accept restriction to preserve the illusion of freedom, which must disappear if they yield to a man. The sylphs who symbolize their psychic and spiritual condition dread physical restriction as the most severe of punishments. The penalty for carelessness, Ariel tells them (II, 123–136), is to be enclosed in vials, wedged in needles' eyes, clogged with "*Gums* and *Pomatums,*" shrunk by the contracting power of alum styptics, fixed like Ixion in fumes of chocolate. But the women they protect are already limited in analogous ways, committed to regimens of cosmetics, perfume, chocolate-drinking, and controlled by their commitments. The eighteenth century has left its records of feminine deaths caused by the use of white lead in cosmetics or attributed to medicines intended for weight reduction: these are only especially dramatic examples of the "limitations" imposed by femininity in a social context.

The imagery of restriction in *The Rape of the Lock* concentrates on the restrictions of artifice, which for women are means to an end in the sexual battle. When Clarissa "opens more clearly the MORAL of the Poem,"[4] she offers an ideal of self-control, labeled "good Humour" and opposed to the self-indulgence of "Airs, and Flights, and Screams, and Scolding" (V, 31–32). Her hearers remain unmoved by her plea: the vision of control as inherent in human nature has little place in Belinda's society founded on vanity and preoccupied with vanities. In *Sober Advice from Horace* Pope returns with bitter energy to the relation between women's willing acceptance of sartorial restriction and their unwillingness to exercise meaningful self-control; this time the point of view is masculine and lascivious:

> Could you directly to her Person go,
> Stays will obstruct above, and Hoops below,
> And if the Dame says yes, the Dress says no.
> (130–132)

The artifices of feminine dress restrict the advances of men as well as the freedom of women. But the real problem is the lack of coherence between outer form and inner content. A few lines later, the speaker asks:

> Has Nature set no bounds to wild Desire?
> No Sense to guide, no Reason to enquire
> . . . what is best indulg'd, or best deny'd?
> (143–144, 146)

The setting of proper bounds, or the acceptance of the bounds implicit in the natural order, is the image for well-advised human choice. A man may resent the obstruction of hoops and stays, may prefer the naked freedom of Mother Needham's brothel, where he can see the goods before buying. But the petticoat's bound can only be condemned if the "looseness" of its wearer contradicts the moral implications of established limits. If lady and dress *both* say no, there is no ground for complaint. As the dress metaphors in the *Essay on Criticism* demonstrated, dress's proper function is to reveal the reality it seems to disguise, and its physical limits should signify the wearer's moral limits.

It is the special problem of women that social forms encourage divergence where there should be harmony—or perhaps it is the emotional nature of women to find proper harmony especially difficult to achieve. The feminine protagonist of *Eloisa to Abelard* both hates and embraces the discipline which, severing her from her lover, encloses her in religious forms; and the reader, receiving no clear indication whether to judge it hateful or valuable, must conclude that from the viewpoint of feminine experience, it is both. Yet such a figure as Martha Blount, evoked in ideal form at the end of *Epistle to a Lady*, exemplifies the proper relation between outer and inner reality, which can convert marriage, too often an exemplification of the tyrannous restrictions imposed on women (287–288), into a state encouraging full expressiveness.

Such words as *expressiveness*, or *form* and *content*, appropriate for defining the problems of women, are even more natural designations for the issues that concern artists. Women are themselves artists, not only in their necessary preoccupation—given the nature of society—with the creation of alluring self-images, but also in the means of creation available to them. Like poets, women depend on style: forms of expression that may be conventional and rigidly controlled, yet expressive of inner truth. Like poets, they find aesthetic issues converting themselves to ethical ones; like poets too, they discover that only through proper control do they achieve meaningful freedom. The pattern exists in nature as well: the "order in variety" that governs *Windsor-Forest* could as well be termed variety in order, the disparate elements being controlled by unifying plan.[5] But nature's control includes within its forms the promise of liberation: "good" laws and kings in *Windsor-Forest* make the desert fertile; the personalized natural principle in *Summer* causes flowers to rise in her tread, forests and mountains to become animate. She is only a fantasy figure, but a fantasy embodying the poet's vision of nature as offering limitless possibilities within its ordered sequence.

Man's ideal relation to nature is exemplified by Burlington, whose architecture and gardening have symbolic force. "He gains all points, who pleasingly confounds, / Surprizes, varies, and conceals the Bounds" (*Epistle to Burlington*, 55–56). It is difficult to organize nature properly, this couplet suggests; and what is true of landscape is true of morality: the bounds should never be ostentatious, and they should always promote rather than obstruct "ease." At the end of the epistle, Burlington is urged to "proceed" with the great works of which he is capable; and the poet finally describes the even greater responsibilities of princes:

> Bid the broad Arch the dang'rous Flood contain,
> The Mole projected break the roaring Main;
> Back to his bounds their subject Sea command,
> And roll obedient Rivers thro' the Land.
> (199–202)

"These," Pope concludes, "are Imperial Works, and worthy Kings" (204). Although they do not comprise the full extent of royal duties or of Burlington's obligations (he is also to protect the arts, erect and repair buildings; the king should build harbors, highways, and churches), they are symbolically as well as literally crucial: they firmly establish the images of containment and control central to the proper relation of man to nature—as to the proper relation of men and women to their own psychic forces.

The king, with his "obedient Rivers," thus becomes, like Burlington, an artist of nature. His achievement suggests what is possible also for the artist of language, whose raw material consists only of his own perceptions. The most crucial focus of Pope's imagery of limits is the poet himself: man using his highest capacities. The *Essay on Man* explored the problem of control for man in general, insisting that reason is the card by which men steer but that only passion's gale makes steering possible. Control and energy are equally necessary. The essay insisted too that self-love both demands discipline and generates the force that creates it, the principle of control thus being contained in what is to be controlled. The artist's problem is a special version of the human problem. From the *Essay on Criticism* to the Horatian imitations and *The Dunciad,* Pope obsessively attempts to define the artist's proper possibility and proper restriction. He is fully aware of the dangers both of freedom and of limitation. And he values and understands the analogies between woman and poet, critic and poet: analogies of double significance. If the poet resembles and can learn from other manipulators of psychic and physical reality, he can also be a model for other strugglers: his solutions, combining as they must the aesthetic with the ethical, should be exemplary.

In the *Essay on Criticism*, that early exploration of wit's problems, the value of laws freely chosen is a recurrent theme. Images suggesting law's importance supplement the poem's direct statement of the idea. Nature, one learns early in the essay, "to all things fix'd the Limits fit, / And wisely curb'd proud Man's pretending Wit" (52–53). Wit is a horse to be curbed, here and elsewhere:

> 'Tis more to *guide* than *spur* the Muse's Steed;
> Restrain his Fury, than provoke his Speed;
> The winged Courser, like a gen'rous Horse,
> Shows most true Mettle when you *check* his Course.
> (84–87)

Wit is, in fact, a horse very like Pegasus: the context of these two couplets, a discussion of the reciprocal roles of wit as an inspiring power and judgment as restraint, suggests that wit itself is "the Muse's Steed." The "wisdom" involved in the curbing function of nature or of judgment increases rather than diminishes the power it controls, a point emphasized by the final stress on the greater "Mettle" of the checked steed.

Politics, not yet the poet's theme, supplies part of the work's substructure and contributes to the essay's imagery of control. Thus, the account of Aristotle explains how the great critic:

> Spread all his Sails, and durst the Deeps explore;
> He steer'd securely, and discover'd far,
> *Led* by the Light of the *Maeonian Star.*
> Poets, a *Race* long unconfin'd and free,
> Still fond and proud of *Savage Liberty,*
> Receiv'd his Laws, and stood convinc'd 'twas fit
> Who conquer'd *Nature,* shou'd preside o'er *Wit.*
> (646–652)

The image of sailing guided by the stars, symbols of natural order, and by the rules of navigation yields to a telling political metaphor, which makes freedom from rule equivalent to savagery. The assumed value of civilization stands behind commitment to law, which alone gives coherence to poetry and life. This same point is made negatively later in the poem, through a similar metaphor: "But *we,* brave *Britons, Foreign Laws* despis'd, / And kept *unconquer'd,* and *unciviliz'd*" (715–716). The point is also relevant to religion, which lends itself equally well to political metaphor: "Heav'n's Free Subjects might their *Rights* dispute, / Lest God himself shou'd seem too *Absolute*" (549–550). In literature, theology, and society, only acceptance of authority's rules makes creativity valuable.

Pope's use of political metaphor recognizes and exploits its complexity, to suggest the ambiguity of commitment to law. In poetry as in politics, higher laws must supersede lower ones. "Great Wits" may sometimes "From *vulgar Bounds* with *brave Disorder* part, / And *snatch* a *Grace* beyond the Reach of Art" (154–155). The bounds often declared so important are "vulgar" in a double sense: they apply to the mass of people, and their value becomes questionable when they are judged by higher (aristocratic) standards. The bravery of disorder is both its courage and its beauty—and the disorder of which Pope speaks is only apparent, involving as it does commitment to higher order. The poet furthers his metaphor's aristocratic implications by pointing out that "the *Ancients* thus their *Rules* invade, / (As *Kings* dispense with *Laws* Themselves have made)" (161–162). But the nature of modern literary aristocracy is different. The modern poet is warned not to transgress the "*End*" of any precept he violates, to deviate seldom from rules, and to justify himself by precedent: "The Critick else proceeds without Remorse, / Seizes your Fame, and puts his Laws in force" (67–68). Modern experience is more fragmented than ancient, in which critics and poets were often united. Modern critics are the new aristocrats, guardians of law. Individual insight, however penetrating, cannot deny the importance of the civilizing order of rules. Although Pope's metaphors support his direct statement that genius is more vital than the rules which try to confine it, they also reveal his recognition that there is no fruitful escape from order: there are only different levels of order, available to different levels of perception.

Some sorts of restriction are unequivocally to be condemned and, if possible, overcome. "The bounded *Level* of our Minds" (221) in youth is the consequence of inexperience; man's view enlarges valuably as he grows. Superstition "enslav'd the *Mind*" as tyranny the body after the fall of Rome (688); the metaphor's clarity supports clarity of judgment. Conversely, metaphors convey how ridiculous, or how shocking, are artistic attempts to escape restriction. The story of Don Quixote and the poet (267–284), in which the knight's professed devotion to the rules of Aristotle gives way to his idiosyncratic insistence that plays must contain tournaments, ridicules the human tendency to sacrifice all systems of order to "one lov'd Folly" (266). More serious is the crime of "Witt's *Titans*," who brave the skies, defying God "with Licenc'd *Blasphemies*" (552–553). Their only virtue is the courage that measures their mindless, sacrilegious opposition to the principle of order.

Although the body of political and legal imagery in the *Essay on Criticism* has complicated implications, the poem's individual images of limitation and control are direct and lucid. The relation of artists to the principle of control seems less problematical than that of women. The critics who in the *Epistle to Miss Blount* were a threat, are in the *Essay on Criticism* useful guides. Society, in whose intricacies both women and artists must live, appears in this poem only as material for metaphor. In the *Epistle to Miss Blount*, the referents of the imagery—the farce, the badly married woman, chains and ties—are simpler than the realities they illustrate; they help to make reality comprehensible, and to justify the complex judgments that must be made on it. The *Essay*, inasmuch as it concerns the problem of control, treats it as a simpler matter. Although restriction may in a given case be either good or bad, there is never much doubt which value judgment applies. The imagery has the same clarity as the subject matter it illustrates. In Pope's mind the law, the social hierarchy, and—at quite a different level—the bounding steed are all comprehensible entities demanding specific kinds of response. In his treatment of them as images, the abstract complexity of legal system and tradition and the concrete simplicity of a spirited horse alike enforce judgment.

The temptation offered the artist by overcommitment to control resembles the temptation to which women often succumb: the lure of pettiness. The great aesthetic and moral appeal of containment is manifest. In *Epistle to Mr. Addison, Occasioned by His Dialogues on Medals,* Pope provides a concrete image for the charm of limitation, describing the great reduced to the minute: "A small Euphrates thro' the piece is roll'd, / And little Eagles wave their wings in gold" (29–30). His recognition of the appeal of vast rivers and violent eagles ordered within a tiny circle provokes yet another discussion of the proper relation between the critic and the art that is his subject: the critic must remain aware of what each limitation expresses and controls; he must beware obsession with medals as self-sufficient objects of value. Value depends on content. Proper restriction derives from precise awareness of what is to be controlled and of the organic laws by which control should operate.

The degree to which excessive control implies lack of awareness and produces pettiness is a subject of *The Dunciad,* where the safeties of containment help to precipitate the uncontrolled and finally uncontrollable triumph of dullness. Here the subject is expanded from the poet to all thinkers, although the bad poet and his bad patrons remain central figures in the argument. Restriction can signify the anticreative forces of society as well as produce the highest creative fusions. Dulness is the "Great Tamer of all human art!" (I, 163) whose restrictive operations are specified in the fourth book. That book begins with images of "*Logic,* gagg'd and bound" (IV, 23), the Muses "held in ten-fold bonds" (35), and only "Mad *Mathesis* . . . unconfin'd, / Too mad for mere material chains to bind" (31–32). In Dulness' reign, severe discipline inhibits the good and perfect freedom looses madness.

References to slavery and bondage support the sense that Dulness is a deity of limitation. She imagines a triumphal procession in which every figure embodying artistic power is physically hampered by one of her representatives:

> A heavy Lord shall hang at ev'ry Wit,
> And while on Fame's triumphal Car they ride,
> Some Slave of mine be pinion'd to their side.
> (IV, 132–134)

The headmaster who speaks immediately after this utterance by Dulness is, like her, concerned with chaining, binding, limiting, and weighing down, but the reference of his metaphors is different. He describes an educational system whose goal is narrowing the mind:

> When Reason doubtful, like the Samian letter,
> Points him two ways, the narrower is better . . .
> We ply the Memory, we load the brain,
> Bind rebel Wit, and double chain on chain,
> Confine the thought, to exercise the breath;
> And keep them in the pale of Words till death.
> (IV, 151–152, 157–160)

The analogies between the educational system and the social system that produces it emerge through the metaphors that evoke them. The elaborated metaphors also suggest why restriction and dullness are allies: narrowing and chains are responses to threat, and reason, wit, thought are clear threats to Dulness' dominion. The political reference made explicit a bit later, as Dulness prays for the return of some pedant king ("For sure, if Dulness sees a grateful Day, / 'Tis in the shade of Arbitrary Sway," 181–182), is implicit here in the insistent imagery of repression. All repression is alike, and all, like perfect license, is allied to Dulness. Aristarchus, with his cement of the mind, and the tutor whose young Aeneas, "freed" from all restrictions, achieves perfect emptiness, while his whore is freed "from sense of Shame" (336), seem to represent opposite pedagogical philosophies, but they produce identical effects: repression of originality and of the operative standards of value, implied in license, alike lead to mediocrity's supremacy.

The close association between Dulness' "freedom" and her slavery emerges in Silenus' speech:

> From Priest-craft happily set free,
> Lo! ev'ry finish'd Son returns to thee:
> First slave to Words, then vassal to a Name,
> Then dupe to Party; child and man the same;
> Bounded by Nature, narrow'd still by Art,
> A trifling head, and a contracted heart . . .

Now to thy gentle shadow all are shrunk,
All melted down, in pension, or in Punk!
(IV, 499–504, 509–510)

Dulness bounds, narrows, contracts, shrinks, and melts down—all metaphors of limitation and diminishment. The natural state of her devotees is to be slaves, vassals, or dupes. The similarity between the two social conditions and the psychic one is revealed by the conjunction; and the fact that the dullard is likely to be "dupe *to Party*" reminds one once more of the political relevance of Pope's themes. Politics supplied metaphors in the *Essay on Criticism;* here it is sinister reality.

The importance of the misuse of intellect becomes clear as the imagery of restriction expands to the metaphysical. Dull philosophers mistreat God in their minds, bragging about how they:

Make Nature still incroach upon his plan;
And shove him off as far as e'er we can:
Thrust some Mechanic Cause into his place;
Or bind in Matter, or diffuse in Space.
Or, at one bound o'er-leaping all his laws,
Make God Man's Image, Man the final Cause.
(IV, 473–478)

To bind or to diffuse is equal violation; but dullness' activity is in essence restrictive. When the dunce o'erleaps the laws of God, declaring his total freedom, he demonstrates its meaning by limiting God to the stature of man. In theology, as in education, literature, and politics, the power of dullness is the power to confine.

In the face of dullness' manifest threats and temptations, the poet must maintain a life of dignity and ease without narrowing his vision to myopia or abandoning the power he should wield. The problem is more of human conduct than of artistic achievement, although the two issues are closely related. The *Epistle to Dr. Arbuthnot* dramatizes the threats to the poet's peace: there are those who would seize the speaker and tie him down in order to force him to judge their work; others would attack in the cause of license.

In the *Imitations of Horace, Epistle* I, vii, declaring his desire for only "Liberty and Ease" (66), the poet-hero develops the paradox that the way to achieve moral freedom is to accept narrow limits:

> Can I retrench? Yes, mighty well,
> Shrink back to my Paternal Cell,
> A little House, with Trees a-row,
> And like its Master, very low.
> (75–78)

Physical shrinkage is a technique of moral expansion. It implies rejection of ostentation and excessive aspiration. Such rejection, and the acceptance implicit in it, are the foundation for more intricate forms of virtue.

The *Imitations of Horace, Epistle* II, ii, uses the imagery of the *Epistle to Burlington*—representation of man's proper physical control of nature—as the basis for establishing a moral and literary ideal of the poet's conduct. The physical domination of the natural world for which the poet admires Burlington is finally futile:

> Link Towns to Towns with Avenues of Oak,
> Enclose whole Downs in Walls, 'tis all a joke!
> Inexorable Death shall level all,
> And Trees, and Stones, and Farms, and Farmer fall.
> (260–263)

Given awareness of such futility, other forms of control become correspondingly more important, as they involve possible survival in the face of death. Literary control and self-control resemble one another:

> But how severely with themselves proceed
> The Men, who write such Verse as we can read?
> Their own strict Judges, not a word they spare
> That wants or Force, or Light, or Weight, or Care . . .
> Prune the luxuriant, the uncouth refine,
> But show no mercy to an empty line;

Then polish all, with so much life and ease,
You think 'tis Nature, and a knack to please:
'But Ease in writing flows from Art, not Chance,
As those move easiest who have learn'd to dance.'
(157–160, 174–179)

The recapitulated couplet from the *Essay on Criticism* reminds one how long Pope had advocated an ideal of "ease," in art as in life, and how long he had associated ease with discipline. The dimensions of the "Art" that produces ease are more distinct here than in the earlier poem. It is an art of pruning, its techniques closely related to those that create man's proper harmony with external nature. Its cutting and control are merciless only to the superflous. The artist's severity, his strict application of law, involves his control of himself as well as his material. His ultimate discipline rejects the importance of poetry for that of life:

To Rules of Poetry no more confin'd,
I learn to smooth and harmonize my Mind,
Teach ev'ry Thought within its bounds to roll,
And keep the equal Measure of the Soul.
(202–205)

Once more, apparent rejection of rule involves commitment to a new level of restriction. The proper bounds of thought and measure of the soul become the poet's preoccupation, in a development anticipating that of *Sailing to Byzantium.* Pope's unstressed metaphors recall the king's rolling of obedient rivers through the land; and the subterranean image of a river of thought heightens the implication of the altered verb "flows" in the couplet slightly changed from the *Essay on Criticism.* In the earlier version, the verb was "comes"; the shift suggests that the poet envisions art, that product of human intellect, as duplicating nature's force and harmony.

Pope's crucial system of analogies reveals the importance of control at all levels of human experience. Although the paradigms of virtuous conduct are numerous, the same lessons emerge from all. The physical references of the idea of control, exploited in imagery, testify to its pervasive relevance and clarify its meaning. The structure of the imagery emphasizes the connection implicit in the ideal of control between the aesthetic and the ethical, a connection always vital in Pope's work, as well as in the thought of his time, and representing an important aspect of the "unifying principle" which underlies that imagery.

Satire is of course Pope's major mode, and the problem of defining positive value in satiric contexts is a knotty one for the poet. Pope's solution depends heavily on the use of imagery, which can provide a significant mode of indirection, making affirmation possible without violating the satiric ambience. Although control is one of Pope's important standards, he often uses the imagery of control for negative purposes, to suggest the dangers of excessive restriction. But he finds other sorts of imagery to convey what is to be upheld even while denouncing its opposite.

John Dryden, who believed as firmly as Pope in the assertion of order against encroaching chaos, who knew with clarity that "The true end of *Satyre,* is the amendment of Vices by correction," supplies a vivid contrast to Pope in some of his ways of evoking positive standards in satiric settings.[6] He and his successor are alike in their commitment to using satire as a positive, not merely a destructive, force; indeed, Dryden insists that "The poet is bound . . . to give his reader some one precept of moral virtue . . . He is chiefly to inculcate one virtue, and insist on that."[7] Pope never defined his position so clearly; but his poetic practice reveals that he too feels that embodiments of good as well as of evil have their place in satire.

It is true that satire cannot exist without some structure of common assumption. In modern times, the difficulty of creating effective satire comes partly from the absence of general standards: it is hard to create satiric exaggeration more fantastic than actuality. What is accepted as satire, in night club acts or on television, is likely to be parochial in the extreme, directed to a limited audience with shared values, or so broad and vague as to lack real bite. Dryden and Pope both wrote when a community of moral assumption still survived, the more real and precious because it was menaced by immediate social and political forces. Although dishonesty and cowardice might be widespread and politically viable, words like *honesty* and *courage* retained value, were assumed to be preferable to their opposites; men felt no cynicism or embarrassment about using them. To recall positive standards in satire, the poet need only mention such words, and his readers could be expected to recognize them as the gauge by which they were to measure the deviations recorded by the satirist.

Both Dryden and Pope employ the terms of value in their satires with manifest confidence that such language has weight, that it affirms what the misdeeds of their satiric targets deny, and that to attach the label of virtue to an act is to coerce the reader into a positive valuation of it. Yet satirists are licensed paranoids: they write with the energy of those who feel themselves surrounded by enemies, and with the paranoid's instinct, they understand the necessity to be clever. Since language itself is threatened by the forces of disorder, labeling is not enough. It is necessary to create meanings while pretending to assume them, to demonstrate what honor is while preserving an apparent assurance that all men know what it is and appreciate its value. Although Dryden and Pope share some techniques of demonstration, their mode of using imagery for the evocation of the "good" in satire is often strikingly different.

For Dryden, the image, when associated with positive forces, may be a means of discrimination:

> Desire of Power, on Earth a Vitious Weed,
> Yet, sprung from High, is of Cælestial Seed:
> In God 'tis Glory: And when men Aspire,
> 'Tis but a Spark too much of Heavenly Fire.
> Th' Ambitious Youth, too Covetous of Fame . . .
> Unwarily was led from Vertues ways;
> Made Drunk with Honour, and Debauch'd with Praise.
> (*Absalom and Achitophel*, 305–309, 311–312)

The poem's characteristic balance of attitudes manifests itself here in a sequence of images that qualify one another and make the reader conscious of the importance of perspective. From a narrow view, desire of power may be "a Vitious Weed," but adequate judgment requires considering its source. Vicious weed versus celestial seed, heavenly glory versus earthly fire:—these pairings affirm both analogies and crucial differences. By the time that the satirist has moved, through conventional metaphors of covetousness and straying from the path, to active images of drunkenness and debauchery, he has prepared the reader for the dual vision which recognizes honor as virtue while perceiving its possibilities as a source for vice.

One of Dryden's favorite devices is to associate virtue, through imagery, with its opposite, and thus to dramatize the ways in which bad men destroy good values:

> Then, Justice and Religion they forswore;
> Their Mayden Oaths debauch'd into a Whore . . .
> But thou, the Pander of the Peoples hearts . . .
> Whose blandishments a Loyal Land have whor'd,
> And broke the Bonds she plighted to her Lord.
> (*The Medal*, 152–153, 256, 258–259)

The effect depends on the reader's unquestioning assumption that justice, religion, and loyalty are to be valued. From this assumption derives the shock value of describing their perversions through an imagery that is just as unquestioningly associated with evil. The technique also lends itself to more subtle forms of qualification:

> Ev'n in the most sincere advice he gave
> He had a grudging still to be a Knave . . .
> At best as little honest as he cou'd:
> And, like white Witches, mischievously good.
> (*The Medal*, 57–58, 61–62)

Again abstract terms—"sincere," "honest," "good"—confidently weighted and assumed as understood, prepare for an image ("white Witches") which sums up the ambiguities implicit in every capacity of an evil man.

The attitudes in these examples are the dominant moral attitudes of the political satires. Dryden is conscious always not only of good and evil but of the subtle relations between them: good turning to evil, good capable of corruption, good contaminated by its own excessiveness. He is aware of ambiguities too subtle for definitive moral judgment. A case in point is the account of David at the beginning of *Absalom and Achitophel.*[8] Although *Macflecknoe* describes a world of people who have simply abandoned real values ("What share have we in Nature or in Art?" 176), the political satires depend on an awareness that real value can be a provocation to those who oppose it. Dryden's moral perceptions center on his sense of process, of the insidious sliding of good toward evil, and the stealthy invasions of evil. But when he wishes to insist on a value for which he cannot assume universal acceptance, he often chooses imagery of solidity:

> If ancient Fabricks nod, and threat to fall,
> To Patch the Flaws, and Buttress up the Wall,
> Thus far 'tis Duty; but here fix the Mark;
> For all beyond it is to touch our Ark.
> To change Foundations, cast the Frame anew,
> Is work for Rebels who base Ends pursue:
> At once Divine and Humane Laws controul;
> And mend the Parts by ruine of the Whole.
> (*Absalom and Achitophel,* 801–808)

Vigorous activity, in this sequence of metaphors, is the source of evil; good exists in the permanence of the object—"fabric" or "ark" —invested with high significance. "None are so busy as the fool and knave," Dryden remarks in *The Medal* (186). The good man exerts force more by his moral "weight" (*Absalom and Achitophel,* 887) than by anything he does. Busy-ness, activity, are inlets for evil. As Dr. Johnson was to say, "the mind can only repose on the stability of truth."[9]

Both the points made by the imagery of moral value and the imagery itself are different in Pope. He, too, sees good threatened by the encroachments of evil, but sees it not as mere spectator:

he presents himself as participant in a ceaseless struggle. "A Horse-laugh, if you please, at *Honesty*," suggests the "Friend" in *Epilogue to the Satires* (I, 38). Pope, like Dryden, expects an automatic response to the idea of honesty, a response that makes the horse-laugh morally as well as physically grotesque. He engages himself in battle against such destructive laughter, against the sneers of "impartial men" at "Sense and Virtue" (*Epilogue to the Satires*, I, 59–60). Sneers and laughter represent moments in a continuing process of menace, menace that may seem trivial or even comic but which can undermine all that is good.

But Pope's imagery for locating virtue does not, like Dryden's, oppose process by stability; rather, it counters action with action. The fable in *Epilogue to the Satires* (II, 150–155) exemplifies Pope's position. It tells of a French marshal's anger at seeing his footman kicked; when he discovers, however, that the kicker is "a Man of Honour," his victim "a Knave," "The prudent Gen'ral turn'd it to a jest, / And begg'd, he'd take the pains to kick the rest." It is almost a definition of the man of honor, in Pope's terms, to say that he is one who kicks knaves. The imagery of virtue concentrates not on stability, but on energy. Even the inanimate—money—acquires value only in action, by being put to use: "In heaps, like Ambergrise, a stink it lies, / But well-dispers'd, is Incense to the Skies" (*Epistle to Bathurst*, 235–236). "Actions best discover man" (*Epistle to Cobham*, 71). Though images of action, Pope emphasizes his vision of virtue. When he uses so conventional an image as the sun (or perhaps the moon) to define the value of "Temper," he stresses function rather than appearance: "Oh! blest with Temper, whose unclouded ray / Can make to morrow chearful as to day" (*Epistle to a Lady*, 257–258). He recognizes that the world judges by superficial standards. People are all too likely to determine saintliness by appearance or social attributes rather than by action: "A Saint in Crape is twice a Saint in Lawn" (*Epistle to Cobham*, 88). Though the saint in black crape gains social stature by acquiring the white sleeves of a bishop, appearance is no adequate index of virtue, for social and moral stature may be at odds. For Pope, as often for Dryden, the most compelling image of goodness is the figure of the good man. Dryden's heroes, however, are defined largely by their attributes; Pope's heroes—the Man of Ross, Bathurst, Burlington, his own father—by their actions.

The difficulty of distinguishing good from evil, implicit in much of Dryden's imagery of virtue, appears in Pope's imagery not to be a practical problem:

> Vice is a monster of so frightful mien,
> As, to be hated, needs but to be seen;
> Yet seen too oft, familiar with her face,
> We first endure, then pity, then embrace.
> (*Essay on Man*, II, 217–220)

Refusing to endure, much less to embrace, vice when he sees it, the satirist retains absolute clarity of distinction. His writing contains no such ambiguous figure as Absalom, since ambiguity is a moral luxury he cannot afford. But like Dryden, he is aware of the ways in which good can be undermined by evil. Dryden exemplifies this process by suggesting how a loyal land becomes a "whore," or how the overturn of laws produces "ruin"; Pope insists more steadily on the degree to which linguistic perversion accompanies moral distortion. His characteristic technique is to employ imagery that demonstrates the degradation of the language of value as well as the actuality. Thus, the imagery often connects Pope's most cherished terms with objects of limited value and nonexistent power, showing not the process of contamination, which interested Dryden, but the accomplished fact. Wit, the great creative force, can be so much excrement (*Epilogue to the Satires*, II, 171–180). Wit's sacred power is parodied when "ten thousand envy and adore" the "Wit of Cheats" (I, 166, 165). Or wit can be a see-saw, "Now high, now low, now Master up, now Miss" (*Epistle to Dr. Arbuthnot*, 324), expressing meaningless force. The satirist's courage as "defender of the faith" is a positive value. Yet spirit and courage, too, may become their own opposites even while retaining honorific labels: "the Courage of a Whore"—courage leading to degraded action—wins admiration in a corrupt world (*Epilogue to the Satires*, I, 165); "spirit" may describe only how a man "drinks and whores" (*Epistle to Cobham*, 189). Temperance can be supported as a virtue by energetic imagery in a satiric setting (*Imitations of Horace, Satire* II, ii, 67–74); but the imagery of temperance may also evoke selfishness and deprivation (*Epistle to Bathurst,* 181–198). The gift of taste becomes a curse from heaven (*Epistle to Burlington,* 17) or an "eternal wanderer" whose aimless activity declares its lack of focus and significance (*Epistle to Augustus,* 312–313). In *The Dunciad* this assumption of terms of value by their opposites is omnipresent, epitomized by the scene early in Book IV where personifications of degraded standards assume the robes and accessories of the values they have displaced.

This technique is not unique in Pope's satiric practice. Dryden too uses it on occasion, as when he describes the "frugal virtue" of Shimei (*Absalom and Achitophel,* 616–628). But Pope's stress on the device calls special attention to its significance, emphasizing the necessity for passionate discrimination—one of Pope's highest poetic gifts, and one of his moral imperatives. The deliberation and balance of Dryden's separation of sinful from heavenly desire for honor do not seem crucial in Pope's moral discriminations (although deliberation and balance are norms of conduct for him, too). The problem, as dramatized in Pope's imagery, is not to define subtle differences between good and bad but to insist that the distinction is absolute, apparent, and vital to defend. Such insistence is part of the defense. With the energy of contempt, Pope dismisses the perversions of courage, spirit, and taste; the passion of his utterance asserts the importance of maintaining the connection between the language of value and what it describes. Dryden's contempt for those who have turned the nation to a whore is as intense as Pope's for those who value the courage of a whore, but the target of their attacks is significantly different. Dryden concerns himself with political reality; Pope, with reality and its mode of presentation. What things are called may be as important as what they are. Pope reminds his readers of the existence of positive values at the same time that he damns their perversions; the act of condemnation is thus itself an act of discrimination.

Militancy can be a mode of containment. For Pope, attack is a way of preserving the standards that establish the limits of human conduct; his poetic vigor supports his mythology of control. Standards must be operative in language as well as in other forms of activity—and the awareness of language as symbolic action is vital in Pope's thought. For this reason the figure of the poet can embody many realized values: he is, by definition, one who fights for the preservation of the good, who defends the integrity of language and of ethical value. The poet-hero of the *Essay on Criticism* reappears in the satiric context of the late Horatian poems, where his role is both aggressive and defensive. Unrealized as character or personality, he gains significance by his activity, itself defined through a rich variety of imagery. In this more general area of defining standards, as specifically in his imagery of limitation, Pope shows by his detailed treatment of poetry as moral force how symbolic he finds the functions of poetry in its union of the aesthetic and the ethical.

Pope's most explicit defense of the poet's role is poetically the weakest. It occurs in the *Epistle to Augustus*, which centers on the poet's responsibility and contains much mocking discussion of poetry's value: verse helps teach foreigners the language, makes country folk pious, and gives children something to memorize. With a sudden shift of tone and technique, and following Horace closely, for this is one of Pope's most literal translations, he defends true poetry:

> Yet lest you think I railly more than teach,
> Or praise malignly Arts I cannot reach,
> Let me for once presume t'instruct the times,
> To know the Poet from the Man of Rymes:
> 'Tis He, who gives my breast a thousand pains,
> Can make me feel each Passion that he feigns,
> Inrage, compose, with more than magic Art,
> With Pity, and with Terror, tear my heart;
> And snatch me, o'er the earth, or thro' the air,
> To Thebes; to Athens, when he will, and where.
> (338–347)

These are Horace's ideas about the poet's power, and in Pope's presentation, they seem automatic and second-hand. Yet they introduce an important aspect of Pope's mythic poet: his extraordinary power, magic or more than magic, involving in this instance the ability to inflict pain, to generate or control emotion, and to transcend the limitations of time and space. If the passage fails to exemplify the power it claims for the poet, it yet provides perspective on the passionate attack that characterizes much of the epistle.

More convincing is the account of the poet in *Imitations of Horace, Epistle* II, ii, where Pope also stays close to his Horatian model but adds a new dimension of religious allusion. The discipline of poets is the subject of the lines:

> not a word they spare
> That wants or Force, or Light, or Weight, or Care,
> Howe'er unwillingly it quits its place,
> Nay tho' at Court (perhaps) it may find grace:
> Such they'll degrade; and sometimes, in its stead,
> In downright Charity revive the dead . . .
> Command old words that long have slept, to wake,
> Words, that wise *Bacon*, or brave *Raleigh* spake . . .
> Pour the full Tide of Eloquence along,
> Serenely pure, and yet divinely strong.
> (159–164, 167–168, 171–172)

The nouns which define the attributes of words give physical reality to language and suggest that to make proper linguistic choices requires conscientious dexterity analogous to that involved in exacting physical manipulation. But what seems a sort of physical exercise soon reveals itself as a moral undertaking: words may find "grace" at court, but their favor in this world opposes the Christian value system that underlies the poet's selectivity, not a matter of dexterity merely but of "downright Charity." The poet revives the dead, awakes sleepers, and generates a pseudonatural "Tide of Eloquence" which shares his implicit attributes of serene purity and divine strength. The poet's "making" resembles physical building, but its creativity is also spiritual. As Thomas Maresca has summed up the implications of this passage, "Poetry becomes . . . the semisacramental act of a morally good man, an almost divinely ordained messenger."[10] Dealing with words, the poet's activity, is analogous to dealing with people, a fact suggested by unstressed but repeated personifications. The sequence of imagery, emphasizing modes of action, heightens the importance of poetry as activity, a concept that stands behind the analogies later in the epistle between the discipline of writing good poetry and that of living a good life.

In the *Epilogue to the Satires* (II) Pope speaks in his own voice, asserting the force of satiric verse as a:

> sacred Weapon! left for Truth's defence,
> Sole Dread of Folly, Vice, and Insolence!
> To all but Heav'n-directed hands deny'd,
> The Muse may give thee, but the Gods must guide.
> Rev'rent I touch thee! but with honest zeal;
> To rowze the Watchmen of the Publick Weal,
> To Virtue's Work provoke the tardy Hall,
> And goad the Prelate Slumb'ring in his Stall.
> Ye tinsel Insects! whom a Court maintains,
> That counts your Beauties only by your Stains,
> Spin all your Cobwebs o'er the Eye of Day!
> The Muse's wing shall brush you all away.
> (212–223)

The association of poetry with truth, sacredness, reverence, honest zeal, and heaven emphasizes the sources of the poet's supernal force. Poetry's grandeur reduces to insignificance the poet's opponents, now identified as enemies of virtue, sleeping mules or spiders to be brushed away by a touch of the muse's wing. The nonpoet is at best a watchman asleep at his post; the poet alone is virtue's warrior, ceaselessly active in the service of the good. But the image of poetry itself is vague: it is a weapon of an unspecified sort used in an undefined way for "Truth's defense." For the idea of poetry to acquire reality and energy depends on its association with the abstract names of virtue rather than on any physical specificity of imagery, and depends also on the energy and vitality of Pope's verse describing it. In contrast, people and forces inadequate to the defense of virtue, or actively opposed to it, are more sharply defined in physical terms: their physicality becomes symptomatic of their spiritual grossness. Watchmen, stalled animals, or insects—their form suggests their moral condition. But the court that values by appearances alone is incapable of discriminating among them: it finds "Stains" equivalent to "Beauties," tinsel as good as gold. And its appearances are fragile: the evanescent glitter of "tinsel Insects" corresponding to the evanescence of the cobwebs they spin.

Far stronger, although at first only sketchily physical, is the muse's power, because it is spiritual rather than physical. By the time the muse emerges as an actual form, she is a figure of light:

> diadem'd, with Rays divine,
> Touch'd with the Flame that breaks from Virtue's Shrine,
> Her Priestess Muse forbids the Good to dye,
> And ope's the Temple of Eternity.
>
> (232–235)

Identified with the flame of virtue and by indirect association with the sun of truth (Pope's own footnote reveals that the "Eye of Day" over which the insects spin cobwebs is a metaphor for truth), she emanates "Rays divine," possessed of all the divine revealing and purifying power of light—the power of Phoebus, god of sun and poetry.

The emphatic images associated in the satiric verse with the positive function of poetry insist on its magic, supernatural, even divine force and oppose it to the energies of moral and social corruption. They make poetry into a mythic agent of good. Less abstract than such qualities as temperance, courage, or reason, it becomes as firmly associated as they with the principle of good. Pope thus separates his role as poet from his fallibility as man; he generates authority for his utterances, insisting on the high function of satire in the act of writing it, with the air of a man reminding his readers of yet another accepted form of virtue. Poetry is the emblem of human possibility. The images' consistent stress on poetry as power reveals the poet as type of man in action, poetry as the height of human achievement.

The absoluteness of Pope's conviction that poetry can and should be the agent of virtue coexists with his awareness that poetry, like other forms of good but perhaps even more than they, is threatened by linguistic and moral decay. Here, too, the name of value may survive without the substance. "The gen'rous God, who Wit and Gold refines" (*Epistle to a Lady*, 289) has imitators, simulacra who bear his name while corrupting his values. The "Harlot form" of Italian opera speaks early in the fourth book of *The Dunciad*, addressing Dulness herself: "Another Phoebus, thy own Phoebus, reigns, / Joys in my jiggs, and dances in my chains" (61–62). The footnote explains, "Not the ancient *Phoebus*, the God of Harmony, but a modern *Phoebus* of French extraction." In the corrupt world of *The Dunciad* the powerful action characteristic of true poetry disappears; the image of dancing in chains both recalls the imagery of power associated with the ancient Phoebus and his devotees, and reveals the distance between true and false.

Whereas Pope uses imagery to convey his sense of poetry's high value and importance, he also renders through images his contempt for the misusers of poetry. *Epistle to Augustus* is especially rich in passages of this sort, existing side by side with passages insisting on poetry's importance. Such conjunctions are typical of this epistle, which keeps its reader in precarious balance, making him aware of the necessity for fine discrimination, but demonstrating at every turn its difficulty.

Here are two capsule accounts of poetry's malfunction, both from the *Epistle to Augustus*:

> No wonder then, when all was Love and Sport,
> The willing Muses were debauch'd at Court;
> On each enervate string they taught the Note
> To pant, or tremble thro' an Eunuch's throat. . .
>
> Now times are chang'd, and one Poetick Itch
> Has seiz'd the Court and City, Poor and Rich.
> (151–154, 169–170)

Both resemble the evocations of true poetry in implying action as the essence of inspiration, but it is action made meaningless—debauchery, castration, the playing of "enervate" strings, the scratching of an itch. The imagery suggests that writing can become mere self-indulgence or perverted self-display.

The poem's most striking image for bad verse is its concluding one:

> And when I flatter, let my dirty leaves
> (Like Journals, Odes, and such forgotten things
> As Eusden, Philips, Settle, writ of Kings)
> Cloath spice, line trunks, or flutt'ring in a row,
> Befringe the rails of Bedlam and Sohoe.
>
> (415–419)

Flattery has been the implicit concern of the entire poem; it becomes an emblem for poetic as well as personal corruption. A specific form of the general subordination of good values to bad, it reduces poetry itself to "dirty leaves." Given ultimate corruption, poetry loses power. The imagery stresses poetry's passivity, its use for trivial purposes, associated with the madhouse and the resort of prostitutes. The transition within a few lines from presenting poetry as able to surmount time and space to the vision of it as "flutt'ring" exemplifies the universal pattern of judgment and force subordinated to expediency. "When I aim at praise, they say I bite," the speaker complains (409). The entire poem supplies the "flattery" to be offered to an unsatisfactory king: its "bite" testifies to the poet's preservation of the energy that is poetry's essence.

Pope's imagery of positive value in the satiric poems reflects his duality of perception: his firm conviction of where value lies and how it must be defended, his consciousness that the enemies of the good may assume the names and appearance of their opposites—a consciousness more sophisticated and cynical than that characteristic of Dryden. More than the direct statements in the didactic poems, the presentations in imagery of embodied values and of their false imitations convey the complexity of his awareness and the intensity of his conviction. And they insist always on the necessary connection between responsible virtue and action: the imagery of value in Pope is almost always imagery of activity. Limits and standards do not simply exist; they must constantly be recreated and defended. Pope's presentation of the good and of its corruptions are repeated actions of preservation and defense.

*Seven*

# To Madness Near Ally'd

> Among the measures taken were those dealing with persons considered socially disruptive. Within this portmanteau category were included a motley group, the members of which were characterized by the fact that they had *overstepped the limits* set by family, social position, religious institutions, the political order, property relations, and the like. These were the people who were sent to houses of correction where they might be brought to their senses. In this way the insane in late seventeenth and eighteenth century France were put into institutions with others who exhibited socially unacceptable or irrational behaviour.[1]

The obvious corollary to Pope's concern with the setting of limits is his interest in those who have overstepped them. Whereas the imagery of discipline, restriction, and control helps to define the proper modes of human behavior and the dangers of excessive preoccupation with propriety, the imagery of madness suggests the pitfalls of the opposite extreme. Moreover, because of the close connection between "socially unacceptable" and "irrational" behavior, such imagery may comment on the state of society as well as the individuals in it. It thus expands the reference of Pope's ethical concerns, reflecting his awareness of both the necessity and the difficulty of living by higher values than society supports, or by different ones.

The eighteenth century's classic account of the complex issues involved in any attempt to locate and evaluate madness in a corrupt society is Swift's "Digression Concerning the Original, the Use and Improvement of Madness in a Commonwealth," which appears in *A Tale of a Tub.* Like much of Pope's treatment of madness, it exists within an intricate satiric matrix. The central problem of madness, as Swift explains it, is the proper relation between the individual and his society. The "Digression" rests on the assumption that self-obsession is the invariable source of insanity. In the essay, a hack writer explains the nature of madness, finding in it the source of "*The Establishment of New Empires by Conquest: The Advance and Progress of New Schemes in Philosophy; and the contriving, as well as the propagating of New Religions.*" As all of these are ways in which individuals can assert their power and enforce their convictions on others, madness is the only conceivable explanation for their desire to do so: "For, the Brain, in its natural Position and State of Serenity, disposeth its Owner to pass his Life in the common Forms, without any Thought of subduing Multitudes to his own *Power*, his *Reasons* or his *Visions;* and the more he shapes his Understanding by the Pattern of Human Learning, the less he is inclined to form Parties after his particular Notions; because that instructs him in his private Infirmities, as well as in the stubborn Ignorance of the People."[2] Swift here speaks in his own voice, enunciating his age's faith in the value of a life passed "in the common Forms," of consciousness informed alike of private and of public infirmities, and of a mind capable of profiting from "the Pattern of Human Learning." Pope's faith is at least intermittently the same, expressed in his commitment to the Horatian ideal of moderate retirement: "Content with little, I can piddle here / On Broccoli and mutton, round the year" (*Imitations of Horace, Satire* II, ii, 137–138). When he declares himself, in his letters and his verse, to be more importantly private man than poet, responsible for the saving of his own soul alone, he reveals the same assurance reflected by Swift.

But assurance soon vanishes from the "Digression." The hack writer's explanation of madness is at first orderly, coherent, comprehensible, and comforting, in its awareness of what is morally wrong with insanity and in its sense of a clear alternative to irrationality. But moral awareness soon disappears. The discussion of delusion leads directly to the famous definition of happiness as "*a perpetual Possession of being Well Deceived,*" which is disturbingly amplified by the further description of "*the Possession of being well deceived*" as "The Serene Peaceful State of being a Fool among Knaves."[3] Happiness and folly, or madness in other words, are virtually identical.

Moreover, the grounds on which madness is to be condemned become increasingly obscure. Society has always judged behavior as mad on the basis of its "style and consistency . . . its orientation to reality, and its consequences."[4] The last point is particularly important. Madhouses are full of those who, in other circumstances, might be considered valuable members of the community. The maniac who "walks duly in one Pace, intreats your Penny with due Gravity and Ceremony; talks much of hard Times, and Taxes, and the *Whore of Babylon;* Bars up the woodden Window of his Cell constantly at eight a Clock: Dreams of *Fire,* and *Shop-lifters,* and *Court-Customers,* and *Priviledg'd Places*" belongs in "the *City* among his Brethren."[5] There he would seem not crazed but sensible, and the consequences of his behavior would be the protection of his property and the establishment of his reputation for prudence. One is considered mad who dreams of shoplifters when he has no shop; but the actual shop-owner who obsessively fears the most minute depletion of his stock is "sane." No moral difference separates the two, yet society pronounces an absolute differentiation.

There is not just satiric exaggeration in the insistence that only arbitrary distinctions divide the mad from the sane, but also truth. To label madness is a social convenience. Empedocles, the hack points out, was called mad because of his suicidal leap; Curtius, who saved Rome by his, was acclaimed a hero. Society establishes and maintains categories that feed collective self-interest. The self-interest of individuals, when it conflicts sharply with what has been declared the general good, must be confined. Happiness depends upon self-deception, but individual self-deception grown too obvious threatens the deceptions of the majority. The "normal" shopkeeper can be allowed his obsession with property because he shares it with so many others.

Swift's discussion of madness thus raises questions about the entire social order. Suggesting the arbitrariness of one kind of social classification, it hints at the possibility that all social organizations and assumptions may be equally arbitrary. A true internal order is possible for the individual only if he commits himself to truth, to an acceptance of "his private Infirmities, as well as . . . the stubborn Ignorance of the People," and if he abandons the search for happiness. A true social order is a more shadowy possibility. Men whom society declares mad reflect and parody the values of their judges; their illusions and obsessions are only slightly more conspicuous than those of the sane. As the world is a vast asylum, it is scant comfort to reflect that its inhabitants are not all equally sick.

Pope at times seems to share this vision of society. It dominates three of the four moral epistles, with their concentration on how the "ruling passion" dominates and distorts human minds. Passion is of course irrational: "On human actions reason tho' you can, / It may be reason, but it is not man" (*Epistle to Cobham,* 35–36). Passion often appears to produce arbitrary action:

> Oft in the Passions' wild rotation tost,
> Our spring of action to ourselves is lost:
> Tir'd, not determin'd, to the last we yield,
> And what comes then is master of the field.
> (*Epistle to Cobham,* 41–44)

Men attempt for their comfort to offer rational explanations for human conduct, but reason provides only a plausible veneer for the chaotic truth:

> Behold! If Fortune or a Mistress frowns,
> Some plunge in bus'ness, others shave their crowns:
> To ease the Soul of one oppressive weight,
> This quits an Empire, that embroils a State.
> (*Epistle to Cobham,* 55–58)

The point, reiterated in Swift's "Digression on Madness" ("The very same Principle that influences a *Bully* to break the Windows of a Whore, who has jilted him, naturally stirs up a Great Prince to raise mighty Armies, and dream of nothing but Sieges, Battles, and Victories"[6]), supports a view of society as founded on arbitrary distinctions, dependent on the reassurance implicit in declaring some of its members insane—a declaration that asserts the reality and potency of defined standards of normalcy despite the fact that these standards can hardly survive examination. In the society Pope evokes, the question of insanity rarely arises; in fact, the disturbing lack of self-examination in the world he describes itself justifies the satirist's probing eye and caustic tongue. Thomas Edwards has described the exemplary characters of the *Epistle to Cobham*: "Their common malady is that a passion for real experience has degenerated into abstract obsessions. As they withdraw from solid actuality into the dream-world of their passionate fancies, life dwindles into a fiction of images wholly divorced from the reality they should represent."[7] This is a description of pathology, of people cut off from reality; but Pope presents them as examples of all humanity. Here are two successive vignettes, representative in their condensation and suggestivity of the poem's narrative technique, and typical in their physical vividness of the way Pope conveys action through image:

> Behold a rev'rend sire, whom want of grace
> Has made the father of a nameless race,
> Shov'd from the wall perhaps, or rudely press'd
> By his own son, that passes by unbless'd;
> Still to his wench he crawls on knocking knees,
> And envies ev'ry sparrow that he sees.
> A salmon's belly, Helluo, was thy fate,
> The doctor call'd, declares all help too late.
> Mercy! cries Helluo, mercy on my soul!
> Is there no hope? Alas!—then bring the jowl.
> (228–237)

The sparrow and the salmon's belly, equivalents for the men who value them, become grotesque images of human self-reduction. The story of the "rev'rend sire" is a tale of the movement from power to helplessness. The sexual potency that fathers an entire "race" almost immediately makes its possessor powerless: that race becomes a metaphor for the crowds of London who jostle and threaten the old man. Lacking grace in the heavenly as well as in the earthly sense, unable and unwilling to bless his unknown progeny, he loses even the upright position that characterizes the human animal and is forced to recognize his inferiority—specifically in sexual power—

to the tiny sparrow. Helluo's drama is similar, its direction being sketched in the first line by the startling conjunction of the mundane and vividly concrete "salmon's belly" with the high abstraction "fate." The high yields inevitably to the low; preoccupation with the soul cannot compete with the temptation of the jowl; and Helluo, comically and pathetically faithful to his true commitment, dies in his gluttony.

The society inhabited by these men pronounces no judgment on them; they exist securely within the range of the "normal." Pope's satiric tone demands that the reader judge the described aberrations by traditional moral standards; but having judged, one realizes that there is no way to separate such aberrations from the others that compose society. "Confronted by a successful satire, we as readers share the satirist's point of view, his emotional strain."[8] The "strain" in this instance is between two perspectives: the moral point of view that isolates and condemns the "madness" of obsession, and the pragmatic viewpoint that recognizes the universality of conduct controlled by obsession. The second view, generating a tone of dispassionate scientific observation, dominates Pope's moral essays, but the poetry's power depends on the tension between the observer's attitude and the moralist's.

For women, according to the second moral epistle (*To a Lady*), social norms are even less demanding, since changeability has become the expected pattern of feminine behavior. Martha Blount's remark that "Most Women have no Characters at all" (2) embodies the poem's typical tension: light and dismissive in tone, it yet contains material for serious moral indictment. The portrait of Atossa demonstrates how the charming frivolities of women can degenerate into what by most human standards might be called insanity:

> But what are these to great Atossa's mind?
> Scarce once herself, by turns all Womankind!
> Who, with herself, or others, from her birth
> Finds all her life one warfare upon earth:
> Shines, in exposing Knaves, and painting Fools,
> Yet is, whate'er she hates and ridicules.
> No Thought advances, but her Eddy Brain

Whisks it about, and down it goes again.
Full sixty years the World has been her Trade,
The wisest Fool much Time has ever made.
From loveless youth to unrespected age,
No Passion gratify'd except her Rage.

(115–126)

Lack of a firm sense of personal identity, emotional chaos, failure of mental balance—a brain become a whirlpool:—these are the characteristics of Atossa's instability, paralleled by the defining traits of other victims of ruling passions. The absence of control in her personality makes her a horror to herself as well as to others. If insanity is the overstepping of social limits, it might also be described as the state of a personality lacking internal principles of control. Despite this woman's frenzied activity, she has no power. Things happen to her: she "finds" her life a warfare, she does not consciously make it one. Inadvertently she becomes what she hates and mocks. Her thoughts, their natural fulfillment denied by the systematic chaos of her brain, can serve no end. The rage that dominates her converts all other emotion to itself; she is doomed by the violence she has generated but cannot restrain.

Her misery is partly that of isolation. The fierce energy of her passions and her inability to discriminate drive people away, and no victory is possible in the "warfare" that engages her. The chronological poles of her experience are "loveless youth" and "unrespected age": never does she find meaningful community. At the end of his description of the sex, Pope generalizes the same point:

See how the World its Veterans rewards!
A Youth of frolicks, an old Age of Cards,
Fair to no purpose, artful to no end,
Young without Lovers, old without a Friend,
A Fop their Passion, but their Prize a Sot,
Alive, ridiculous, and dead, forgot!

(243–248)

This summary draws serious attention to the harmless social activities characteristic of women. The metaphor in the first line suggests that many women share with Atossa an involvement in life as warfare. They survive their battles, never confronting the triviality or purposelessness of their lives, to confront Atossa's fate as well as her instability. Lacking love in youth, friendship in age, respect in life, or remembrance after death, for all their frenzied social activity, they too can achieve no real community.

Though it is possible to argue that the description of Atossa implies a psychosis, no one would be likely to maintain that women who spend their youth in frolics, their old age in card-playing, are therefore mad. Their conduct, fully sanctioned by society, actually establishes the norms by which women are commonly evaluated. Yet the horror of their lives and destinies is hardly less than of Atossa's: they participate in society's madness.

This point is not explicit in *Epistle to a Lady,* so that to suggest it may seem a critical imposition. But the third moral epistle directly asserts the possibility of understanding society as insane, and the perspective thus created seems relevant also to the two preceding epistles. This epistle's subject is money, which is closely linked with madness in a capitalistic society. The *Epistle to Bathurst* explores that relationship. The opposed polarities which the good man must avoid are those "Of mad Good-nature, and of mean Self love" (228). Neither epithet is casual. The insanity of failed control masquerading as good feeling is the opposing counterpart of self-obsession's avarice. The horror of one kind of self-love is self-limitation; that of the opposite kind is the absence of limits. Money goes alike "to the Fool, the Mad, the Vain, the Evil" (19), a grouping that suggests the identification of madness with moral failure and the way in which money attaches itself to and intensifies moral weakness of all kinds.

The *Epistle to Bathurst* contains two developed images of madness in action. One is fantasy, the other purports to be realistic, although the Twickenham note to Pope's account of Cutler points out that it "is quite unhistorical."[9] Both disturbingly imply the difficulty of distinguishing sanity from insanity in a corrupt society and question the assumption that normality should be the operative standard of sanity.

First is the description of Worldly "crying coals from street to street" (50) in a fantasized social order where goods have replaced currency as the medium of exchange. His avarice thus expresses itself so conspicuously that it cannot be ignored. The most charitable hypothesis to explain his moral condition is that he is "some poor tradesman craz'd" (52), but this "mistaken" interpretation reveals the truth: his monetary obsession, reducing him to the level of tradesman, is truly a form of insanity. Yet only Worldly's "wig so wild, and mien so maz'd" (51) distinguish him significantly from Sir Morgan "Astride his cheese" (49), "His Grace" leading a bull to White's (55), or "soft Adonis" who drives "to St. James's a whole herd of swine" (61–62)—all aristocrats whose conduct is acceptable because it conforms to imagined social norms. The norms themselves appear ridiculous to the reader, the poem argues, only because the abstract (here money in its modern forms) has been made concrete, a conversion which not only provides an image for the poet's method, but also creates satiric effect by giving reality to what is usually conveniently vague. It is easy to conclude that the whole of society, as here imagined, is "mad," and if so, that the world it imitates and exaggerates is mad as well. The standard of judgment by which Worldly is singled out and labeled insane in a society of madmen is one of appearance: when moral substance vanishes, standards can hardly be substantial. The image of Worldly both exemplifies the moral inadequacy of capitalistic values and reveals the arbitrary nature of judgment in an amoral world.

Cutler's parsimony evokes a more serious image of madness:

> Cutler saw tenants break, and houses fall,
> For very want; he could not build a wall.
> His only daughter in a stranger's pow'r,
> For very want; he could not pay a dow'r.
> A few grey hairs his rev'rend temples crown'd,
> 'Twas very want that sold them for two pound.
> What ev'n deny'd a cordial at his end,
> Banish'd the doctor, and expell'd the friend?
> What but a want, which you perhaps think mad,
> Yet numbers feel, the want of what he had.
>
> (323–332)

Cutler's "want" is his madness. As the word is reiterated, it accumulates meaning, defining an interior lack while seeming to describe various lacks of money. The final couplet introduces the explicit idea of madness very tentatively. The imagined reader, or Bathurst himself, may be capable of judging such a man mad, but the speaker's assurance of such a judgment is shaken by the fact that Cutler's mode of madness is widespread. Because "numbers feel" what Cutler felt and enact their fantasies in similar ways, the possibility of firm negative judgment is diminished. Cutler reverses or perverts many fundamental human assumptions. Loyalty, parental love, even vanity disappear under the pressure of his compulsion. Such "mean Self-love" drives out ordinary kinds of self-interest, denying even the basic life-wish and a sense of community by rejecting medical aid and friendship at the end. But even such dramatic forms of perversity are only "perhaps" called mad: as madness multiplies, it becomes less discernible.

Hannah Arendt has written, "But anger, and above all Lessing's kind of anger, reveals and exposes the world just as Lessing's kind of laughter . . . seeks to bring about reconciliation with the world. Such laughter helps one to find a place in the world, but ironically, which is to say, without selling one's soul to it."[10] Anger and laughter are the satirist's traditional weapons, and the functions Arendt suggests—exposure and ironic reconciliation—are relevant to Pope's use of them. The metaphor of madness is particularly useful to convey simultaneously a comic and a tragic understanding of life. The portraits of Worldly and Cutler define extreme attitudes: Worldly is a comic figure, Cutler a horrifying one. The poet laughs at his first victim, finds the existence of the second morally intolerable. Madness was in the eighteenth century still considered a comic spectacle, but it was also felt to be a tragic reality. By implying the view that society is mad, the poet both expresses his anger at the existing state of things and suggests the terms on which he can continue to live in such a world—on the basis of an ironic perception of reality.

•

Madness is not only a social phenomenon; it exists in individuals as well. Such modern thinkers as R. D. Laing, agreeing that society is sick, conclude that individuals declared psychotic may in fact be those whose insights are truer and deeper than the world can tolerate.[11] Pope drew no such conclusions. His presentation of social insanity rests largely on accumulated portrayals of obsessed individuals, and madness is for him fundamentally a matter of individual moral failure. This view is more than a useful satiric device.

When Dryden wrote, "Great Wits are sure to Madness near ally'd; / And thin Partitions do their Bounds divide," he defined a problem that was to vex the eighteenth century.[12] He "proved" his point, in relation to Achitophel, by this evidence:

> Else, why should he, with Wealth and Honour blest,
> Refuse his Age the needful hours of Rest?
> Punish a Body which he coud not please;
> Bankrupt of Life, yet Prodigal of Ease?
>
> (165–168)

Disregard for the body's welfare is an index of moral failure, a failure that turns out, in this instance as in many others, to resolve itself into the classical sin of hubris. Achitophel's greatness and his madness are "near ally'd" because the line between proper aspiration, signifying human possibility, and improper ambition, Adam's sin and Lucifer's, is often difficult to discern. The madness of great men is their desire for more—which is also the source of their greatness.

From one point of view, madness is universal, inherent in man's fallen nature. When "a sober sage" cries, responding to the fantasies of spreading evil in *Epistle to Bathurst*, "All this is madness," the poem's speaker inquires, "But who, my friends, has reason in his rage?" (153–154). He alludes to the "rage" caused by the spread of avarice, specifically perhaps to the "Party-rage" (151) which Blount wished to eliminate or to the fact that Blount's brain was "fir'd" (147) with a desire "To buy both sides, and give thy Country peace" (152), but also to the "rage" that drives him as poet to indict the misdeeds he observes. No one escapes humanity's madness. The sage suggests that the universal insanity derives from the inevitable presence of the ruling passion, but his interlocutor points out that there are various levels of madness. The ruling passion may direct itself toward some end, or it may be altogether aimless. To Warburton, Pope wrote, "concerning the Extravagant Motives of Avarice, I meant to show those wch were Real were yet as mad or madder than those wch are Imaginary."[13] Irrationality is everywhere; yet the possibility of making distinctions must remain. To characterize all the world as mad may itself be a form of moral obtuseness, an avoidance of the need to discriminate; but Pope's treatment of madness in individuals demonstrates that one can see the world as a madhouse, yet distinguish among its inmates.

In its every appearance in Pope's verse, madness is a version of self-love, reflecting a failure of moral judgment and of discipline. This view had historical sanctions. The shift in attitudes toward insanity from the Middle Ages to the Renaissance was in part a change from the belief that madness was essentially diabolical, reflecting perhaps—in the most horrifying version of possibility—a madness of the universe. Such cosmic implications diminished in the Renaissance, and madness became an image of the "subtle rapport that man maintains with himself."[14] Madmen were to be locked up, not for punishment exactly, though Bedlam and the jail often appear together in literary references (including Pope's verse), a combination which suggests a persistent mental association between crime and insanity, that interior form of crime. Self-love, part of every man, must be controlled. The command of God "bade Self-love and Social be the same" (*Essay on Man*, III, 318); at his most optimistic, Pope can assert, "Ev'n mean Self-love becomes, by force divine, / The scale to measure others wants by thine" (II, 291–292). But observation tells him that in practice the relation between self-love and social love is often tenuous, that the insanity of self-obsession is a danger for everyone, and that the function of satire is to "lash the madness of a vicious age."[15] Vice is madness from the viewpoint of moral assurance, and madness vice.

Both forms of excess lead to self-destruction. An image for the process is the piling of Ossa on Pelion:

> Oh sons of earth! attempt ye still to rise,
> By mountains pil'd on mountains, to the skies?

Heav'n still with laughter the vain toil surveys,
And buries madmen in the heaps they raise.
(*Essay on Man*, IV, 73–76)

This is the paradigmatic action of madness, encompassing such a career as that of Alexander the Great, who can be dismissed as "Macedonia's madman" (*Essay on Man*, IV, 220). Even such a virtue as courage can become madness: "Who wickedly is wise, or madly brave, / Is but the more a fool, the more a knave" (IV, 231–232). But forms of excess are apparent in all human desire and action. "Mad Vain-glory" draws the monarch's sword (*Epilogue to the Satires*, II, 229); "wild desire," for wealth or women, unites its possessor with "the maddest" (*Imitations of Horace, Epistle* I, vi, 67–80); avarice and love are different forms of that "Fever of the soul" (*Epistle* I, i, 55–58) which lies in wait for all.

The individual shape of a man's madness depends on the nature of his self-image. Men may take false comfort from awareness that they are unthreatened by one mode of irrationality, only to fall prey to another. In *Epistle* II, ii, the point is explicit, as a man responds smugly to a discussion of avarice:

'But why all this of Av'rice? I have none.'
I wish you joy, Sir, of a Tyrant gone;
But does no other lord it at this hour,
As wild and mad? the Avarice of Pow'r?
Does neither Rage inflame, nor Fear appall?
Not the black Fear of Death, that saddens all?
With Terrors round can Reason hold her throne,
Despise the known, nor tremble at th' unknown?
(304–311)

In the original of this passage, Horace focuses on vice rather than madness. Although he too is capable of viewing the world as an asylum, he here introduces neither madness nor the opposing power of reason in his discussion of the interior evils that threaten man. Pope's language, more emotive than that of his classic source, reminds one steadily of the emotional power of those dark forces that possess men's minds. If one defines madness simply as mental imbalance, its inevitability becomes apparent: no one has the strength to possess himself in perfect poise. Reason holds her throne precariously, threatened by emotion, superstition, and the fundamental facts of human existence. One emotional tyrant is "As wild and mad" as another; the good man strives to oppose them all, but his relation to an ideal of humanity is apt to be highly theoretical.

Although the "individuals" implied in such a presentation are symbolic rather than literal human beings, Pope's characteristic employment of human figures in the landscape of social chaos reflects his belief that the only meaningful salvation is individual, not social. Like Swift, he conveys a sense of madness, only faintly metaphorical, brooding over mankind; but his stress is different. Swift as a satirist concerns himself with the ways in which men organize their corruption. At his most metaphysical, in the fourth book of *Gulliver's Travels*, he moves toward concentration on the individual soul, but *A Modest Proposal* and *A Tale of a Tub* are more representative in their stress on evil organized and consolidated.[16] Pope attends more consistently to the sources of social evil in the individual soul. The hack finds no significant difference between Bedlam and the world outside it; Pope finds no important distinction between the rationality of one mind and another. The only difference is that implied by the domination of different tyrants.

The awareness of precarious mental poise that generates the imagery of mad tyranny, black fear, flaming rage, and trembling Reason underlies most of Pope's references to madness, metaphoric and literal. Such references, however lightly developed, have the effect of images because an underlying integrity of attitude gives substantiality to even casual allusions. This technique of creating images is important in Pope. It bears some affinities to the mode of personification, which at its eighteenth century best also achieves physical suggestivity by resting on intellectual and moral assumptions so clear and powerful that a mere hint is enough to remove them from the realm of abstraction. Madness may be a physical fact, with physical manifestations, but it is also, and primarily, a mental and moral one. Pope's imagery of madness is often not physical, yet its force is that of the concrete.

The *Epistle to Dr. Arbuthnot,* over whose world "The Dog-star [which presides over and was thought to cause madness] rages!" (3), provides an unusual degree of physical objectification for its imagery of madness. Insanity here is a metaphor both for social disorganization and for the threats to individual integrity of which the poet, more than other men, is conscious. The close association between madness and poetry exemplifies the precariousness of the poet's psychic existence:

> nay 'tis past a doubt,
> All *Bedlam,* or *Parnassus,* is let out:
> Fire in each eye, and Papers in each hand,
> They rave, recite, and madden round the land.
> (3–6)

Bedlam and Parnassus are interchangeable localities of confusion and of "inspiration," which may or may not bear any meaningful relation to reality. But the nature of reality itself is questionable: despite the opposed emotional responses traditionally accorded to Bedlam and to Parnassus, it is difficult to tell which is which. The poet's reciting and the madman's raving are indistinguishable; because the poet is a bad poet, both activities symbolize the lack of clear operative values in society, which tolerates mania because incapable of recognizing it.

The madman-poet, whether literally or figuratively mad, prizes his madness as the source of his distinction:

> Is there, who lock'd from Ink and Paper, scrawls
> With desp'rate Charcoal round his darken'd walls?
> All fly to *Twit'nam,* and in humble strain
> Apply to me, to keep them mad or vain.
> (19–22)

The first couplet contains the most specific and sympathetic image in Pope of the madman's physical fate; but sympathy for the desperation of the maniac driven to express himself by scrawling on walls becomes disgust when he begs for support in the madness that alone makes his poetry possible. Madness is a threat to true poetic as well as social values; it is also, even from without, a threat to the personal integrity of the genuine poet, whose goal in life is to "Maintain a Poet's Dignity and Ease" (263). To both, the madmen lay siege. Their flattery is destructive: "Of all mad Creatures, if the Learn'd are right, / It is the Slaver kills, and not the Bite" (105–106). The poet's dismissive reduction of his flatterers to animals suggests madness' ultimate horror, its destruction of reason, the human prerogative. Men who deny their reason by commitment to flattery's irrationalities willfully make themselves subhuman: like the mad poets, they embrace their insanity as a source of advantage; worse than the poets, they actually *choose* it. They threaten the speaker of the *Epistle to Dr. Arbuthnot* by what they exemplify, subhuman irrationality, as well as by what they do. And madmen of various sorts surround the speaker: Dennis raves (153); critics, like poets, publish out of madness (155); the poet does not combat them because he will not wage "war with *Bedlam*" (156). Those who claim his friendship and then reject it are "The dull, the proud, the wicked, and the mad" (347); this line's hierarchical order sums up the moral intolerability of madness.

All except the last two of these allusions to insanity involve physical objectification of madness. The poem's introductory images vividly evoke the swarm of poetasters whose "madness" is attested by the later Bedlam detail; the moral contempt conveyed by the conjunction of their pitiable confinement with their presumption in demanding Pope's attention to their verse supports their reduction to mad dogs. Dennis' "raving" is a physical metaphor for his rant in print. Such glimpses of mad men and animals in action reinforce the mere list of moral and intellectual qualities with which the poet finally conveys his judgment of those who persecute him by means of their own inadequacies. The value of dignity and ease as humane ideals emerges partly through the clarity with which their opposites are embodied, and references to madness create one form of that embodiment.

In the Horatian imitations, however, the embodiment is largely moral rather than physical. The most vivid exception is a little story in *Epistle* II, ii, which serves an equivalent function to the corresponding tale in Horace, but is significantly altered in substance. Horace tells (126–140) of a man of Argos who imagined himself watching the acting of tragedies and happily applauding in an empty theater. Yet he filled all his domestic responsibilities and behaved otherwise with perfect self-possession. When his relatives finally managed to cure him of his delusion, he complained that they had provided death rather than deliverance, robbing him of pleasure and depriving him of his soul's dearest illusion.

Pope's version concerns a member of the House of Lords who believed Parliament to be functioning even when it was not, and "tho' the House was up, delighted sate, / Heard, noted, answer'd, as in full Debate" (186–187). He too was a model citizen in other respects; and he too complained when cured:

> My Friends? he cry'd, p-x take you for your care!
> That from a Patriot of distinguish'd note,
> Have bled and purg'd me to a simple *Vote*.
>
> (195–197)

The analogy, in Horace and Pope, is to the plight of the poet who believes it necessary to give up versifying in order to harmonize his mind, but who finds the writing of verse more pleasant than the alternative of maturity. Horace's character is obsessed with a passive role; Pope's, with an active one. The eccentric lord, in preserving his illusion, preserves his self-image as a "distinguish'd" figure, whereby the analogy to the poet's situation is exact and penetrating. A man's self-image is always at the heart of his madness. A madman may see himself through romantic identification with a literary model; he may resemble Don Quixote. Or he may identify himself as having whatever qualities he admires, "by means of a delusive attachment that enables him to grant himself all the qualities, all the virtues or powers he lacks."[17] Horace's madman is merely deluded; Pope's is deluded in a way that exemplifies the treacheries of self-concern. The mad nobleman believes himself to fill an important public function; the poet, believing the same thing, thereby suggests his own "madness" (though Pope and Horace both elsewhere claim the public importance of their poetry). According to

Pope, in resigning himself to concern with "the equal Measure of the Soul" (205) rather than the measure of a line, a man resigns himself to public insignificance, accepting the fact that all men die alone, that public concerns must at last yield to private, and that the belief that any man can greatly affect the world is only illusion. His resemblance to the cured lord is poignant. The analogy implies the seriousness with which Pope takes madness as a metaphor for the human condition. The story of the deluded lord underscores the insidious and omnipresent sources of madness as well as its manifestations.

The poet-speaker swears in *Epistle to Dr. Arbuthnot* that he will not be "Lucre's Madman" (335), but it is more difficult—as Horace and Pope testify—to avoid the madness inherent in a commitment to writing. The following observations on Pope's behavior are illuminating: his "sister, Mrs. Rackett said—'For you know, to speak plain to you, my brother has a maddish way with him.' Little people mistook the excess of his genius for madness. 'Igad that young fellow will either be a madman or make a very great poet' (Rag Smith, after being in Mr. Pope's company when about fourteen)."[18] Madness and poetry are closely allied. In the *Imitations of Horace* the poet-speaker declares mental incoherence to be one of his characteristics (see *Epistle* I, i, 165–176); and he recognizes that devotion to true value does not forestall it—may indeed produce it:

> Thus good, or bad, to one extreme betray
> Th' unbalanc'd Mind, and snatch the Man away;
> For Vertue's self may too much Zeal be had;
> The worst of Madmen is a Saint run mad.
>
> (*Epistle* I, vi, 24–27)

In the same epistle Pope asserts that "all Men may be cur'd, when'er they please" of mental disease (59). But in another of these poems, treating the composition of verse as madness, he comments that the poet who swears to give up writing is likely to wake "in a raging Fit" and find himself versifying once more (*Epistle* II, i, 179–180).

As the imagery of limitation and control finally concerns itself with the problems and prerogatives of poetry, so the imagery of madness in the late poems focuses on the figure of the poet. Horace imagines old age and death as threats to his writing; Pope adds a vision of the darkened room and the whitened wall on which he may scribble with a skewer: Bedlam is another natural form of the poet's nemesis (*Satire* II, i, 97–99). The commitment to poetry must always be in part a version of that ruling passion which Pope sees as causing almost universal, and necessarily incurable, mental imbalance. The poet-satirist presents himself as guardian of public morality, truth's defender, vice's enemy. In the poems dealing with satire's function and value, the allusions to madness counterbalance this kind of self-presentation and depict the poet's sobering consciousness of his own inherent human limitations and what they mean.

The theory of the ruling passion codifies Pope's interest in the obsessions of which human beings are capable. Though men and women driven by their passions beyond eccentricity into perversity may be, like the deluded lord, "not quite" mad (190), Pope's insistent presentation of mental imbalance conveys a truly classical view of the dangers of experience. The Greek Dionysiac cult, for example, paid homage to the sinister possibilities of the passions. "To resist Dionysus is to repress the elemental in one's own nature; the punishment is the sudden complete collapse of the inward dykes when the elemental breaks through perforce and civilization vanishes."[19] Awareness of the dangers of repression is both a very modern idea and a very ancient one; and Pope seems on the whole more conscious of repression's value than of its evil. He believes that it is necessary to resist Dionysus. But his portraits of perversity also reveal his belief that the structures of civilization are fragile and delusive, that neither outer dikes nor inward ones can be altogether trusted, and that only by a generous tolerance can men judge themselves and each other to be meaningfully sane.

Yet he rarely calls any described individual insane. That he does not label the absence of control madness is crucial to his poetic effect, suggesting the final, subtle way in which his technique balances that of *A Tale of a Tub*. Swift supplies a discussion and a description of madness, then blandly asks how different the world of sanity is from that of insanity. Pope shows the manias of "normality," the conduct of real or imaginary symbolic figures who demonstrate how life is actually lived in the world. He does not discuss madness in detail; he only alludes to it. But the allusions add up to an evocation of madness as a constant threat, to society and to individuals. It is a threat from without, in that madmen persecute the sane by their activities and demands, but also from within: Bedlam is a prospect that even the most virtuous man should contemplate as a personal possibility. The world is full of, perhaps even dominated by, persons whose activities, as described by a master of balance and control, seem dangerously close to insanity. Swift suggests that madmen are much like other people; Pope, even more disturbingly, reveals that "other people" are much like madmen. "The ruling Passion, be it what it will, / The ruling Passion conquers Reason still" (*Epistle to Bathurst*, 155–156). Since all possess, or are possessed by, a ruling passion, the primacy of reason is dubious indeed. By his imagery of madness Pope suggests that man is, at best, only *rationis capax*.

The problem of repression and its effects on psychic process is central in two of Pope's early poems about women, *The Rape of the Lock* and *Eloisa to Abelard*. Both deal with neurosis; both suggest that external controls, even controls assented to by their victims, can hardly bound, may even encourage, the excesses of narcissism. Like the allusions to madness, these poems manifest Pope's interest in the relation between limitation and excess and in the value of both.

Belinda is self-obsessed, which she could hardly avoid being, since when she smiles, the world is gay. Her power derives from the radiance of her beauty; the force of her smile reminds one that she is her society's "sun," a point made repeatedly through metaphor. But her smile's force, her position as "sun," are also functions of her self-conception. Gay herself, she can neither imagine nor perceive absence of gaiety in others. The wretches who hang are remote from her mind, as are the judges and jurymen who hang them. The "sacred Rites of Pride" (I, 128) which begin her day provide the appropriate focus for judging her. She sees in the mirror "A heav'nly Image" (125), the object of her adoration. Her perception, as many critics have pointed out, is both accurate and misguided:

she is indeed almost divine in her beauty, a benign power in the poem, but she is also trivial and limited in her self-obsession. She sees others as subordinate to herself, society as controlled by her emotions; here, too, she is both right and wrong. As unquestioned queen of her milieu, she exercises emotional control over her companions; her inability to comprehend psychic states different from her own gives her the strength of obtuseness and fortifies her sense of power. Her dreams tell her that she is the "distinguish'd Care / Of thousand bright Inhabitants of Air!" (27–28); "reality," as here rendered, substantiates dream and objectifies Belinda's fantasies. The vision of an earthly lover lurking at her heart is enough to nullify the sylphs's power; this detail confirms the repeated—although not constant—implication that the poem's mythology and society are alike reflections of Belinda's mind.

Yet society, if it seems a projection of Belinda's imagination, also controls that imagination: it limits what a woman can see, what she is likely to think, and what she can do. Making appearances crucial, it thus destroys substance. Frowning on obvious sexual indulgence, it encourages substitutions and fantasies. Dominated by women, it magnifies the trivial and diminishes the significant. "The ancient Poets," Pope comments, "are in one respect like many modern Ladies; Let an Action be never so trivial in it self, they always make it appear of the utmost Importance."[20] The enlarging effect, which obscures the nature of reality but accurately renders emotional response to it, is an important manifestation of Belinda's mental process.

Here is a portrait of the heroine in action:

> *Belinda* now, whom Thirst of Fame invites,
> Burns to encounter two adventrous Knights,
> At *Ombre* singly to decide their Doom;
> And swells her Breast with Conquests yet to come.
> Strait the three Bands prepare in Arms to join,
> Each Band the number of the Sacred Nine.
> Soon as she spreads her Hand, th' Aerial Guard
> Descend, and sit on each important Card.
> (III, 25–32)

The operations of Belinda's mind and feelings give significance to the minutiae of card-playing. The swelling of her breast, like her burning thirst of fame, testifies to the high dignity that she feels in such a pursuit. For her, each detail of procedure has meaning: the number of cards in each hand, the arranging of high cards. The sylphs, reflecting her view of the world, guard her important cards, their role being in part to embody what she feels and believes.

There is little evidence that Belinda suffers—certainly none that she knows she suffers—from any repression. The perfect reciprocal poise between her and her social environment makes its forms and restrictions seem "natural" in her. Yet Pope calls attention to the striking disparity between the degree of Belinda's feelings and the ways in which she is allowed to channel them. He seems comically to justify his heroine's emotion by associating her activities with splendid traditions: the grandeur of knighthood, "the Sacred Nine." At the same time he provides the satiric reminders inherent in mock epic of the disparity between present and past and, in this instance, between cause (a card game) and effect (burning thirst of fame, swelling breast). These manifestations of emotion are clearly sexual in origin, but not explicitly so in expression: the forms of the society are not adequate to the emotional content of individuals in it. Belinda is unaware of this fact: the sexual feeling is hers, knowledge of it only the poet's. Her lack of insight makes her and her society appropriate objects for mockery because the enlarging action of her sensibility, sanctioned and encouraged by the social world, obscures reality, while the narrator's perception penetrates it.

The lines describing Belinda's reaction to the rape of her lock provide an even more striking example of the relation between her sensibility and the poet's:

> Then flash'd the living Lightning from her Eyes,
> And Screams of Horror rend th' affrighted Skies.
> Not louder Shrieks to pitying Heav'n are cast,
> When Husbands or when Lap-dogs breathe their last,
> Or when rich *China* Vessels, fal'n from high,
> In glittring Dust and painted Fragments lie!
>
> (III, 155–160)

The exaggerated response here described is once more Belinda's; her expressive reactions dramatize her evaluation of what has happened and epitomize the permitted release of extravagant emotion, given a socially sanctioned pretext. She sees herself, larger than life-size, as a heroine of epic or tragedy, and behaves accordingly. The poet's language seems to concur in her self-evaluation, but undercuts it as well. The "living Lightning" which flashes from her eyes recalls the "keener Lightnings" that "quicken in her Eyes" (I, 144); those earlier flashes, like the "purer Blush" with which they are connected (143), are the result of cosmetic manipulations. The association of ideas emphasizes the staginess of her emotive response, which is, like many aspects of Belinda, simultaneously "real" and artificial. The attribution of emotion to skies and heaven, like the comparison between the number of cards and of muses, stresses the disproportion of effect to cause; yet since it is true that Belinda's "beauty and feminine graces, of which this poem makes so much, actually are a light of daily living and one of the ordering forces of the world," the destruction of beauty involved in the destruction of a curl is in fact symbolically almost as important as Belinda thinks.[21] Nor are the lap-dogs and china, key symbols throughout the poem of society's values, merely pieces of trivia. On the contrary, the systematic association of lap dogs with men, which deprecates men, elevates the importance of dogs; and china vessels symbolize chastity, to be taken very seriously indeed.[22] Since human beings require emotional outlets, a world that restricts emotional possibility also makes arbitrary attributions of value which provide pretexts for the expression of feeling. Belinda, unaware of any gap between pretext and reality, undercuts her own dramatic performance by her blindness; Pope, through the full awareness of his elevating language, undercuts it further.

The Cave of Spleen passage makes more explicit than any other part of the poem the degree to which *The Rape of the Lock* concerns itself with psychic landscape, particularly with the mechanisms of repression and release. Here each individual image objectifies some neurotic distress. The living teapots and bottles, the fiends and snakes and lakes of liquid gold, reflect specific states of mind, although not any particular person's immediate condition. When the goddess grants her petitioner a bag containing "the Force of Female Lungs, / Sighs, Sobs, and Passions, and the War of Tongues" (IV, 83–84), when the gnome empties the bag over Belinda's head, the imagery of spleen clearly signifies the hysteria of false valuation which opposes the "good Sense" and "good Humour" Clarissa advocates. R. K. Root has suggested that "The first half of the poem draws its central comic idea from the lack of good sense . . . [in the second half] the theme becomes the lack of good humour."[23] Both lacks involve the presence of their opposites. The symbolic representations of Belinda's states of mind—the serene self-absorption of the period before the "rape," the hysterical self-indulgence afterward—generate not only comedy but serious meaning.

The conscious and willful indulgence in bad temper that characterizes the general feminine response to the violation of a lock is not merely, as Clarissa seems to suggest, a failure of proper self-control. The response is as ambiguous as the "rape." Belinda is enraged because it was not a real rape—the Baron failed to seize "Hairs less in sight" (IV, 176)—even though Thalestris argues that the rape was as real as anything else in this world of appearances. In a deeper sense, Belinda's rage is self-justifying, and the severing of the lock provides only the excuse for emotion. Although Dionysus has seemed to have no place in this society, the Baron's act unleashes the furies, and the subsequent indulgence in rage is Dionysian in abandon and sexual implication, expressing emotion in all its ambiguity for men as well as for women: "Nor fear'd the Chief th' unequal Fight to try, / Who sought no more than on his Foe to die" (V, 77–78). It is clear why Clarissa's admirable advice has no effect: she advocates inner control to a woman suffering too much from the effects of artificial external controls. The virtues of good sense and good humor are far less appealing than the immediate pleasure of unrestrained passion—a passion that has at last found a socially condoned form, given the Baron's act of violation.

Yet the passionate self-indulgence into which the characters fling themselves is almost as far removed from the true realities of their feeling as their earlier decorum. Arbitrary repression is the emotional foundation of this society, its loopholes allowing release for the forces of sexual feeling, but making those forces ridiculous by the imposition of distorting forms. The poet's mock epic presentation clarifies the folly of excessive commitment to the norms of high society. Pope resolves the comic battle by removing the pretext for emotion. Beginning his discussion of the possible fate of the lock (V, 113), he moves away from concentration on Belinda's psychic states to a more distant and "objective" point of view. The final declaration of poetry's power to preserve beauty asserts the necessity of psychic distance to create the possibility of accurate judgment and proper appreciation, which can exist only beyond the insistent pressures of social conformity, the forces of repression that create the necessity for release, however ludicrous its forms.

In *Eloisa to Abelard,* the forces of repression are more serious than those of *The Rape of the Lock.* Whereas society justifies its restrictions in the name of decorum, grace, and pleasure, the restrictions of a nunnery have higher justifications. Yet their effect, too, may be to explode the passions they purport to control. The drama, the emotion, the high rhetoric of this poem all derive from an internal conflict that the poet contemplates with morbid enthusiasm. Although it is true that "Eloisa is rather the exemplification of a theme than an imaginatively realized person," it is also true that the theme she exemplifies cannot be adequately rendered in abstract terms.[24] The poem concerns the conflict between nature and grace—between the human desire for emotional expression and the imposition of restriction in the name of God—as that conflict might be experienced by a human being. The human reality of Eloisa, in other words, is crucial to the poem; yet the result of Pope's insistent antithesis is that human reality often disappears. Reuben Brower, describing the "Ovidian poetry of sharp oppositions between values and logical positions, between emotions, or characters, or scenes," has added, "The adjectives that come to mind after reading *Eloisa to Abelard,* however sympathetically familiar we may be with the Ovidian tradition, are 'remarkable' and 'fine,' not 'how moving' or 'how convincing.' "[25] It is a curious fact that a poem manifestly concentrating on emotion and its conflicts should evoke so little emotional response in most of its readers.[26]

Since all of the action in the poem takes place in Eloisa's memory or imagination, or is formed by a mixture of the two, the heroine's sensibility determines the reader's knowledge and understanding of the facts of her experience. One is offered no point of view but hers; and her point of view is the most important fact supplied. Like Belinda, Eloisa sees herself as the center of her world:

> Canst thou forget what tears that moment fell,
> When, warm in youth, I bade the world farewell?
> As with cold lips I kiss'd the sacred veil,
> The shrines all trembled, and the lamps grew pale:
> Heav'n scarce believ'd the conquest it survey'd,
> And Saints with wonder heard the vows I made.
> (109–114)

Her world is not only social but cosmic: she sees herself as cause for wonder in "heav'n" and "Saints" as well as in other men. The intensity of her emotion is the focus of her self-esteem:

> Unequal task! a passion to resign,
> For hearts so touch'd, so pierc'd, so lost as mine.
> Ere such a soul regains its peaceful state,
> How often must it love, how often hate!
> How often, hope, despair, resent, regret,
> Conceal, disdain—do all things but forget.
> But let heav'n seize it, all at once 'tis fir'd,
> Not touch'd, but rapt, not waken'd, but inspir'd!
> (195–202)

Her implicit claim that such a soul as hers is worth struggling for, because of her special capacity for feeling, dominates the poem.

Brendan O Hehir has argued convincingly that the apparent instances of pathetic fallacy in *Eloisa to Abelard* actually represent accurate and naturalistic reporting. The trembling shrines and paling lamps Eloisa describes, he suggests, are the natural result of tear-filled eyes and the shadowing effect of her literal "taking the veil."[27] However naturalistic the explanations for what Eloisa sees, the fact remains that she herself perceives the world as subordinate to her emotions. She states this perception directly when she admits that the convent's surroundings are no longer restful:

> But o'er the twilight groves, and dusky caves,
> Long-sounding isles, and intermingled graves,
> Black Melancholy sits, and round her throws
> A death-like silence, and a dread repose:
> Her gloomy presence saddens all the scene,
> Shades ev'ry flow'r, and darkens ev'ry green,
> Deepens the murmur of the falling floods,
> And breathes a browner horror on the woods.
> Yet here for ever, ever must I stay.
>
> (163–171)

A modern historian of madness comments on eighteenth century attitudes toward the effect of strong religious commitment: "Religious beliefs prepare a kind of landscape of images, an illusory milieu favorable to every hallucination and every delirium . . . Too much moral rigor, too much anxiety about salvation and the life to come were often thought to bring on melancholia."[28] Melancholia, "the English malady," as Dr. Cheyne labeled it, is never far from Eloisa, although she is also capable of manic self-absorption; and her melancholy is fostered, if not produced, by the religious images with which her mind is stored and which her surroundings constantly reinforce. Although she objectifies "Melancholy" in a fashion that lessens its emotional immediacy for modern readers, the meaning of her account is unambiguous. She states that melancholy is inherent in her environment, full of traditional associations of death and unworldliness, but also that her feelings distort her perception of that environment. Not only is there self-indulgent pleasure in her account of the darkness of every green, the "horror" of the woods, but the same pleasure is apparent throughout the poem. It is perhaps an oversimplification to define this pleasure as Eloisa's delight in the intensity of her own feelings, yet certainly her sense of herself as a dramatic heroine is vivid throughout, and her memories of the past, her account of the present, and her fantasies of the future all reflect a sense almost of awe. The fact that Eloisa finds such enormous emotional power in her own experience may make it difficult for the reader to find as much.

This is by no means the full explanation, though, for the

poem's emotional inadequacy as a literary experience. The reader's lack of a full response may be partly conditioned by his inability to know what is expected: the uncharacteristic lack of "placing" in this poem. Its intent is clarified by its participation in Ovidian tradition, which assumes the self-sufficient interest of extravagant emotion. Yet it is difficult to accept Eloisa at her own evaluation, even for the space of the poem: one expects the intervention of a judging voice. By eighteenth century and modern standards alike, Eloisa displays a mental distress amounting to imbalance. Here is a comment by a twentieth century psychoanalyst on a psychotic patient: "The scenes that take place around her are now undissociated from the patient's inner world; nor is the ego independent in its own right, but is broken up in the objects themselves. It is for this reason that Renee hears her own protest, her own suffering and hostility in the sigh of the wind and the rustling of trees."[29] One would not care to subject Eloisa to Freudian analysis, but the description of this patient is suggestively accurate as an account of Pope's heroine. The poet's voice, however, indicates no awareness of anything wrong with his central figure. On the contrary, at the only point in the poem where one feels his existence as separate from Eloisa's, he explicitly identifies himself with the value system that dominates her. Her defining characteristics are her tendency to subordinate all reality to her emotional responses, and her belief that emotional response is self-justifying. The "bard" whose presence is felt at the end of the poem suffers, like Eloisa, from the absence of a loved one; his justification for telling her story is contained in the poem's final line: "He best can paint 'em [the woes of the sad lovers], who shall feel 'em most" (366). The verse epistle displays not only the feeling of its heroine but that of its author, who appears to accept the thesis that emotion is self-justifying and self-sufficiently interesting.

Comparison of the poem with *The Rape of the Lock* makes one aware of what is missing. *Eloisa to Abelard* too depends on an effect of magnification, but without satiric purpose, and hence, without counterpoint or commentary. To complain that Pope wrote in other genres than satire would be unreasonable. But it is surely relevant to note that in *Eloisa to Abelard* he appeared unable to replace the complexity of satire with any other real complexity: the alternations of an emotional seesaw involve only shifts of attention, not of perspective. Whether Eloisa directs her longings to God or to Abelard, her concentration remains focused on her own feelings:

> Still on that breast enamour'd let me lie,
> Still drink delicious poison from thy eye,
> Pant on thy lip, and to thy heart be prest;
> Give all thou canst—and let me dream the rest. . .
> Oh grace serene! oh virtue heav'nly fair!
> Divine oblivion of low-thoughted care!
> Fresh blooming hope, gay daughter of the sky!
> And faith, our early immortality!
> Enter each mild, each amicable guest;
> Receive, and wrap me in eternal rest!
>
> (121–124, 297–302)

The appeal to her lover is rather more convincing than the invocation of heavenly virtues, but both display the same willful intensity of self-obsession. The fact that they are so similar is one of the poem's main sources of interest: one becomes absorbed in the operations of a sensibility incapable of making real distinctions, yet torn by the sense that the making of distinctions is crucial. But the poem is confined by the sensibility it records. As one would hardly wish to be trapped in Belinda's mind without a glimpse through other eyes, it is ultimately no more interesting to be trapped in Eloisa's.

*The Rape of the Lock* concludes with the lock's, and Belinda's, achievement of transcendence through the distancing and heightening of art:

> When those fair Suns shall sett, as sett they must,
> And all those Tresses shall be laid in Dust;
> *This Lock,* the Muse shall consecrate to Fame,
> And mid'st the Stars inscribe *Belinda's* Name!
>
> (V, 147–150)

*Eloisa to Abelard* ends with Eloisa's plea for a poet to immortalize her:

Such if there be, who loves so long, so well;
Let him our sad, our tender story tell;
The well-sung woes will sooth my pensive ghost;
He best can paint 'em, who shall feel 'em most.
(363–366)

But the heightening of art is not so effective with Eloisa as with Belinda, partly because the poet chooses rhetorically to identify himself with his subject and consequently is unable fully to exploit the values that his kind of verse embodies. Murray Krieger has commented perceptively on "the glaring inappropriateness of Pope's epigrammatically contrived heroic couplet to the would-be spontaneity of Eloisa's outpourings . . . I think we can see the impropriety of form as symptomatic of Pope's general problem in the poem: His classic need for order must override whatever chaotic tendencies there may be in his materials, however existentially resistant they prove to be . . . Pope imposes his rhetorical structure upon the recalcitrant materials he has let loose from the well-springs of Eloisa's mind, imposes it with the very rigor we find in the careful couplets that package (and inhibit) her passionate cries."[30] The inappropriateness of rigor to passion symptomizes Eloisa's problem as well as Pope's. The heroine resolves it by pretending the two are identical: the "order" of convent life provides an opportunity for the refocusing of her tempestuous feelings. It does not control the forces of "nature," only redirects them. Although the passionate woman recognizes at least verbally the necessity of discipline, she never accepts its value; nor does anything in the poem, except the couplet form itself, imply true awareness of that value.

In *The Rape of the Lock,* as in all Pope's great work, form reiterates content. The importance of beauty, grace, and delicacy, the positive qualities embodied by Belinda and her guardian sylphs, emerges in the grace of the couplets, which also reveal the possibility that beauty can coexist with integral discipline, the aesthetic equivalent of that ethical control which Clarissa recommends but cannot impose. What Belinda cannot accomplish in life, the poet can achieve through art; and his manifest affection for his heroine depends partly on the fact that she is purified and elevated by being contained in a poem. Eloisa, in contrast, is inadequately contained. Pope's "careful couplets" are not careful enough: the kind of feeling they render, the necessities of the first-person point of view, produce flaccidity of verse as well as of sentiment. The two sets of couplets last quoted are in this respect representative of the poems from which they come. The lines from *The Rape of the Lock* contain a single adjective; those from *Eloisa* include ten adjectives and adverbs. These modifiers reiterate a single point: the insistent emotionalism of the story. Though semicolons separate the lines, there is no sense of forward movement, only a rather aimless circularity. Eloisa's tone is tentative, hopeful, self-indulgent; it creates little authority. In contrast, the absolute clarity and conviction of the two couplets from *The Rape of the Lock* are striking. Verbs carry the weight of meaning, which moves inevitably forward to the exclamation point at the end. A lucid point of view creates verse of lucidity.

The problem of discipline versus expressivity, in other words, is fully worked out in *The Rape of the Lock,* in action and language. Eloisa, however, is unable to resolve this problem for herself, and the poet does not resolve it in his verse. Both poems use narcissistic heroines to explore the values and the dangers of repression, external and internal; but only one of them carries the exploration to a meaningful resolution.

"There are more metaphors of the mind and references to mental institutions in the literature of this century than literary critics have noticed—indeed the artist's personal struggle to define himself in relation to the world of sanity or insanity is so pervasive that it may be called a leitmotif."[31] The concern with the prevalence of mental instability and with the nature of psychic well-being explicit in *Epistle to Dr. Arbuthnot* and *Epistle to Bathurst,* implicit even in such a *jeu d'esprit as The Rape of the Lock* (" 'Tis a sort of writing very like tickling"[32]), comes to fruition in *The Dunciad,* in which the problem of madness becomes a metaphysical issue. The satire thus suggests how "the artist's personal struggle to define himself in relation to the world of sanity or insanity" may expand its implications far beyond the personal.

Erasmus, in his account of human folly, describes a symbolic dance in which Madness, or Folly, leads a throng of human weaknesses: "*Philautia* [Self-Love] is the first figure Folly leads out in her dance, but that is because they are linked by a privileged relation: self-attachment is the first sign of madness, but it is because man is attached to himself that he accepts error as truth, lies as reality, violence and ugliness as beauty and justice."[33] Such a state of affairs can be social as well as individual; in *The Dunciad* it is both. The poem's initial setting is "Close to those walls where Folly holds her throne, / And laughs to think Monroe would take her down" (I, 29–30). Folly, closely linked to the anarchic power of dullness, broods over the dullards' world, laughing at the pretensions of Bedlam's doctor, who fancies himself able to triumph over the goddess Dulness. That laugh echoes hollowly through *The Dunciad,* aimed also at the pretensions of the poet who thinks he will locate and effectually attack the operations of folly and dullness. "For as when madmen are found incurable, wise men give 'em their way, and please 'em as well as they can," Pope wrote in an early letter, "so when those more incorrigible things, poets, are once irrecoverably be-mused, the best way both to quiet them, and to secure ourselves from the effects of their frenzy, is to feed their vanity, which indeed for the most part is all that's overfed in a poet."[34] Vanity is always the problem; the special attachment of folly and self-love operates at all intellectual and social levels. *The Dunciad* is a series of studies in solipsism and its spreading effects: corrupt values, then madness.

To connect dullness, self-love, and madness as operative forces in *The Dunciad* is not mere word-play. Insanity is a steady, hidden metaphor of the poem, emerging sometimes in clear references. In a detailed and concrete way, Pope is describing a world gone mad. He is thus suggesting the special ineluctability of Dulness' power, the impression that all her arguments, both verbal and enacted, are unanswerable: there is no place to stand and answer. She rules the mind "In native Anarchy" (I, 16); hers is the natural mental state, conquered with difficulty, prevented from new dominion only by ceaseless effort. At the beginning of the poem there is Bedlam; at the end, all is darkness: the destruction of the good of intellect spreads from asylum to universe.

Madness often displays itself through an individual's commitment to a personal system of imagery. "Thinking [exclusively] by symbol and image [is] a type of thinking primarily self-centered."[35] Involving concentration on private symbols of meaning, such thinking may reject the discipline of systematic logic and syntax to produce an incoherent phantasmagoria of references whose relevance to one another and to reality remains obscure; or the madman's imagery may display frightening coherence, predicated on false assumptions but consistent within its limits. *The Dunciad* supplies both kinds. Books II and IV, especially, contain duncelike systems of imagery conspicuous for their logic, their sense of inevitability. Books I and III make heavier use of chaotic sequences that demonstrate another mode of Dulness' operations.

Book III, like Book I, begins with Bedlam:

> Then raptures high the seat of Sense o'erflow,
> Which only heads refin'd from Reason know.
> Hence, from the straw where Bedlam's Prophet nods,
> He hears loud Oracles, and talks with Gods.
>
> (III, 5–8)

Bays is led toward the underworld by "A slip-shod Sibyl . . . In lofty madness meditating song" (15–16). The vision he there sees is his because he is, as Settle points out, "born to see what none can see awake!" (43): his mental equipment makes dreams easier than reality for him to absorb. It is relevant that Bays's "folly," here exemplified by his predilection for dreams, can also—as in the long tradition of the literature of folly—produce wisdom, although he himself is unable to make use of it. The ambiguity about the truth or falsity of the vision in Book III reflects the ambiguity of the fool's position; his very lack of perceptual capacity may enable him to see what wiser men cannot, since the "wide awake" men of the world are often blind to the reality of dreams.

The dream version of reality that comprises most of the book is a view of chaos, given an illusory facade of order:

> Jacob, the scourge of Grammar, mark with awe,
> Nor less revere him, blunderbuss of law.

Lo P—p—le's brow, tremendous to the town,
Horneck's fierce eye, and Roome's funereal Frown.
Lo sneering Goode, half malice and half whim,
A Fiend in glee, ridiculously grim.
Each Cygnet sweet of Bath and Tunbridge race,
Whose tuneful whistling makes the waters pass:
Each Songster, Riddler, ev'ry nameless name,
All crowd, who foremost shall be damn'd to Fame.
Some strain in rhyme; the Muses, on their racks,
Scream like the winding of ten thousand jacks:
Some free from rhyme or reason, rule or check,
Break Priscian's head, and Pegasus's neck;
Down, down they larum, with impetuous whirl,
The Pindars, and the Miltons of a Curl.
  Silence, ye Wolves! while Ralph to Cynthia howls,
And makes Night hideous—Answer him, ye Owls!
(149–166)

The illusion of order comes from the guide's air of rationality and plausibility; his syntax is that of a man locating salient features of a comprehended panorama. His cries of "lo" and "mark" demand the viewer's comprehension. By his use of "each," "all," and "some," he classifies what he shows, and his tone insists that the appropriate response is a sight-seer's wonder. A further superficial impression of unity is provided by the fact that all the men named are writers; they therefore "belong" together.

But the jarring sequence of images counteracts the passage's surface plausibility. In eighteen lines, one finds a scourge, a blunderbuss, a fiend, swans, racks (for torture or for cooking), roasting jacks, Pegasus, wolves, and owls. Although many of these images have in common associations of destructiveness, cygnets and cooking implements, Pegasus and owls, violate this principle of consistency. The principle, indeed, seems to be one of inconsistency, supported by violations of logic and probability in the actions and appearance of the figures evoked. A man may be named "Goode" yet compounded of malice and whim, his glee fiendish, his grimness ridiculous. The whistling of cygnets mysteriously affects waters.

Writers vie for the privilege of being damned, muses scream, those who might aspire to ride Pegasus break his neck, the poet of night makes his subject hideous. There is no "rhyme or reason, rule or check" to offer a principle of control; this is the madness of a literary life without discipline. The meaningless noise of a blunderbuss—screaming, "laruming," howling, whistling—adds the final note of chaos, threatening total disorder.

The organizing function of imagery is vital in Pope's poetry, but so are imagery's possibilities for disorganization. Bays's dream, reflecting his mind, is chaotic. Like Adam, he will wake to find it truth, revealing what underlies civilization's apparent order. Bays's dream is the poet's nightmare, its deliberate incoherencies displaying the madness that Pope sees everywhere in his society. The descriptions of theatrical extravagance which provide the most obvious exemplification of the possibilities of disorder within Bays's mind are no more bizarre than the simple facts of literary life as lived and perceived.

Mental disorder is madness. It reduces men to animals; or it may be understood as demonic possession. Both metaphors for madness prevail in *The Dunciad's* presentation of the real world, where men resemble wolves, owls, or baby swans, but reveal their fiendishness in action and appearance. The "demonic" imagery that Northrop Frye has described as characteristic of the ironic mode also suggests "the world that desire totally rejects: the world of the nightmare and the scapegoat, of bondage and pain and confusion . . . the world also of perverted or wasted work, ruins and catacombs, instruments of torture and monuments of folly . . . [It] is closely linked with an existential hell, like Dante's *Inferno*, or with the hell that man creates on earth."[36] Confusions, wasted work, monuments of folly—these are the hellish emblems of a world gone mad, and of the diabolical nature of its possession by dullness.

Books II and IV are in some ways most emphatic in their image-making. Book II, closely unified by its concentration on the parody of heroic games, provides particularly striking images of two kinds. There are the large images of grotesque action, as of Lintot in the footrace:

lab'ring on, with shoulders, hands, and head,
Wide as a wind-mill all his figures spread,
With arms expanded Bernard rows his state.
(II, 65–67)

Another is Osborne in the urinating contest:

First Osborne lean'd against his letter'd post;
It rose, and labour'd to a curve at most . . .
A second effort brought but new disgrace,
The wild Meander wash'd the Artist's face.
(II, 171–172, 175–176)

And there are presentations of individual human beings who seem literally reduced to images, imitations of reality rather than living people:

See in the circle next, Eliza plac'd,
Two babes of love close clinging to her waist;
Fair as before her works she stands confess'd,
In flow'rs and pearls by bounteous Kirkall dress'd . . .
Fast by, like Niobe (her children gone)
Sits Mother Osborne, stupify'd to stone!
(II, 157–160, 311–312)

Both kinds of imagery have the flavor of madness.

The sense of madness in the imagery of action depends on the apparent madness of the participants, on their mindless dedication to grotesque and ridiculous activity, their insane competitiveness for worthless prizes, their lack of emotional response to enveloping ugliness, and their excessive response to offered rewards. Lintot, like a giant bird, "rows" along, a comic but horrible figure, to be defeated by the power of excrement. His defeat, like his effort, is funny; and the account of it displays Pope's penetrating, judging wit. Yet one's pleasure in comedy and wit is modified by the horror of the grotesque. Each bit of action is precisely, pictorially imagined. Pope demands that the reader see Lintot, see the details of the urinating contest. Though the imagination recoils from the scenes, it is yet forced to dwell on their details. And the details—Lintot's outstretched arms and laboring shoulders, Osborne's laboring stream of urine, blown back into his face—insistently define a world gone comically awry.

The sense of madness inheres in the large panorama as well as in the psychological states of its participants. Book II has a striking cumulative effect, the result of the repeated impact of a multiplicity of images. The participants in the games comprise an entire society. Though they do different things, their differences add up to an identity. As the mind struggles to make sense of the diverse and distasteful details, it is forced to generalize. The spectacle of chaos demands lucidity, which illumines and judges what it sees, finding it subhuman, mindless, diabolical—mad. Only by this sort of generalization can one deal with the disorderly sequence of ludicrous yet horrifying activity presented.

Throughout Book II one encounters people who are really phantoms of air, or versions of their own frontispieces, or figures in a tapestry, or men turned to stone who have thereby effected no real alteration in their condition. The meaning of such figures is like that of mindless action: they exemplify the subhuman nature of their own commitments. But their imaginative impact is separable from their ideational meaning. As individual images, varied but repetitive, they create a strange depopulated world—depopulated despite the fact that it is filled with frenzied activity. On the level of abstraction, one can say that Curll's delight at seeing himself depicted in full ignominy is an example of his lack of discrimination:

> Himself among the story'd chiefs he spies,
> As from the blanket high in air he flies,
> 'And oh! (he cry'd) what street, what lane but knows,
> Our purging, pumpings, blankettings, and blows?'
> (II, 151–154)

But the more immediate effect of the vivid evocation of the earless, cudgeled, "flagrant" (148) misdoers as depicted in tapestry is to suggest that they are "realer" in this rendition than in their actual lives. And since it is tempting to draw analogies between one form of art and another, this fact is relevant to the situation of bad writers being given permanency in *The Dunciad.* As Pope himself suggested—and Dr. Johnson after him—many of his victims owe their immortality to his attacks. Curll's pleasure in seeing himself preserved in cloth reflects his subliminal awareness of the lack of substantiality in his nature and his fame. Phantom poets seem as valuable as real ones to such publishers; the woman as mere frontispiece-image is a prize to be eagerly sought; and the noble lord whose power derives from his passivity is an object of respect. The reality of these men as human beings seems hypothetical; their unreality is far more striking.

The questioning of reality conveyed by and through the dunces implies a pseudometaphysic that suggests how the force of dullness, operative in individual minds, finally darkens the universe. The metaphor of madness offers a fruitful approach to understanding this questioning in relation to Pope's other work. The dunces, whose reality is self-created, are logical developments from the self-obsession of Eloisa, or Helluo, or Atossa: they represent the ultimate consequence of self-love. A poet so centrally concerned with the establishment and preservation of effective limits—æsthetic, intellectual, ethical, and social—must fear the result of limits ignored or violated; and the consequence of violated intellectual controls is dullness or madness. Or perhaps the two are identical: certainly those whom Pope labels "dull" often act psychotic. To charge that the poets, educators, noblemen, and scientists whom society honors are mad is to imply again that society itself is sick, and thus to explain its lack of discrimination, its inability to separate true from false, real from unreal, human being from inanimate object. This view unites the world of *The Dunciad* with that of the *Moral Epistles* and of the *Epilogue to the Satires,* in which unreasoning masses duplicate the mindless motion of the dunces in rushing to worship at the shrine not of Dulness but of Vice. It recalls the discussion in *Epistle to Dr. Arbuthnot* of the ways madness threatens the preservation of the good, and Pope's many accounts of the precariousness of moral and mental sanity. The sinister significance of the darkened mind is apparent if such darkness is insanity.

As the similarity of Dulness' role and Vice's suggests, Pope's discriminations between the sane and insane are as much moral as intellectual; the metaphor of madness enforces his belief in the ultimate moral significance of setting limits in all areas of human activity. The aesthetic control of the couplet, the intellectual control of proper education, the social control of established hierarchy—all alike respect the imperatives of moral insight, aware of consequences, demanding discipline. Conversely, *The Dunciad's* world of vanished or arbitrary limitation is one of moral incoherence.

*The Dunciad*'s madness seems total, and threatening. Like the visions of insanity, this picture of the world has a weird persuasive power, and like most insane visions, it makes one feel how intolerable would be its reality. So the reader rejects it, laughs at it, remarks its grotesque exaggerations; the fundamental premises of this society seem almost as unacceptable as the assumption that it is conceivable to eat children. The poem's coherence of structure and, even more, the rational intelligence implicit in literary imitation and parody, assure one that this is not a madman's view of the world, but a satirist's. Yet the threat implicit in the satirist's view is a version of the threat of madness. By placing his society slightly askew, exaggerating the details he observes, he reveals the menace of total irrationality implicit in the erosion of standards demonstrated in conduct and judgment.

As Aubrey Williams and Alvin Kernan in different ways have shown, Book IV is the most tightly organized section of *The Dunciad*, conveying a sense of inexorable movement, purposeful in its purposelessness, toward ultimate denial of all positive values.[37] The systematic organization of the characters into those who misuse and misvalue things and those who do the same with words controls the imagery. But the imagery of this book has a special quality because it belongs to a world explicitly declared to have yielded to madness:

> Now flam'd the Dog-star's unpropitious ray,
> Smote ev'ry Brain, and wither'd ev'ry Bay;
> Sick was the Sun, the Owl forsook his bow'r,
> The moon-struck Prophet felt the madding hour.
> (IV, 9–12)

Among the banished, bound, or murdered abstractions of value, "Mad *Mathesis* alone was unconfin'd, / Too mad for mere material chains to bind" (31–32): madness qualifies its possessor for successful (that is, "unconfin'd") existence in this decayed society, whose inhabitants dramatize through speech and action the meaning of a civilization without controls, in which form and content have become divorced.

At one extreme is Bentley, "that awful Aristarch" (203), consumed with a sense of his own grandeur. Here is the final passage of his long speech:

> What tho' we let some better sort of fool
> Thrid ev'ry science, run thro' ev'ry school?
> Never by tumbler thro' the hoops was shown
> Such skill in passing all, and touching none.
> He may indeed (if sober all this time)
> Plague with Dispute, or persecute with Rhyme.
> We only furnish what he cannot use,
> Or wed to what he must divorce, a Muse:
> Full in the midst of Euclid dip at once,
> And petrify a Genius to a Dunce:
> Or set on Metaphysic ground to prance,
> Show all his paces, not a step advance.
> With the same Cement, ever sure to bind,
> We bring to one dead level ev'ry mind.
> Then take him to devellop, if you can,
> And hew the Block off, and get out the Man.
>
> (IV, 255–270)

Bentley explains how education has become a mere form, whose content contradicts its purpose. He shows his total contempt for students and for study: metaphors of tumblers and prancing horses are appropriate descriptions of intellectual accomplishment; the highest achievement of the aspiring scholar is to "plague" or "persecute"; the educator at his best achieves petrifaction of his victims and creates a block where none existed before. The educator's artistry destroys humanity. The contrast between the verbs identifying the student and those applied to his teachers exemplify the poles of intellectual activity. The teachers are manipulative to no purpose, or to destructive ends: at best they "let" the fool indulge in his folly; at worst they "furnish what he cannot use" or "petrify" him or "set" him on the ground where he can only prance. The student is vigorous in degrading activities: he threads the maze of science, runs through the schools, touches nothing in his frenzy of motion. He can plague, persecute, or divorce, but he cannot use what is valuable. If he is to turn into a man, it will be by the efforts of others, not his own; his own efforts are meaningless, a paradigm of the meaningless intellectual activity throughout *The Dunciad*. Bentley reveals by his imagery how matters of the utmost importance are converted to insignificance.

At the other extreme is the devotee of butterflies:

> Of all th' enamel'd race, whose silv'ry wing
> Waves to the tepid Zephyrs of the spring,
> Or swims along the fluid atmosphere,
> Once brightest shin'd this child of Heat and Air.
> I saw, and started from its vernal bow'r
> The rising game, and chac'd from flow'r to flow'r.
> It fled, I follow'd; now in hope, now pain;
> It stopt, I stopt; it mov'd, I mov'd again.
> At last it fix'd, 'twas on what plant it pleas'd,
> And where it fix'd, the beauteous bird I seiz'd:
> Rose or Carnation was below my care;
> I meddle, Goddess! only in my sphere.
>
> (IV, 421–432)

His concerns are transcendentally insignificant, but his language and imagery lend them apparent dignity. The allusion to *Paradise Lost* not only points to the self-love implicit in this naturalist's limited perceptions, but also calls special attention to the elevating power of language. The pastoral grace of the opening couplets makes one accept for the moment the speaker's evaluation of the object of his pursuit. By the time it becomes a "beauteous bird," the valuation attached to it is manifestly false; but poetic diction has enabled the speaker to avoid ever calling his object by its proper name, and has lulled the reader into temporary complacency equivalent to the butterfly hunter's. The next line of his speech is, "I tell the naked fact without disguise": a fine irony. The delicacy, the total lack of satiric bite in the imagery itself, contribute to the ultimate satiric purpose, reiterating the obscurantism implicit in all Dulness' activities. The misleading use of language is part of the misleading attitude toward objects, and the two are finally inseparable. Whereas Bentley degrades large concerns, the butterfly lover elevates petty ones, and both have the same effect.

Like the visions of earlier books, the total picture of Book IV is a construct of madness. Though I have been using the idea of madness as a loose metaphor for all kinds of disturbing imagery and concepts, it is in fact a serious symbol of what is going on in *The Dunciad.* According to a modern historian, the eighteenth century theory of madness depended on the linkage of false images with rational forms: "Madness fills the void of error with images, and links hallucinations by affirmation of the false. In a sense, it is thus plenitude, joining to the figures of night the powers of day, to the forms of fantasy the activity of the waking mind; it links the dark content with the forms of light. But is not such plenitude actually *the culmination of the void*?"[38] In the fourth book of *The Dunciad,* the plenitude of dullness, the total envelopment at the end, is a plenitude of vacuity. The grotesque images of madness, in a frighteningly logical context, reveal the laws of their nature; the dark content of the poet's fantasies of ultimate horror is linked with "the forms of light," of rational discourse. Pope's demonstration of disparity between form and content presents the world as seen by a madman, and as populated by madmen.

Perhaps it is one of the peculiar energies of satire to produce such effects. Swift's *Modest Proposal* makes readers feel that either the projector is mad or they are; only such language adequately describes the extremity of emotional effect. Given such an effect, such a reaction, one seeks desperately the evidence of rational control implicit in coherent satiric purpose. The reader becomes vulnerable, in other words, to the satirist's serious intent because he has been made to feel that the alternatives are to believe the satirist mad—a remote possibility, given a writer of such control as Pope—or to believe the world is mad. Because madness is realer than demonology to the twentieth century, it is perhaps more relevant to understand the characteristic image patterns of satire as "insane" rather than "demonic." The insane is in fact more than demonic. It combines the terror of the nonrational with that of the supernaturally powerful, suggesting the power of animal noncomprehension in combination with the power of superhuman insight and penetration. The force of *The Dunciad* depends on its capacity to terrify, to invoke the reader's nonrational fears as well as his rational commitments. At best it presents a nightmare, from which one may hope to wake; its terror derives from its suggestions that there may be nothing else to wake to.

Pope's interest in madness, as metaphor and as point of reference, reflects the concern with the relation of form to content manifest everywhere in his work. His characteristic coherence of technique, the way in which the aesthetic disciplines of his verse reflect the ethical standards he advocates, is a display of sanity; but his insistence, in poetry and in prose, that poets and madmen are closely allied may explain the compulsiveness of that display. Satire provides a permissible release for the maddest energies of poetic impulse, disciplined by the necessities of logic and of form. The satirist can use his wildest fantasies to social ends, can fearlessly indulge in extravagant visions. Critics disturbed by Swift's misanthropy have persistently invoked insanity as the explanation for it; the fact suggests that satire at its most forceful may seem to its readers frighteningly close to madness.

Pope never sufficiently relaxes the control he advocates to allow anyone the critical hypothesis that insanity might be the source of his visions. His use of the imagery of madness exemplifies not only his control but also his capacity to take risks, for the suggestion that mental imbalance is omnipresent might provide a convenient pretext for dismissing his condemnation of social and individual corruption as one more instance of distorted rationality. And his images of the world as inhabited by madmen vividly reveal the sense of the unity of *ethos* and *pathos* that underlies all his work. Concerned with conduct as he and his contemporaries characteristically were, he was also interested in the emotional significance of action.

James Harris, around the middle of the eighteenth century, concluded that poetry was superior to painting as an art, "In as much as no Subjects of Painting are *wholly superior* to Poetry; while the Subjects, here described [manners, passions, sentiments], *far exceed the Power* of Painting—in as much as they are of *all* Subjects the most *affecting*, and *improving*, and such of which we have the strongest Comprehension."[39] Harris' point is that poetry has other resources than the visual imagery to which painting is confined. But Pope, while making full use of those other resources, also demonstrates how manners, passions, and sentiments, always his concern, can be rendered and judged through poetic imagery. The imagery of madness is valuable because it evokes strong emotional response, forces readers to feel as the poet wishes about the moral deviations he depicts. Action is a proper cause for feeling; feeling leads in turn to action. Only in *Eloisa to Abelard* does Pope present pathos as self-sufficiently interesting. Elsewhere, he exploits emotional possibility through imagery, characterization, and commentary, requires emotional response, and implies that right feeling must produce right thought and action. Images of madness are the most extreme examples of his imagery's emotional demands. They exemplify the extraordinary ambition of Pope's poetic effort: to discipline passion without destroying it; to display the aesthetic and moral values of both passion and control.

Notes

Index

# Notes

## One: The Controlling Image

1. Erik H. Erikson, *Gandhi's Truth: On the Origins of Militant Nonviolence* (New York: W. W. Norton, 1969), p. 34.

2. Samuel Johnson, *The Vanity of Human Wishes,* ll. 345–346, *Poems,* ed. E. L. McAdam, Jr., with George Milne, The Yale Edition, vol. VI (New Haven: Yale University Press, 1964), pp. 107–108.

3. Pope, *Epistle* I, i, 167–168, *Imitations of Horace,* ed. John Butt, The Twickenham Edition, vol. IV (New Haven: Yale University Press, 1961), p. 291. Succeeding references in the text to Pope's poems are also to the Twickenham Edition.

4. Martin Price, *To the Palace of Wisdom: Studies in Order and Energy from Dryden to Blake* (Garden City: Doubleday, 1964), pp. 144, 148.

5. Pope, *Imitations of Horace,* ed. Butt, p. 9.

6. The play metaphor is Pope's contribution. Horace at this point uses the image of a feast.

7. Price, *To the Palace of Wisdom,* p. 225.

8. Philippe Ariès, *Centuries of Childhood: A Social History of Family Life,* trans. Robert Baldick (New York: Random House, 1962), p. 25.

9. Maynard Mack, *The Garden and the City: Retirement and Politics in the Later Poetry of Pope, 1731–1743* (Toronto: University of Toronto Press, 1969).

10. Pope to Allen, July 6, 1738, *The Correspondence of Alexander Pope,* ed. George Sherburn (Oxford: The Clarendon Press, 1956), IV, 108–109.

11. Pope and Bolingbroke to Swift, [March 1731/2], *Correspondence,* III, 276.

12. Pope to Arbuthnot, Sept. 3 [1734], *Correspondence,* III, 431.

13. Pope to Fortescue, August 23, 1735, *Correspondence,* III, 486.

14. Samuel Johnson, *Lives of the English Poets,* ed. George Birkbeck Hill (Oxford: University Press, 1905), III, 247.

15. Dryden, "Dedication of the Aeneis," *Essays of John Dryden,* ed. W. P. Ker (Oxford: The Clarendon Press, 1900), II, 161.

16. *Spectator* #420, July 2, 1712, in *The Spectator*, ed. George A. Aitken (London, 1898), VI, 116–117.

17. *Spectator* #421, July 3, 1712, in Aitken, VI, 121–122.

18. Dryden, "The Author's Apology for Heroic Poetry and Poetic License," *Essays of John Dryden*, I, 186.

19. John Aikin, *An Essay on the Application of Natural History to Poetry* (Warrington, 1777), p. 95.

20. Meyer Abrams, *The Mirror and the Lamp: Romantic Theory and the Critical Tradition* (New York: Norton, 1958).

21. *Spectator* #411, June 21, 1712, in Aitken, VI, 72.

22. Thomas Tickell, "De Poesi Didactica" (1711), in Richard Eustace Tickell, *Thomas Tickell and the Eighteenth Century Poets (1685–1740)* (London: Constable, 1931), p. 201.

23. William Duff, *An Essay on Original Genius* (London, 1767), pp. 146–147.

24. G. Wilson Knight, *Laureate of Peace: On the Genius of Alexander Pope* (New York: Oxford University Press, 1955), p. 24.

25. W. J. Bate, *The Burden of the Past and the English Poet* (Cambridge, Mass.: Harvard University Press, Belknap Press, 1970), pp. 20–21.

## Two: Wit Governing Wit: *An Essay on Criticism*

1. Byron to Murray, March 1821, in G. Wilson Knight, *Laureate of Peace: On the Genius of Alexander Pope* (New York: Oxford University Press, 1955), p. 140; T. E. Hulme, *Speculations: Essays on Humanism and the Philosophy of Art*, ed. Herbert Read (New York: Harcourt, Brace, 1924), p. 134.

2. See Aubrey Williams' Introduction to *An Essay on Criticism* in Pope, *Pastoral Poetry and An Essay on Criticism*, ed. E. Audra and Aubrey Williams, the Twickenham Edition, vol. I (New Haven: Yale University Press, 1961), pp. 212–218.

3. For wit's various meanings to Pope, see Williams' Introduction in Pope, *Postoral Poetry*, pp. 212–218; William Empson, *The Structure of Complex Words* (Norfolk, Conn.: New Directions, 1951), pp. 84–100; E. N. Hooker, "Pope on Wit: The *Essay on Criticism*," in *The Seventeenth Century . . . By Richard Foster Jones and Others Writing in His Honor* (Stanford: Stanford University Press, 1951), pp. 225–246.

4. Pope, *The Iliad of Homer*, ed. Maynard Mack, the Twickenham Edition, vol. VII (New Haven: Yale University Press, 1967), p. 188.

5. See Maynard Mack's Introduction to Pope, *The Iliad*, VII, xlvi-xlvii; Williams' Introduction in Pope, *Pastoral Poetry*, p. 214.

6. Pope's Preface to *The Iliad*, VII, 9.

7. Jacob H. Adler, "Balance in Pope's *Essays*," *English Studies*, 43

(1962), 438–439.

8. Williams' Introduction in Pope, *Pastoral Poetry,* p. 224.

9. Donald Greene, "'Logical Structure' in Eighteenth-Century Poetry," *Philological Quarterly,* 31 (1952), 330.

10. Horace, *Ars Poetica,* ll. 60–69, *Satires, Epistles and Ars Poetica,* with an English translation by H. Rushton Fairclough (London: William Heinemann, 1929), pp. 454–457.

11. Maynard Mack, ed., *The Augustans* (Englewood Cliffs, N.J.: Prentice-Hall, 1961), pp. 22–23.

12. See also Mack, ed., *The Augustans,* p. 23; William Bysshe Stein, "Pope's 'An Essay on Criticism': The Play of Sophia," *Bucknell Review,* 13 (1965), 73–86.

13. John Aden, "*'First* Follow Nature': Strategy and Stratification in *An Essay on Criticism,*" *Journal of English and Germanic Philology,* 55 (1956), 604–617.

14. Meyer Abrams, *The Mirror and the Lamp: Romantic Theory and the Critical Tradition* (New York: Norton, 1958), *passim.*

15. Richard Harter Fogle supports this point in connection with Pope's Coleridgean metaphors. Fogle, "Metaphors of Organic Unity in Pope's *Essay on Criticism,*" *Tulane Studies in English,* 13 (1963), 51–58.

16. Pope, *The Iliad* XIV, 457, Twickenham Ed., VIII, 186.

17. *Spectator* #253, December 20, 1711, in *The Spectator,* ed. George A. Aitken (London, 1898), IV, 10.

18. *The Works of John Sheffield . . . Duke of Buckingham,* 2nd ed. (London, 1729), I, 128–129.

19. Rosemond Tuve, *Elizabethan and Metaphysical Imagery* (Chicago: University of Chicago Press, 1947), p. 183.

20. Pope, *The Dunciad,* ed. James Sutherland, The Twickenham Edition, vol. V (New Haven: Yale University Press, 1963), pp. 205–206.

21. Caroline F. E. Spurgeon, *Shakespeare's Imagery and What It Tells Us* (New York: Macmillan, 1936), p. 9.

22. Boileau, *L'Art Poétique,* IV, 121–124, *Oeuvres Poétiques,* ed. F. Brunetière (Paris: Librairie Hachette, 1918), p. 225. Translation mine.

23. Thomas R. Edwards, Jr., *This Dark Estate: A Reading of Pope* (Berkeley: University of California Press, 1963), p. 18.

24. Williams identifies a source for this idea in Quintilian, in his Introduction in Pope, *Pastoral Poetry,* p. 231.

25. Pope, *The Iliad* V, 1054, Twickenham Ed., VII, 317.

26. Empson, *Structure of Complex Words,* p. 84.

27. Pope to Wycherley, April 10, 1706, *The Correspondence of Alexander Pope,* ed. George Sherburn (Oxford: The Clarendon Press, 1956), I, 16.

28. Pope to Cromwell, December 17, 1710, *Correspondence,* I, 109–110.

29. Pope to Wycherley, November 20, 1707, *Correspondence*, I, 34.

30. Abraham Cowley, "Ode. Of Wit," ll. 33–40, *The Complete Works in Verse and Prose*, ed. Alexander B. Grosart (Edinburgh, 1881), I, 135–136.

31. Tuve, *Elizabethan and Metaphysical Imagery*, p. 61.

32. Reuben Arthur Brower, *Alexander Pope: The Poetry of Allusion* (Oxford: The Clarendon Press, 1959), p. 200.

## Three: Word and Vision: Donne's *Anniversarie* Poems and *An Essay on Man*

1. Martin Kallich, *Heav'n's First Law: Rhetoric and Order in Pope's* Essay on Man (DeKalb, Ill.: Northern Illinois University Press, 1967).

2. Josephine Miles, "Toward a Theory of Style and Change," *Journal of Aesthetics and Art Criticism*, 22 (1963), 64.

3. Kenneth MacLean, *John Locke and English Literature of the Eighteenth Century* (New Haven: Yale University Press, 1936), p. 13.

4. John Newbery, *The Art of Poetry on a New Plan* (London, 1762), I, 47.

5. Thomas Tickell, "De Poesi Didactica" (1711), in Richard Eustace Tickell, *Thomas Tickell and the Eighteenth Century Poets (1685–1740)* (London: Constable, 1931), pp. 199, 203.

6. Pope, *An Essay on Man*, ed. Maynard Mack, The Twickenham Edition, vol. III i (New Haven: Yale University Press, 1958), p. 7.

7. J. M. Cameron, "Doctrinal to an Age: Notes Towards a Revaluation of Pope's *Essay on Man*," in Maynard Mack, ed., *Essential Articles for the Study of Alexander Pope*, rev. and enl. ed. (Hamden, Conn.: Archon Books, 1968), p. 366.

8. Pope, *An Essay on Man*, p. lv.

9. Ernest Lee Tuveson, *The Imagination as a Means of Grace: Locke and the Aesthetics of Romanticism* (Berkeley and Los Angeles: University of California Press, 1960), p. 22.

10. William Bowman Piper, *The Heroic Couplet* (Cleveland, Ohio: The Press of Case Western Reserve University, 1969), p. 131.

11. Kallich, *Heav'n's First Law*, p. 17.

12. Piper, *The Heroic Couplet*, p. 137.

13. Pope, *An Essay on Man*, p. 7.

14. Carol Johnson, *Reason's Double Agents* (Chapel Hill: The University of North Carolina Press, 1966), p. 28.

15. John Donne, *The First Anniversarie: An Anatomy of the World*, l. 37, *The Anniversaries*, ed. Frank Manley (Baltimore: The Johns Hopkins Press, 1963), p. 68. All succeeding references in the text to Donne's poems are from this edition.

16. Johnson, *Reason's Double Agents*, p. 43.

17. Maynard Mack, " 'Wit and Poetry and Pope': Some Observations on His Imagery," in James L. Clifford, ed., *Eighteenth-Century English Literature: Modern Essays in Criticism* (New York: Oxford University Press, 1959), p. 24.

18. Rosemond Tuve, *Elizabethan and Metaphysical Imagery* (Chicago: University of Chicago Press, 1947), p. 175.

19. John Donne, *Sermons*, VI, 333, quoted in *The Anniversaries*, p. 134.

20. *Spectator* #62, May 11, 1711, in *The Spectator*, ed. George A. Aitken (London, 1898), I, 320–324.

21. Francis Bacon, *Of the Proficience and Advancement of Learning, Divine and Humane* (London, 1605), Book II, fol. 47r.

22. John Barton, *The Art of Rhetorick Concisely and Compleatly Handled* (London, 1634), p. 16.

23. Jean Hagstrum, *The Sister Arts: The Tradition of Literary Pictorialism and English Poetry from Dryden to Gray* (Chicago: University of Chicago Press, 1958), p. 140.

24. Joseph Spence, *Observations, Anecdotes, and Characters of Books and Men*, ed. James M. Osborn (Oxford: The Clarendon Press, 1966), I, 187.

25. *Spectator* #411, June 21, 1712, in Aitken, VI, 72.

26. Milton Allan Rugoff, *Donne's Imagery: A Study in Creative Sources* (New York: Russell and Russell, 1962), p. 240.

27. John Gay, Fable XLIX, "The Man and the Flea," 11. 41, 45–46, *The Poetical Works*, ed. G. C. Faber (London: Oxford University Press, 1926), p. 273.

28. John Dennis, *Advancement and Reformation of Poetry*, Epistle Dedicatory, *The Critical Works of John Dennis*, ed. Edward Niles Hooker (Baltimore: The Johns Hopkins Press, 1939), I, 202.

29. Bacon, *Of the Proficience and Advancement of Learning*, Book II, fol. 18r.

30. Daniel Webb, *Remarks on the Beauties of Poetry* (London, 1762), p. 56.

31. Reuben A. Brower, *Alexander Pope: The Poetry of Allusion* (Oxford: The Clarendon Press, 1959), p. 206.

32. William Wordsworth, "The Tables Turned," 11. 21–24, *The Poetical Works*, ed. E. de Selincourt and Helen Darbishire, vol. IV (Oxford: The Clarendon Press, 1947), p. 57.

33. Rebecca Price Parkin, *The Poetic Workmanship of Alexander Pope* (Minneapolis: University of Minnesota Press, 1955), p. 228.

34. Sir William Temple, "Of Poetry," in J. E. Spingarn, ed., *Critical Essays of the Seventeenth Century* (Oxford: Oxford University Press, 1908–1909), III, 81.

35. Donne, *The Anniversaries*, pp. 46–49.

36. Martin Price, *To the Palace of Wisdom: Studies in Order and Energy from Dryden to Blake* (Garden City, N.Y.: Doubleday, 1964), p. 134.

37. Brower, *Alexander Pope*, p. 236.

38. Pope, *An Essay on Man*, p. 89.

## Four: Worlds of Unreason: *The Dunciad* and *The Waste Land*

1. Aubrey Williams, *Pope's Dunciad: A Study of Its Meaning* (London: Methuen, 1955.)

2. George Berkeley, *A Treatise Concerning the Principles of Human Knowledge*, in *The Works of George Berkeley, Bishop of Cloyne*, ed. A. A. Luce and T. E. Jessop, vol. II (London: Thomas Nelson, 1949), pp. 42, 48, 56.

3. George Berkeley, *Three Dialogues between Hylas and Philonous*, in *The Works of George Berkeley*, II, 238.

4. Williams, *Pope's Dunciad*, p. 123.

5. Edwin Fussell, *The Rhetorical World of Augustan Humanism: Ethics and Imagery from Swift to Burke* (Oxford: The Clarendon Press, 1965), p. 92.

6. Alvin Kernan, *The Plot of Satire* (New Haven: Yale University Press, 1965), p. 113.

7. William Wordsworth, "Lines Composed a Few Miles above Tintern Abbey," 11. 104–107, *The Poetical Works*, ed. E. de Selincourt, vol. II (Oxford: The Clarendon Press, 1944), p. 262.

8. Pope to Gay, October 23, 1730, *The Correspondence of Alexander Pope*, ed. George Sherburn (Oxford: The Clarendon Press, 1956), III, 142–143.

9. Pope to Swift, October 15, 1725, Swift to Pope, September 29, 1725, *Correspondence*, II, 333, 325.

10. Martin Price, *To the Palace of Wisdom: Studies in Order and Energy from Dryden to Blake* (Garden City, N.Y.: Doubleday, 1964), pp. 225, 226.

11. Pope, *The Dunciad*, ed. James Sutherland, The Twickenham Edition, Vol. V (New Haven: Yale University Press, 1963), p. 270.

12. Carol Johnson, *Reason's Double Agents* (Chapel Hill: The University of North Carolina Press, 1966), p. 75.

13. Tony Tanner, "Reason and the Grotesque: Pope's *Dunciad*," *Critical Quarterly*, 7 (1965), 152.

14. Petrus Berchorius, quoted in Erwin Panofsky, *Studies in Iconology: Humanistic Themes in the Art of the Renaissance* (New York: Harper and Row, 1962), p. 109.

15. Jay Martin, "T. S. Eliot's *The Waste Land*," in Jay Martin, ed., *A Collection of Critical Essays on "The Waste Land"* (Englewood Cliffs,

N.J.: Prentice-Hall, 1968), p. 7.

16. T. S. Eliot, *The Complete Poems and Plays, 1909–1950* (New York: Harcourt, Brace, 1952), p. 54.

17. Quoted in Ernest Jones, *The Life and Work of Sigmund Freud*, ed. and abridged by Lionel Trilling and Steven Marcus (Garden City, N.Y.: Doubleday, An Anchor Book, 1963), p. 333.

18. Hannah Arendt, *Men in Dark Times* (New York: Harcourt, Brace and World, 1968), p. 193.

19. Arendt, *Men in Dark Times*, pp. 193–194.

20. Mario Praz, *Mnemosyne: The Parallel Between Literature and the Visual Arts* (Princeton: Princeton University Press, 1970), p. 192.

21. George T. Wright, *The Poet in the Poem* (Berkeley and Los Angeles: University of California Press, 1960), p. 63.

22. F. R. Leavis, *New Bearings in English Poetry: A Study of the Contemporary Situation* (London: Chatto and Windus, 1942), pp. 93–94.

23. Jacob Korg, "Modern Art Techniques in *The Waste Land*," in Martin, ed., *A Collection of Critical Essays*, p. 92.

24. Pope to William Bowyer, Jr., November 13, 1742, *Correspondence*, IV, 426.

25. Maynard Mack has suggested that "there was more at stake in the term 'brazen' . . . than a happy but mistaken epithet," and that it may have been yet one more of Pope's allusions to Robert Walpole. Mack, *The Garden and the City: Retirement and Politics in the Later Poetry of Pope, 1731–1743* (Toronto: University of Toronto Press, 1969), p. 157.

26. "The Publisher to the Reader," *The Dunciad*, p. 205.

27. Pope letter referred to in Morris Golden, "The Imagining Self in the Eighteenth Century," *Eighteenth-Century Studies*, 3 (1969), 30. I have been unable to locate this letter.

28. Pope to Hugh Bethel, January 1, 1741/2, *Correspondence*, IV, 377.

29. Pope to John Caryll, Jr., December 5, 1712, *Correspondence*, I, 163.

30. See Thomas R. Edwards, Jr., *This Dark Estate: A Reading of Pope* (Berkeley and Los Angeles: University of California Press, 1963), pp. 112–131.

31. "Ricardus Aristarchus of the Hero of the Poem," *The Dunciad*, p. 256.

32. Fabricated letter of Pope to Robert Digby, December 28, 1724, *Correspondence*, II, 281.

33. Hugo M. Reichard has commented, "The 'temperance' and 'prudence' of the seedy men of letters to be found in the *Dunciad* contain vastly more earnest than jest; they bear in upon us the truth that material privation and insecurity warp the moral and intellectual development of human beings." Reichard, "Pope's Social Satire: Belles-Lettres and Busi-

ness," in Maynard Mack, ed., *Essential Articles for the Study of Alexander Pope* (Hamden, Conn.: Archon Books, 1968), p. 760.

34. "Hints of confusion and abortion point to the metaphorical centre of the poem in the pervading image of chaos, 'the mighty maze without a plan,' which stands in contrast to the Great Order of Nature." Reuben A. Brower, *Alexander Pope: The Poetry of Allusion* (Oxford: The Clarendon Press, 1959), p. 328.

35. Rebecca Parkin, *The Poetic Workmanship of Alexander Pope* (Minneapolis: University of Minnesota Press, 1955), p. 118.

36. George Sherburn has mentioned Pope's recurrent food metaphors as instances of the fact that "from first to last his satires are full of images that might occur to a modern realistic painter or poet." Sherburn, "The *Dunciad*, Book IV," in Mack, ed., *Essential Articles*, p. 740.

37. See Williams, *Pope's Dunciad*, pp. 131–158.

38. Delmore Schwartz, "T. S. Eliot as the International Hero," in Robert E. Knoll, ed., *Storm over The Waste Land* (Chicago: Scott, Foresman, 1964), p. 91.

39. Schwartz, "T. S. Eliot," p. 91.

40. Cleanth Brooks, "The Beliefs Embodied in the Work," in Knoll, ed., *Storm over The Waste Land*, pp. 78–79.

41. Yvor Winters, *On Modern Poets* (Cleveland and New York: World Meridian Books, 1963), pp. 39, 63.

## Five: Forms of the Human and Superhuman

1. Henry Home, Lord Kames, *Elements of Criticism* (Edinburgh, 1762), III, 65.

2. William Melmoth, *Letters on Several Subjects by the Late Sir Thomas Fitzosborne, Bart.*, 2nd ed. (London, 1748), II, 228.

3. Thomas Parnell, *An Essay on the Different Stiles of Poetry* (London, 1713), p. 25.

4. Hugh Blair, *Lectures on Rhetoric and Belles Lettres* (Dublin, 1783), I, 331.

5. Marshall McLuhan, *The Gutenberg Galaxy: The Making of Typographic Man* (New York: New American Library, A Signet Book, 1969), p. 148.

6. E. R. Dodds, *The Greeks and the Irrational* (Berkeley and Los Angeles: The University of California Press, 1968), pp. 41, 185.

7. This phrase by Bacon is quoted by Pope in "The Design," prefaced to *An Essay on Man*, ed. Maynard Mack, the Twickenham Edition, vol. III i (New Haven: Yale University Press, 1958), p. 7.

8. For a detailed study of the characterization, see James M. Osborn, "Pope, the Byzantine Empress, and Walpole's Whore," in Maynard Mack, ed., *Essential Articles for the Study of Alexander Pope*, rev. and enlarged ed. (Hamden, Conn.: Archon Books, 1968), pp. 577–590.

9. Osborn, "Pope, the Byzantine Empress, and Walpole's Whore," p. 588.

10. Quoted in Osborn, "Pope, the Byzantine Empress, and Walpole's Whore, p. 580.

11. Earl R. Wasserman, *Pope's* Epistle to Bathurst: *A Critical Reading with an Edition of the Manuscripts* (Baltimore: The Johns Hopkins Press, 1960), p. 17.

12. Milton Rugoff, *Donne's Imagery: A Study in Creative Sources* (New York: Russell and Russell, 1962), p. 21.

13. William Flint Thrall and Addison Hibbard, *A Handbook to Literature,* rev. and enlarged by C. Hugh Holman (New York: The Odyssey Press, 1960), p. 232.

14. Alvin Kernan, *The Plot of Satire* (New Haven: Yale University Press, 1965), p. 149.

15. Note to Pope, *The Odyssey* IX, ed. Maynard Mack, The Twickenham Edition, vol. IX (New Haven: Yale University Press, 1967), p. 299.

16. Samuel Johnson, *Poems,* ed. E. L. McAdam, Jr., with George Milne, The Yale Edition, vol. VI (New Haven: Yale University Press, 1964), pp. 90–109.

17. A note in the Yale Edition points out that "there is an echo of Pope" in these lines, from *Odyssey* XI, 747: "Here hovering ghosts, like fowl, his shade surround, / And clang their pinions with terrific sound." Johnson, *Poems,* p. 93.

18. Carol Johnson, *Reason's Double Agents* (Chapel Hill: The University of North Carolina Press, 1966), p. 53.

19. C. Day Lewis, *The Poetic Image* (London: Jonathan Cape, 1947), p. 54.

20. Pope, *Epistles to Several Persons,* ed. F. W. Bateson, The Twickenham Edition, vol. III ii (New Haven: Yale University Press, 1961), p. 67.

21. Benjamin Boyce, *The Character-Sketches in Pope's Poems* (Durham, N.C.: Duke University Press, 1962), p. 75.

22. Irvin Ehrenpreis, "The Cistern and the Fountain: Art and Reality in Pope and Gray," in Howard Anderson and John S. Shea, eds., *Studies in Criticism and Aesthetics, 1660–1800: Essays in Honor of Samuel Holt Monk,* (Minneapolis: University of Minnesota Press, 1967), pp. 156–175.

23. Daniel Webb, *Remarks on the Beauties of Poetry* (London, 1762), p. 81.

24. See Maynard Mack, "The Muse of Satire," in Richard C. Boys, ed., *Studies in the Literature of the Augustan Age: Essays Collected in Honor of Arthur Ellicott Case* (Ann Arbor, Mich.: Distributed for the Augustan Reprint Society by The George Wahr Publishing Co., 1952), pp. 218–231.

25. William Butler Yeats, *Essays and Introductions* (London: Macmillan, 1961), p. 509.

26. Dodds, *Greeks and the Irrational*, p. 9.

27. Pope to Gay, October 1730, *The Correspondence of Alexander Pope*, ed. George Sherburn (Oxford: The Clarendon Press, 1956), III, 138.

28. Joseph Spence, *Observations, Anecdotes, and Characters of Books and Men*, ed. James M. Osborn (Oxford: The Clarendon Press, 1966), I, 269.

29. Peter Dixon, *The World of Pope's Satires: An Introduction to the Epistles and Imitations of Horace* (London: Methuen 1968), p. 112.

30. I have explored *The Vanity of Human Wishes* more thoroughly in "From Satire to Description," *Yale Review*, 58 (1969), 232–248.

31. John Aden, *Something Like Horace: Studies in the Art and Allusion of Pope's Horatian Satires* (Nashville, Tenn.: Vanderbilt University Press, 1969), pp. 117, 119.

32. See Maynard Mack, *The Garden and the City: Retirement and Politics in the Later Poetry of Pope, 1731–1743* (Toronto: University of Toronto Press, 1969).

33. Thomas R. Edwards, Jr., *This Dark Estate: A Reading of Pope* (Berkeley and Los Angeles: University of California Press, 1963), p. 110.

34. Pope to Jacob Tonson, Sr., June 7, 1732, *Correspondence*, III, 290.

35. *Correspondence*, III, 419n5.

36. Pope to Arbuthnot, July 26, 1734, *Correspondence*, III, 419.

37. Pope to John Caryll, January 1732/3, *Correspondence*, III, 340.

## Six: Freedom Through Bounds

1. Erwin Panofsky, *Studies in Iconology: Humanistic Themes in the Art of the Renaissance* (New York: Harper and Row, 1962), pp. 5, 7.

2. Reuben A. Brower, *Alexander Pope: The Poetry of Allusion* (Oxford: The Clarendon Press, 1959), p. 149.

3. Brower, *Alexander Pope*, p. 149.

4. Pope, *The Rape of the Lock*, in *The Rape of the Lock and Other Poems*, ed. Geoffrey Tillotson, The Twickenham Edition, vol. II (New Haven: Yale University Press, 1962), p. 199.

5. See Earl R. Wasserman, *The Subtler Language: Critical Readings of Neoclassic and Romantic Poems* (Baltimore: The Johns Hopkins Press, 1959), *passim*.

6. John Dryden, "To the Reader," prefaced to *Absalom and Achitophel*, in *The Poems of John Dryden*, ed. James Kinsley (Oxford: The Clarendon Press, 1958), I, 216.

7. John Dryden, "Discourse Concerning the Original and Progress

of Satire," *Essays of John Dryden*, ed. W. P. Ker (Oxford: The Clarendon Press, 1900), II, 104.

8. For an economical account of the ambiguities, see Anne Davidson Ferry, *Milton and the Miltonic Dryden* (Cambridge, Mass.: Harvard University Press, 1968), pp. 81–84.

9. Samuel Johnson, *Preface to Shakespeare*, in *Johnson on Shakespeare*, ed. Arthur Sherbo, The Yale Edition, vol. VII (New Haven: Yale University Press, 1968), 62.

10. Thomas Maresca, *Pope's Horatian Poems* (Columbus, Ohio: Ohio State University Press, 1966), p. 127.

## Seven: To Madness Near Ally'd

1. George Rosen, *Madness in Society: Chapters in the Historical Sociology of Mental Illness* (New York: Harper and Row, Harper Torchbooks, 1969), p. 167. My italics.

2. Jonathan Swift, *A Tale of a Tub*, ed. A. C. Guthkelch and D. Nichol Smith (Oxford: The Clarendon Press, 1920), pp. 162, 171.

3. Swift, *A Tale of a Tub*, pp. 171, 174.

4. Rosen, *Madness in Society*, p. 101.

5. Swift, *A Tale of a Tub*, p. 177.

6. Swift, *A Tale of a Tub*, p. 165.

7. Thomas Edwards, *This Dark Estate: A Reading of Pope* (Berkeley and Los Angeles: University of California Press, 1963), p. 50.

8. Edward A. and Lillian D. Bloom, "The Satiric Mode of Feeling: A Theory of Intention," *Criticism*, 11 (1969), 117.

9. Pope, *Epistles to Several Persons*, ed. F. W. Bateson, The Twickenham Edition, vol. III ii (New Haven: Yale University Press, 1961), p. 119.

10. Hannah Arendt, *Men in Dark Times* (New York: Harcourt, Brace and World, 1968), p. 6.

11. See, e.g., R. D. Laing, *The Divided Self* (Baltimore, Md.: Penguin Books, 1969).

12. Dryden, *Absalom and Achitophel*, 11. 163–164.

13. Pope to Warburton, quoted in Bateson, ed., *Epistles to Several Persons*, p. 106.

14. Michel Foucalt, *Madness and Civilization: A History of Insanity in the Age of Reason*, trans. Richard Howard (New York: Pantheon Books, 1965), p. 26.

15. John Gay, "On a Miscellany of Poems to Bernard Lintot," 1. 22, *The Poetical Works*, ed. G. C. Faber (London: Oxford University Press, 1926), p. 172.

16. Edward Rosenheim has argued, in relation specifically to Swift, that only an attack with a specific historical reference should be called

satire. Rosenheim, *Swift and the Satirist's Art* (Chicago: University of Chicago Press, 1963), *passim*.

17. Foucalt, *Madness and Civilization*, p. 29.

18. Joseph Spence, *Observations, Anecdotes, and Characters of Books and Men*, ed. James M. Osborn (Oxford: The Clarendon Press, 1966), I, 13.

19. E. R. Dodds, *The Greeks and the Irrational* (Berkeley and Los Angeles: University of California Press, 1968), p. 273.

20. Pope, "To Mrs. Arabella Fermor," *The Rape of the Lock and Other Poems*, ed. Geoffrey Tillotson, The Twickenham Edition, vol. II (New Haven: Yale University Press, 1962), p. 142.

21. Rebecca Price Parkin, *The Poetic Workmanship of Alexander Pope* (Minneapolis: University of Minnesota Press, 1955), p. 112.

22. See Aubrey Williams, "The 'Fall' of China and *The Rape of the Lock*," in Maynard Mack, ed., *Essential Articles for the Study of Alexander Pope*, rev. and enlarged ed. (Hamden, Conn.: Archon Books, 1968), pp. 284–300.

23. R. K. Root, *The Poetical Career of Alexander Pope* (Princeton: Princeton University Press, 1941), p. 86.

24. Root, *The Poetical Career of Alexander Pope*, p. 100.

25. Reuben A. Brower, *Alexander Pope: The Poetry of Allusion* (Oxford: The Clarendon Press, 1959), p. 83.

26. There are, however, exceptions. The range of responses is summarized in Henry Pettit, "Pope's *Eloisa to Abelard:* An Interpretation," in Mack, ed., *Essential Articles*, p. 320.

27. Brendan O Hehir, "Virtue and Passion: The Dialectic of *Eloisa to Abelard*," in Mack, ed., *Essential Articles*, pp. 333–349.

28. Foucalt, *Madness and Civilization*, p. 215.

29. Marguerite Sechehaye, *Autobiography of a Schizophrenic Girl*, trans. Grace Rubin-Rabson (New York: Grune and Stratton, 1951), p. 114.

30. Murray Krieger, " 'Eloisa to Abelard': The Escape from Body or the Embrace of Body," *Eighteenth-Century Studies*, 3 (1969), 45.

31. G. S. Rousseau, "Science and the Discovery of the Imagination in Enlightened England," *Eighteenth-Century Studies*, 3 (1969), 115.

32. Pope to Mrs. or Miss Marriot, February 28 [1713/14], *The Correspondence of Alexander Pope*, ed. George Sherburn (Oxford: The Clarendon Press, 1956), I, 211.

33. Foucalt, *Madness and Civilization*, p. 26.

34. Pope to Caryll, January 25, 1710/11, *Correspondence*, I, 114.

35. Sechehaye, *Autobiography of a Schizophrenic Girl*, p. 147.

36. Northrop Frye, *Anatomy of Criticism: Four Essays* (Princeton: Princeton University Press, 1957), pp. 147, 151.

37. Aubrey Williams, *Pope's Dunciad: A Study of Its Meaning*

(London: Methuen, 1955); Alvin B. Kernan, *The Plot of Satire* (New Haven: Yale University Press, 1965), *passim.*

38. Foucalt, *Madness and Civilization*, p. 106.

39. James Harris, *Three Treatises* (London, 1744), pp. 91–92.

# *Index*